Important Nonsense

Essays in Philosophy

Steven Brutus

Daimonion Press ◆ Portland, Oregon

Copyright © 2012 Steven Brutus
All rights reserved.
ISBN: 0615608809
ISBN-13: 978-0615608808 (Steven Brutus)

Preface

This work explores a number of themes in the psychology of philosophy. I am investigating the emotions that incite philosophy, the emotions that sustain philosophy, and the emotions in which philosophy results. My subjects include suffering, which I think of as an important beginning for philosophy; *philalethes*, or love of truth, which I see as animating the practice of philosophy; and hope, which I think of as an important outcome of philosophy.

One of the main ideas of this work is that suffering upsets the meaning we give our lives. We cannot live without meaning. Philosophy responds to moral crisis and struggles to heal what suffering has injured. The high calling of philosophy has the humble purpose of enabling us to reenter the world and act. My study of suffering and of philosophy that struggles with it leads me to the conclusion that resilience in the face of suffering is a choice. There is no explanation for human strength greater than the decision to be strong. Suffering incites philosophy and philosophy emboldens hope. My study of hope and of philosophy that awakens it leads me to the conclusion that human beings can only understand what is directly in front of them by imagining it into a still unrealized future. The core function of thinking is a kind of hoping forward. This hope meets one obstacle after another and is repeatedly dashed and rekindled. Philosophy is therapy for this restless, knocked-about, rising and falling, core function of hope. This book examines several such offers of therapy, narrates several case histories, and assesses the benefits of philosophic interventions. All these cures propose to liberate us from the past and all count on the power of choice. But their recommendations are quite different – they answer different problems – they advocate different lives. Some try to talk us down. They look for peace, calm, unknowing. Some try to psych us up. They try to get us back in the fight, and to love something worth fighting for. We have to question all these strategies, thinking beyond them, to pose the question about philosophy and the role it should play in our lives.

The title of this book is drawn from Frank Ramsey's 1929 essay entitled "Philosophy." Ramsey thought that we are driven to philosophize because we do not know clearly what we mean. Philosophy therefore is a reflection on meaning. It tries to make sense of things and cut away nonsense. But he wondered whether philosophy itself is nonsense. He added that, if this is our finding, we should not trick ourselves into thinking that philosophy is important nonsense.

I am also trying to understand philosophy by wondering whether philosophy is nonsense, and what drives us to it, and what it is trying to accomplish, and whether it is in any way important.

Important Nonsense

Suffering   1

Hope   47

Striving   82

Peace   162

Important Nonsense   187

--

notes   219

Suffering

I am trying to get to *wisdom* that comes out of suffering and set it down as clearly as I can.

My strategy for arranging many thoughts stirring in me on this difficult topic is to begin with some of the Buddha's ideas about suffering and then to look at some ideas from Greek sources; then to explore some of the theology of suffering and the theodicy problem; then to explore some relations between suffering and culture; then to find some common themes – some ideas that cut across culture – ideas that appear in many if not in all cultures. I consider some arguments that counsel us *not* to think about suffering. I try to separate what suffering feels like and what it does to our thoughts. In formulating a conclusion to this study, I am trying to set down what I can say *I know* about suffering and fill up a thimble full of wisdom about suffering.

Beginning with the Buddha

The Buddha did not begin his teaching by talking about the ecstasy of life but about suffering.

His followers have not always taken this tack. Thinkers in the Buddhist tradition sometimes say less about suffering and more about happiness. Asanga and Vasubandhu (fourth century CE) taught that suffering belongs to the world of illusion. People should treat it as if it were real and act accordingly to lessen it. But (they argue) it is more important to choose happiness than to examine sorrow.

This reasoning makes it appear that we can take up different attitudes about suffering and that some attitudes may help whereas others may hold us back. It's good to remind ourselves that we have choices about the way we look at a thing – even at indisputable facts – since so much depends on how we look at things and the efforts we make.

However, perhaps before presuming much about freedom, it makes sense to begin by stating clearly what is the case.

The Buddha taught "the four noble truths" – the first is called "the noble truth of suffering" – but in fact all *four* truths are about suffering – thus it appears that suffering is not only the place to begin thinking but also the main subject of thinking and even the last word – thinking about life is thinking about suffering – philosophy is about suffering – that is, we are trying to single out suffering as *the* problem of thought and begin to think through some of our response to it.

The Pāli Canon, an early Buddhist standardization of tradition, preserved in the Pāli language, and the first to be written down, is datable to 29 BCE. The Canon cites the first truth as the *dukkha ariya sacca*, "the noble truth of suffering." The second truth is the *dukkha samudaya ariya sacca*, "the noble truth of the arising of suffering." The third truth is the *dukkha nirodha ariya sacca*, "the noble truth of the cessation of suffering." The fourth truth is the *dukkha nirodha gamini patipada ariya sacca*, "the noble truth of the way leading to the cessation of suffering." Thus (reading from this ancient source) the whole teaching is about *dukkha* and about trying to bring *dukkha* to some kind of conclusion.

The Pāli term *dukkha* is usually translated into English as 'suffering' and is thought to derive from earlier Sanskrit terms like *duskha* (meaning 'difficult') or *dusstha* ('frustrating'), probably terminating at the root *du* ('difficult to endure'), e.g. according to *The Oxford Sanskrit-English Dictionary* of 1899. Many other translations have been proposed, e.g., Chögyam Trungpa proposes 'misery,' 'restlessness' and 'pain,' Stephen Batchelor translates 'anguish' and Francis Story says 'dejection,' 'worry,' 'despair,' 'fear' and 'dread.' Jeffrey Po comments on the difficulty of translating this philosophical word and argues that we should think of *dukkha* as something like "the reality of living" or "the process of living, with all its pleasurable and painful moments." Some of the ancient commentaries say 'vulnerable,' 'liable to suffering,' 'impermanent.' These translations are all alike in pointing to *subjective* experience.

All the commentators cited bring out the point that *dukkha* is something that cuts deep in us – it comes of having a mind and feelings to register anything at all – in this sense *dukkha* was made for us or is ours or is something human, since there is no *dukkha* for a stone. This seems right, since a stone cannot be ignorant (*avijja*) or have cravings (*tanha*).

Some writers take the translation out of the subjective realm (getting away from personal feelings) and point to ideas such as variability (as a blank characteristic of life) or, simpler still, change (as a condition of all being). *Dukkha* is part of anything with a 'dependent origination' (*paticca samuppada,* also translated as 'conditioned genesis') even if it seems especially concerned with human beings. (The idea of dependent origination is an important one in Buddhist philosophy. One way of stating this idea is that 'all phenomena arise in a mutually interdependent web of cause and effect.' Another is the idea that 'there is no first cause.')

Walpola Sri Rahula (a Buddhist monk, scholar and writer from Sri Lanka, who died in 1997) recommends that we not translate the term *dukkha* at all but leave it in its original tongue because worries about translation (and about misunderstandings that might arise from it) get us off the subject. The subject is stated in the first noble truth which is literally *saabe sankhara dukkha* for which some translations are "all life is suffering" or "everything that exists is suffering" or "everything that is compounded (made up of parts) is suffering." The Buddha expressed his teaching in sermons such as his first sermon (*dhamma cakka pattana sutta*, "Setting in Motion the Wheel of Truth") and his second sermon (*aditta pariyaya sutta,* literally "Fire Discourse Sermon"). "The Fire Sermon" contains lines like these:

Everything in our experience is on fire.
The eyes are on fire, and what they see;
The mind is on fire, and the object it thinks;
Everything we feel is on fire.

This line of thinking moves us in the direction of the second noble truth, which offers the Buddha's explanation as to why all life is suffering and his discussion about desire (*tanha*) and related terms such as wanting, longing, greed, lust, clinging, clutching, craving, hunger, thirst, all pointing to a human neediness that sooner or later is frustrated in the course of experience and thus gives rise to *dukkha*, suffering. This makes translations of *dukkha* such as writers like Trungpa, Story and Batchelor offer (anguish, dread, worry) ring true, since the Buddha is directing our attention to subjective, personal, human experience.

Early Buddhist teaching suggests that there are different kinds of suffering – *dukkha dukkha*, *viparinama dukkha* and *sankhara dukkha*. These are, first, shocks of experience, physical and mental pain as actually felt, e.g. a broken heart or the loss of a loved one; secondly, the passage of time, experience of the vicissitudes of life, e.g. growing old, becoming sick or infirm; and, lastly, the breaking up of compounded things – i.e., things that have been put together. The Buddha refers to this third idea in what has come down to us as the last words he spoke. His last saying is *vyadhamma sankhara appamadena sampadetha*. Some traditional translations of this last saying are: "All things must pass – but keep on working" and "Conditioned things are impermanent – but strive on heedlessly" and "It is the nature of determinations to disappear – but struggle on vigilantly" and "Things fall apart – but keep going – stay focused and undisturbed" and "What you see before you is transient – but try to accomplish your aim with diligence."

The story goes that the prince and heir to the Shakya crown, Siddhartha Gautama, renounced his wealth, position and family and became a wandering ascetic because he became aware of suffering and set himself to solve the problem of suffering. After wandering for most of a decade and reflecting on the teachings of famous ascetics, holy men and thinkers, he reached a conclusion in his examination of suffering. He reasoned that he had solved the problem of suffering and so pronounced himself enlightened, calling himself and afterwards known as *the Buddha*, which is literally 'the Awakened One.' "Setting in Motion the Wheel of Truth" – his first sermon and first teaching about *dukkha* – ends with these words:

"When my grasp of knowledge became fully clear and I understood the reach of the four noble truths, I claimed to have realized perfect enlightenment. A grasp of knowledge rose up in me. My heart's deliverance became unassailable. This was the last birth. Now there is no more becoming in me."

The Buddha says that he has exited the "jungle of opinions" and that he speaks from the standpoint of knowledge – he is able to say "I know" – he has caught hold of a guiding truth and lets it guide him. But this restricts his claim very severely. He is not talking about God. He is not talking about words like *soul, eternity, sin, last judgment, redemption, angels, beforelife or afterlife* or *reincarnation*, or any other supernatural or miraculous thing – he calls these "questions which tend not to edification" – he says that whatever is true of God or soul or hell or reincarnation, or any idea, there is suffering.

Let us take the Buddha at his word that the only thing that he claims to know about is suffering.

Suffering (he teaches) is made for us, is ours, we make it; since it is ours we can renounce it, we can unmake it. Suffering is always in our power. The problem is suffering and here is the solution: what we have made, we can unmake; what we have learned, we can unlearn; what we have troubled, we can quiet.

We still have the problem of living our lives – we still have to work – to strive on diligently – but pain, time, and things falling apart are in front of us right where we can see them – at least we can see *part of the way* ahead of us, since we have set ourselves against ignorance and craving. We have set ourselves against violence that comes out of confusion or grasping at things. But we have not come *all of the way* – since we still have the problem of living our lives – we see, we set ourselves against many things, but we do not see everything, we are still ignorant and must practice. This is the problem of living our lives – where to direct our energy or heart or love, what to do – how to live within knowledge and without greed.

The core idea is self-possession. The idea is to prepare oneself for the meeting with suffering. I should try to possess myself and stand against ignorance and greed. I should try to endure suffering and also come back from adversity. In the end I have to rely on myself. But I am not acting for myself. I am acting for a value against suffering. I am what I take responsibility for, what I have the strength to be and carry through, what I aim for and make real. This value that I am acting for is as real as I can make it.

If we become aware of suffering and draw the conclusion that we cannot wish it away, we can call ourselves 'realists.' If we follow through with this realism, then we will also gain some humility about what we can accomplish. How do I accomplish good in the world? – By working on myself, by making some progress with myself, by trying to overcome my own ignorance and greed, by seeing clearly but also striving on diligently, by setting this example. Much of this idea is expressed in Gandhi's powerful words, "to be the change you want to see in the world."

Nietzsche and Schopenhauer

The Buddha discovers suffering, frames it as a problem and devotes himself to solving it. Nietzsche presents a useful opposite to this strategy in that he expressly attacks the idea that suffering is a problem. Nietzsche holds that suffering is obvious and ineradicable; the issue is our response to it. Nietzsche thinks he sees a hidden history at work in our thinking about suffering. The natural response to suffering is to fight against it. The strong get stronger and the weak fall in its wake. Wishing for happiness in this world is a fool's errand. The world is on fire, exactly as Buddha taught. But if happiness is impossible, at least we can be noble – we can be heroic – we can laugh rather than cower – and if we are still alive at the end of fighting, then we are stronger. Nietzsche holds that suffering is not a problem but a condition of life. To make it a problem is a sign that we have backed away from life – a sign of weakness. In the course of history, with a twisted logic, this weakness calls itself virtue. Nietzsche's judgment is, here is a virtue for cowards; here is a morality for slaves. Coward-virtue counsels us to stop fighting in the world and start fighting in ourselves. It counsels us to withdraw from the world and take aim at ourselves as the cause of suffering. Nietzsche draws several conclusions: we are seeking meaning for suffering, and we actually provide suffering a meaning by making ourselves its cause (e.g. suffering punishes us for our sins; suffering is an expiation of our sins). The sufferer, in making himself the cause of suffering, offers a religious interpretation of suffering, and this interpretation actually succeeds in alleviating suffering (believers are in fact comforted by their beliefs). But at a deeper level there is a universal principle at work that takes new forms as it adapts to new challenges. This force is at work equally among the strong and the weak. The idea that Nietzsche has caught hold of is that when we turn inward to discover ourselves at the origin of suffering, this is also an attempt to become *master of ourselves*, an intent to gain control and thus an example of the universal process inherent in all being, *the will to power*.

Nietzsche has a kind of empirical thesis running alongside this metaphysical view about reality or its supposed "inner core of willing." The empirical idea is that the aggressive instincts, which were originally allowed to vent themselves on others, get turned inward, become poisonous, and thus create a kind of illness that every human being is bound to contract "under the stress of the most fundamental change that human beings have ever experienced" – "that is, when they found themselves finally enclosed within the walls of society and at peace" (*Genealogy of Morals*, II, 16).

Nietzsche concludes that we are wrong to want to abolish suffering. He laments what he calls the "new Buddhism" that makes suffering into a problem that it tries to solve. He says that this really is a kind of fear – a coward's ethic – because hatred of suffering is hatred of life (*Beyond Good and Evil*, §202, 225).

Some of the prehistory of this idea lies in Nietzsche's encounter with his predecessor Arthur Schopenhauer, the subject of Nietzsche's youthful work *Schopenhauer as Educator*. Schopenhauer writes: "Life is a miserable thing. I have decided to spend my life thinking about it." Suffering – Schopenhauer thinks that our life is made for it – we should address one another as "fellow sufferers" – we must smile at the idea of being happy in this world. Nietzsche praises Schopenhauer as someone who wakes a young person out of his sleep and makes him ask himself "what have you loved up to now? what has it really cost you? what sacrifice have you made? what are you about as a person? and what scar do you have to show for it?"

On Nietzsche's reading, Schopenhauer is a truthful spirit, but he also seems to despair of the truth. Schopenhauer draws a great darkness around him and speaks in a ghostly voice. Still – he has found something – he has gotten hold of something, he has managed to discover something within the chaos we all live in – here at least is *sincerity*, here is the voice of a person who is not trying to cover over anything, not trying to hide. Schopenhauer says exactly what he thinks is true and also finds a way to express his very evident strength of mind. His thinking is so strong that it makes him laugh. Nietzsche feels a kind of life-force pulsing in Schopenhauer's ideas, a strength of conception and lively dynamism, a warming cheerfulness, "cheerful the way a god is cheerful beside the monster he has slain," "cheerful from the deepest thoughts," cheerful as a spark of life lit in darkness that awakens for a moment as conscious being and "must love whatever is most alive."

This cheering thing is laid down in very ancient writings about suffering – Schopenhauer directs the reader's attention to the ancient past, to the *Upanishads*, "a priceless gift to our still young century" (first published in Europe in 1804, this comment from 1818) – a writing "which has been the solace of my life and will be the solace of my death" – a copy lay open on his table and often was his study before sleep:

While we are still here, we have come to know *atman*.
If you do not know it, your destruction will be great.
Those who know it — they become immortal.
As for the rest — suffering awaits them.
Brihad-aranyaka Upanishad, 4,14

When a man sees things rightly
He sees no death, no sickness, no suffering.
When a man sees things rightly
He sees everything, he wins everything, wholly and completely.
Khāndogya Upanishad, 21,4

Schopenhauer calls himself a "Buddhaist" but also calls upon Meister Eckhart to carry his message, which is that "the steed to carry you to perfection is suffering" and that wisdom is won by a bitter trial. This is a harsh wisdom that sees human being fated to suffer. Schopenhauer explains that "In my seventeenth year, without any learned school education, I was gripped by the misery of life, just like Buddha in his youth, when he saw sickness, pain, aging and death." Reaching this conclusion and seeing the futility of all willing, you set yourself to cease willing. Taking the "high mountain road" of philosophy, you reach a place where nothing can alarm or move you any more – you reach a perfect detachment that takes in everything – you arrive at the standpoint of the observer even about your own will – you leave everything behind you, you reach a point where everything lies below you "engulfed in dead of night"— you escape from *willing* entirely – and thus finding a way to dwell outside the world, you discover something eternal. Schopenhauer describes this realization as a return to the deeply cheering wisdom discovered in India many ages ago (*The World as Will and Representation*, II, 603 ff; *Parega and Paralipomena*, 143; *Manuscript Remains*, 20).

Schopenhauer speaks for, Nietzsche against the Buddha – but arguably in both cases the issue is not what the Buddha taught but the idea of the active human will. Schopenhauer teaches that suffering – our own suffering and our observation of suffering in the world – if we understand it and even if we don't – leads us to find the thing in us that wants to live the most – the thing in us that *wants* – in order to kill this thing. Suffering is the cost of loving, and experience burns love out of us. That is: life itself, working in us, is intent on extinguishing itself. The experience of suffering frees us from the life-instinct and makes us actively oppose our indwelling *will to live*. Weariness lifts us out of the circus of emotional attachment and disappointment. So doing, it draws us closer to peace – to rest, quiet, tranquility – to calm rationality.

Nietzsche and Schopenhauer face each other over this weariness. Schopenhauer takes it as a cue to make a retreat from life. Nietzsche sees it as a symptom of exhaustion. He wants to rouse us back again to life.

Nietzsche teaches that we can no more pull suffering apart from life than good from evil, since they are bound up together. Rather than denying our own inhering *will to live*, we should follow and perfect this instinct. Human life is not about exiting the field or achieving an objective standpoint. Human life is exactly this gritty stuff that Schopenhauer despises – power, strife, work, pain – will to enter the *agon* (contest) and try to prevail. Nietzsche considers this idea an explanation of our attempts to master ourselves, of human behavior generally and even of nature as such. The will to power is "the doctrine preached by life itself to everything that is alive" – it is "the fundamental character of reality" (*Beyond Good and Evil*, §239, *The Will to Power*, § 125).

//

Studying this brief chapter in German philosophy, the inquirer is led to the conclusion that suffering prompts different kinds of reactions in different people – also, different kinds of reactions in the same person, varying with time and circumstance. But the common element is easy to see. It is true that suffering transports a person *from* a given place *to* a given place. In some cases the inciting event transports the sufferer to an otherworldly place – in some cases the sufferer faces a reality here and now. The otherworldly place, however, is *in us*, or we must discover it in us. It is our problem to discover it. Likewise, the reality here and now is *in us*. It is laid out in our view of the world and in our ability to stay present in it. Therefore: the common element is captured in the phrase 'in us.'

Whatever is to be done with suffering – whatever we are to learn from it – however we are to take it in and go on, the problem takes place 'in us.' This is *our* problem. We cannot give it away. We must find the way on our own.

Ancient Greece

In the Homeric world there is a double audience: gods and men. There is a double audience in Greek theatre: the actors in the play, who are not in on the secret, and we the audience, who are.

The stark contrast between life and death, the sharp break and sudden transition, the chasm between god and man, Olympus and the earth – the magic and careless world of the gods laid out behind the world of suffering and death – this is the double image – these are the two worlds. The poets' sketch of the divine background represents another kind of 'solution' to the problem of suffering.

The Greek scholar Jasper Griffin explains that greatness and fragility need one another. "Suffering enables mortal men to establish a claim on the serious interest of the gods" – even more, "a divine gaze is fixed upon those who suffer the most." Griffin is thinking especially of the Oedipus story – famous Oedipus, who marries his mother, kills his father, blinds himself and, after many years of wandering, finally reaches a kind of understanding about the enormous suffering he has had to endure. We all know the story. Watching the play unfold on stage, the audience already knows what the actors will do; what matters is *how* the actors comport themselves. The actor may play a shameful part and cower from his fate. Or he may rise to the part of the hero. Accepting suffering "ennobles and transforms the mere necessity of having to endure it" (*Homer*, 1982).

The Stoic thinker Seneca expresses this idea in his motto "fate leads if you assent, drags if you resist." Nietzsche's saying is *amor fati*, "love of fate."

Thus in face of suffering it is possible to turn inward and fight the desire that makes suffering into suffering – the desire that creates the loss – as it were, *internalizing* the struggle. Another solution, pushing the struggle *outwards* into the world, is to accept suffering and then try to endure it – to respond by acting in the world.

What is the purpose of suffering? The tragic or comic calamity in the play has a purpose because it leads the actor to a recognition that grows out of suffering. He can no longer *believe* something or he can no longer deny his *feeling*; some illusion is swept away or some emotion is purged; a feeling is brought out of darkness into the light where it can be seen. The character learns what it is like to live without the thing that mattered most.

The heroic ethic shows itself in bravery and strength and so is bound up with suffering to test human steel. The heroism can show itself in a fight, but also in steady purpose not susceptible to distraction; or in self-respect and lack of self-pity; or by looking squarely at misfortune and facing it without any hint of evasion. The common element comes out in expressions like these: accepting, facing, facing up to, believing, believing in spite of, taking it in, taking it on, taking responsibility for, deciding, acting.

//

Initially, it is possible to distinguish four different sorts of approach to suffering. These are: the ethic of self-possession; the ethic of fiery will; the ethic of blowing out the flame; and the heroic ethic.

We pay attention to things that hurt. Then the four reactions: We try to not mind them hurting. We try to hurt them back. We try to get away from them. We try to prove ourselves by them.

The world seems differently conceived in each of these approaches. We try to make a name for ourselves in the world; we try to be the change we want to see in the world; we try to change the world; we try to leave it.

Stepping back from the survey of ideas about suffering, a few first tentative hypotheses come into focus. There is the big idea that the response to suffering has to do with giving consent, accepting, having the wherewithal to come back from suffering with a strength bigger than the shock of the event. This appears to be a complicated process, but we can make out a few words in the language.

The event comes first. This is fate, necessity, the accident – the storm, the fire – disaster, horror, crime – i.e., the event that brings suffering. Accepting (if it comes at all) follows. This gets worked out in terms of meaning and spirit. That is: we cannot live without meaning; suffering upsets the meaning we give our lives; the injury sets us the task of restoring meaning. The formula is: man responds to meaninglessness by making meaning; he looks for a purpose in suffering; he creates. With the term 'spirit' I am trying to capture the idea of being bigger than suffering, having something left over after suffering has done its work, outlasting or growing beyond or enduring suffering. In a word: resilience. Spirit can be bigger than suffering; the heart can be bigger than this; faith can be bigger; grace, elegance, belief, courage, imagination can be bigger; thankfulness for life, love of life can be bigger than suffering, pain and anger. My hypothesis is that this is a truth of experience. It emerges, and is valid, cross-culturally.

Human beings respond to suffering with human 'stuff' – like meaning and spirit – human beings respond to the inhumanity of suffering with their humanity – they get a chance to show what humanity is like – suffering is bound up with something like 'grace' that comes from enduring pain.

The Greek inheritance, e.g. the Oedipus story, also brings out another theme. This is the idea that when suffering comes up there is a kind of challenge to humility. Somehow the game is to see that the self is unimportant; part of the truth-seeking response to suffering is to get the big ego out of the way and let suffering do its work (the work of purging the self of greed, ignorance, lust and arrogance). Probably a better way of putting this idea is that *we* do this work, not suffering, though we do it at the call of suffering (or in the face of suffering). The ancient stories point to the complexity of ideas about the self: seeing that the self is nothing; getting the self out of the way; purging the self; working on the self; hardening the self; forging the self.

People respond to moral crises with very different histories, characters and results. Those to whom evil is done do evil in return – *sometimes*; sometimes this is not the response. The fact that people who experience horrible things sometimes do horrible things shows that suffering is not a teacher just by itself. If it is a truth of experience that spirit can be bigger than suffering, then this is the kind of truth that we have to make for ourselves. It's not just 'out there' somewhere for us to bump into. The learning process, the teaching moment, metamorphosis or moral growth – the kind of change that has to do with giving consent and facing the challenge to humility – e.g., the subject-matter of Sophocles' play *Oedipus at Colonus* – it seems to have precedents, but it also seems to be an explicit choice. There is no explanation for human strength greater than the decision to be strong. Human fate is the kind of fate that can be taken over; this is the truth that Seneca and Nietzsche are trying to point us to. It's as if you made a law for yourself and then (as a new step) you discipline yourself to keep it. This is one of the things I am trying to look out for in studying ideas about suffering from around the world – i.e., what kind of decision this is. It seems to have something to do with 'being bigger than suffering' or 'having something left over' or 'finding a way to come back from suffering' (e.g. being bigger in feeling and in thought – being fearless enough to feel and patient enough to think; or working through the response step by step; or being driven to look for something, and to take some time with it). This is the kind of thing I am trying to point to in talking about 'spirit' or 'resilience.'

Homer shows us what a soldierly resilience looks like – what a heroic response looks like – but he also shows the responses of many different kinds of characters. He shows us 'playing the part bravely'; he shows us 'being able to take it'; he shows us what resilience looks like in a world in which conflict is a daily reality. He shows us characters who confront suffering and are ennobled by it. But he also paints cowardice, blood-lust and despair; he shows what *not* allowing oneself to feel looks like; also, being unhinged by feeling; also, shutting down, made numb by feeling. He shows both thoughtful and thoughtless responses, and many conditions of moral imagination, including indifference, family-feeling, camaraderie, and a sense of brotherhood and common fate even with the enemy.

Thus we can make out several different responses to suffering; several different ethical positions; several different big ideas; many kinds of human characters; and perhaps a truth of experience. It is possible to be bigger than suffering. It is possible to suffer and not lose your dignity, your values, the things you stand for. It is possible to suffer and not lose your humanity.

Ancient Japan

The *Kojiki*, or "Record of Ancient Events," the earliest chronicle of Japanese history, is thought to date from the year 712. The history begins in the fourth century CE as the ruling clan, which had established itself in the Yamato region, sought to subdue the entirety of the Japanese countryside. Emperor Keiko sends his son Takeru to march out of the city into distant provinces, "in order to subdue the rough gods in the mountains, and the malicious gods in the plains, who bar the highways and obstruct the roads, causing much suffering to our people." The Emperor goes on to say that among the eastern savages the most powerful are the Emishi.

What is interesting about this passage is that it makes no distinction between supernatural creatures and the primitive tribesmen who worship them. The passage seems to say: the people are the gods they worship, and the gods are the people who worship them.

Human beings wander from the cradle to the grave. Myth recounts these journeys in a language of dreams. A mythic background and explanation for suffering puts suffering into some larger context. In some cases the gods send suffering to men simply to amuse themselves. In some cases the gods send suffering as a punishment, or as a path to redemption. Something in the story, a dramatic context or meaning, a small detail, drives the story to an unexpected conclusion, and at the end of the story suffering may not even look like suffering any longer.

If gods and men are mixed up together and can stand for one another, then human suffering can attract a divine interest, and divinities can suffer with human beings or even for them. Suffering can become mystic suffering or ecstatic suffering. Suffering can become sacred pain, or God can become our fellow sufferer. God can become first sufferer, suffering servant, sacrificial lamb, divine offering. The dying god can be the problem of suffering writ large. Human suffering becomes *visible*; it begins to be seen and begs to be understood.

Being human means becoming responsible for fulfilling the meaning-potential in every life situation, including the advent of suffering; as it were, suffering is a kind of experience that calls up the resources of human sensibility, calling upon human beings to act humanly, calling upon human beings to show what humanity can bring to life; and if men and gods are mixed up together, then telling stories, or retelling the myth, or making the sacred sign, offering the sacrifice or the prayer, become ways in which people wrestle with suffering. The predicament of suffering gets turned into an achievement. It becomes a chance for human beings to show what human sensibility is like.

Thus we think of God as a spirit who sees our suffering and understands our suffering and comforts us. God may take on our suffering and free us from it. Or in another idiom God is silent – as Bonhoeffer said, "the God in us is the God who has forsaken us" – God comes to us even in the death of God. In a case like this we wrestle with suffering by talking about God's absence.

I think there is a profound idea in the Japanese chronicle dated many centuries ago – the idea that *we are our gods* and that *our gods are us*. The idea is: we are our ideals and we suffer from them; they suffer with us; if they are true, they bring us through suffering; if they are false, then they will fail us – they bring us nothing and will pass away. Our hope is that they outlast us and show how we have borne up under suffering.

Ancient Israel

The prophets of ancient Israel create a new language to contrast the divine realm and the world of men. The magic and careless world of immortal Titans, set against the world of suffering and death, is replaced by a vision of a God of justice, a righteous God, set against a weak and sinful failure, man.

God is the inexorable creator of the universe. He sits above the circle of the earth, he stretches out the heavens like a curtain, heaven is his throne, the earth is his footstool, he looks down upon the inhabitants of the earth like grasshoppers. The Creator is a mighty power such as is worshipped in many lands, but among the ancient Hebrews, running through a long and complex history, the worship of Greatness becomes focused on living the law and doing justice for man. "He who oppresses a poor man insults his Maker, he who is kind to the needy honors Him" (*Proverbs* 14:31).

Man lies at the other end of creation and has no standing. "Can a mortal man be righteous before God? Can a man be pure before his Maker?" (*Job* 4:17); "Shall a faultfinder contend with the Almighty?" (*Job* 40:2); "For there is no man who does not sin" (*I Kings* 8:46); "Surely there is not a righteous man on earth who does good and never sins" (*Eccles.* 7:20); "Enter not into judgment with Thy servant; for no man living is righteous before Thee" (*Psalm* 143:2).

Man toils under the sun, a wisp, forgetful, inconstant, treacherous, a fool, lewd, full of iniquity, unclean. Yet God said "let us make man in our image" (*Genesis* 1:26) and man alone in Creation bears this likeness; man bears his fate alone in creation and is unlike any other thing. Man is made weak or (as it were) weakness was made for man, since there is no weakness for a stone. "For affliction does not come from the dust, nor does trouble sprout from the ground; but man is born to trouble as the sparks fly upward" (*Job* 5:6-7). "I knew that from birth you would deal very treacherously, and that from birth you were called a rebel" (*Isaiah* 48:8).

Strangely, God loves man – greatness loves weakness – even stranger, God wants love from this weak fool. "For I desire love, not sacrifice, attachment to God rather than burnt offerings" (*Hosea* 6:6). "Attachment to God" is a translation of *daath elohim*: this could also be 'knowledge of God' or 'sympathy for God' or 'together with God.' The verb *yada*, the origin of many later terms in Semitic languages, also signifies sexual union ("Now Adam knew Eve his wife" *Genesis* 4:1); also mental or spiritual union, a communion of hearts or minds.

But God is like a faithful, loving, but forsaken husband, and Israel is like a wanton wife, a harlot, a whore. "A day will come when you call Me 'my husband' and I will betroth you to Me in righteousness and in justice, in love and in mercy" (*Hosea* 2:16). God told Hosea to marry a girl named Gomer, the daughter of Diblaim. They were happy for a time – then she betrayed him – then she was sent away as an adulteress. But against the law, God tells Hosea to go out and find Gomer and bring her back home. "Renew your love for her, even as the Lord loves Israel, though she turns to other gods" (*Hosea* 3:11).

In the Greek world, the bond between god and man never becomes so close that it could be expressed by a possessive pronoun – human beings excite some interest in "the god" or "the gods" – offering some amusement for Immortal Power; and suffering is like a fact attaching to the state of man. As the Greek scholar Walter Burkert says, "it is left for men to endure as long as they are able." The Hebrew formula is wildly different – the Jew prays to "my God" or "the God of my fathers" – likewise man's suffering is not a fact, but is his own fault. The Hebrew scholar Abraham J. Heschel explains that greatness and fragility are bound tightly together as "man defying God" and "God seeking man" to reconcile with him.

God wants man's love – God is in search of man – God is testing man – God is turning man to the light. "The Lord reproves him whom He loves, as a father the son in whom he delights" (*Proverbs* 3:11).

Behold, I have refined you, but not like silver;
I have tried you in the furnace of affliction.
Isaiah 48:10

On man's side, man fails, man breaks the law, man does injustice, man is weak, man is a fool, man strays from the path. Men worship power instead of right. History is a kind of nightmare in which justice itself suffers defeats. But the prophets look forward to a reconciliation – "Many nations will join themselves to the Lord on that day, and be My people" (*Zech.* 2:15); "My house shall be called a house of prayer for all people" (*Isaiah* 56:1-7). Thus, taken all together, human suffering is bound together with man's guilt, his shame, but also his capacity for repentance.

Heschel summarizes some of this logic of this thinking in his examination of the figure of the prophet. The prophet speaks for God – here is a human being with a supreme confidence in what he is saying – he is the anger of God, the justice of God, God's love, God's heart.

Surely the Lord God does nothing
Without revealing his secret
To his servants the prophets.
Amos 3:7

Heschel held that "the prophet is a person who, living in dismay, has the power to transcend this dismay" (*The Prophets*, 1962). The prophet shouts the blast of God – God's anger – God's rage against sin, willfulness and violence. The prophet makes the call to repentance, remorse, shame – he *is* this call and lives in it, and lifts the people by his actions – he becomes God himself witnessing our times, shouting out what we believe in, trying to wake us from our sleep – and on His side, by His love of man, God Himself is ashamed, He takes back His harsh judgment, He repents and says "It shall not be" (*Amos* 7:3).

Thus God is able to model human suffering. God can become the problem of suffering writ large. Oppositely God is able to model human repentance. God can embody becoming responsible for the fulfillment of meaning. God can be the spirit larger than suffering that finds a way to bring meaning to pain.

Theodicy

The term *theodicy* sometimes refers to a proposed vindication of God, sometimes to a branch of theology that defends God's justice in the face of suffering (a coinage of Leibniz from the year 1710). Hume, two generations later, by contrast, set himself against God, arguing that the existence of a good and supreme being is incompatible with the powerfully evident existence of suffering; there can be no theodicy.

There are many traditions of justification, at least as many as there are worlds of belief. The justification or vindication is especially for the believers themselves, because faith is bound to collide with experience. Ritual, myth, tradition, faith or belief is bound to collide with suffering, reality, impermanence, the unexpected. Justification offers to help believers return to their belief. Atheism is also for believers, and is fairly well meaningless outside the framing community. Looking at theodicy is another way to get at the way human beings come back from suffering.

Adorno said that philosophy became impossible after Auschwitz. On the same reasoning, philosophy is always becoming impossible, because there is always a new horror. Even so, people try to defend God – "to justify the ways of God to man" – people try to go on with the project of meaning. People continue to wrestle with suffering and typically make opposite kinds of mistakes, believing either too much or too little.

Gandhi coined the term *satyagraha* to help get hold of this predicament. "Its root meaning is *holding on to truth*, hence *force of righteousness*. I have also called it love force or soul force. In the application of *satyagraha*, I discovered in the earliest stages that pursuit of truth did not permit violence being inflicted on one's opponent, but that he must be weaned from error by patience and sympathy. For what appears truth to one may appear error to the other. And patience means self-suffering. So the doctrine came to mean vindication of truth, not by the infliction of suffering on the opponent, but on one's self" (*Statement to the Disorders Inquiry Committee*, January 5, 1920).

Gandhi's concept of *satyagraha* draws many ancient strains of thinking about suffering together – the idea of fighting against injustice, the idea of turning inward and fighting oneself, the idea of getting above fighting, the idea of being strong enough to receive a blow, of aiming high and reaching something eternal. It appears to incorporate the idea of becoming the value that you are trying to uphold, and thus uniting the means of achieving the goal with the valued goal itself. It also includes the novel recognition that different peoples see the world very differently.

Gandhi is trying to discover a species of reasoning that has exited all trace of sectarianism. This was an immediate problem for him, because he did not claim to have reached any kind of special absolute.

Gandhi said "there is no God higher than truth." And he proposed a form of social action that he called *holding on to truth*. These thoughts seem to imply that he thought he had caught hold of a truth – that he could say 'I know' – very interestingly, he does not say this. He says, my vindication of truth is directed at me – as it were, *I* become the sacrifice – I become the offering. I am not ready to claim that you are nothing; I am much more ready to claim that I am nothing. I make myself suffer; that is, rather than inflict suffering, it is better to receive it; but I am here.

Martin Luther King, Jr. reasoned that the kind of suffering that Gandhi underwent – suffering that is chosen and undeserved – has a redemptive power, and proves itself to be a force for social progress. Dr. King was initially skeptical about the strategy of meeting hate with love. Gandhi's approach appears so high-minded – but how can this work in practice – how can idealism foster progress? Gandhi did not just want to win – to overcome the opponent – he wanted to convert him. He wanted to draw the opponent into the moral universe, where the right course of action would emerge for everyone. To do this, he arms the resister with moral force, rather than physical force. He argues for the strength of forgiveness and against the weakness of punishment. King says that he gradually understood that Gandhi's approach was not idealism, but skepticism – a deep skepticism aimed primarily at human nature – a skepticism that always has to begin with the self. The first opponent must always be one's own demons, fears and insecurities. Impatience, barbarism and intolerance betray a lack of faith in one's own cause. We have to burn these away in order to serve the cause rather than our own vanity. King was especially impressed by Gandhi's discussion of the "law of suffering" (*Young India*, June 16, 1920). Gandhi says:

"Suffering is the mark of the human tribe. It is an eternal law. The mother suffers so that her child may live. Life comes out of death. No country has ever risen without being purified through the fire of suffering... It is impossible to do away with the law of suffering which is the one indispensable condition of our being. Progress is to be measured by the amount of suffering undergone... the purer the suffering, the greater the progress."

Gandhi accepts suffering as a condition of life (as Nietzsche taught) and takes it on as the crucible of moral growth (as taught by the Hebrew prophets). Dark impulses are always there, but when one takes aim at them in one's own being and endures, the force or power of self-suffering shines through what one does and ultimately transforms the conflict and even the opponent. It becomes self-suffering that lives in the public space – witnessed especially by man, rather than God – where it lives and grows and gradually facilitates a transfer of power. The strong become weaker, the weak stronger. Wrong is undone and good is revived.

Enduring suffering and emerging from it intact has a kind of Biblical import – "I have tried you in the furnace of affliction" (*Isaiah* 48:10). It strips a person down to elemental strength. A person has a chance to discover reservoirs of inner strength. It is a chance to connect to a powerful, guiding purpose. For an individual this is something like 'honestly facing oneself' but also 'coming to grips with trauma.' Taking on the injury, or burning away one's own vices, stores up *tapas* (a Sanskrit term whose meaning is something like 'spiritual power gained by austerities'). The process also works for society – hardship offers the prospect of a new context. Historical crises are also political opportunities in which societies sometimes find reservoirs of solidarity and common purpose through shared hardship. But Gandhi and King both remarked that suffering is *merely* an opportunity – for the self and for society – it is a chance that may still founder. Suffering does not guarantee anything. In the end we have to make a choice.

The Language of Suffering

The language of suffering presents a jumble of metaphors that get at the idea from many angles.

The English term *suffering* derives from the Latin *sufferre*, to undergo, *ferre*, to bear; from the Greek *pherein*, to bear; ultimately to the hypothetical Indo-European root, *bher-^{1}*, to bear, to take, to take on, to carry, to carry over, to bring, to convey across.

The English, Latin, Greek and Sanskrit terms – many Indo-European roots generally – appear to address the idea of suffering with the metaphor of bearing a heavy weight across some distance.

The Mandarin verb form *sho-koo* (受苦) joins the two characters 'take upon' and 'bitterness.' This is usually translated 'suffers' or 'is suffering.' The noun form is *koo-nan* (苦難), literally 'bitterness' + 'difficulties, troubles.' This is usually translated 'suffering.' Both forms refer to the sense of taste.

The Japanese noun for suffering is based on the same form, *khoo* (苦), bitterness. The Japanese expression *mono no aware* is translated into English using the Greek word *pathos*. *Mono no aware* is 'the *pathos* of things.' The Japanese scholar and translator Ivan Morris explains this expression as follows: "(this is the) central theme in traditional Japanese aesthetics...an instinctive sympathy with the fate of the failed hero, whose defeat dramatically exemplifies the confrontation of all living creatures with adversity, suffering, defeat and death" (*The Nobility of Failure*, 1975). The Greek term (*pathos*) that Morris uses to translate this Japanese expression (*mono no aware*) has at least three senses: suffering; the human capacity to feel anything at all (the emotions are the *pathei*), but especially the sense of compassion; and being affected, the reality of feeling, the personal or emotional element of art, as opposed to *ethos* – the point of the artwork or the moral judgment it tries to express. *Mono no aware* as a whole complex is something like 'life-hurt inspires, transpires and expires in a transitory art-space.'

The root idea of the Greek term *pathos* is receiving – i.e., it is not *erga* (works) or *poesis* (doing), but has to do with being treated as an object – not being the actor but just suffering whatever happens.

The Hebrew term *anah* (הנע), suffering, affliction, also in forms like *anah arak*, 'long suffering' (afflict, make suffer + defer, draw out, lengthen, prolong), the source of Aramaic, Syriac and Arabic terms such as *atsab* (be in pain, cause pain, torture) and *tsarar* (to bind, to tie, to oppress), all probably originate in the same hypothetical Semitic root *nqs*. The root has senses like humble, abase, bow down, be humbled, be put down, be cast down, be downcast. It is related to Amharic and Ethiopic terms for kings and great men who look down on their subjects. These are all terms of position, in which the idea suffering is captured by expressions such as 'knocked down' or 'laid low.' Some related terms are *anan, anur*, cloud, shadow, darkness, suggesting the idea of being without *owr, nwr, nur*, light.

To bear the weight, to carry the weight, to taste bitterness, to feel and be overcome with emotion, to have no power, to be cast down, to be in darkness, to become a thing.

Novalis said that looking at word histories stands to philosophy in the same relation that experiment stands to science. Philosophy itself is a kind of sustained intellectual experiment. The idea is to capture the root forms of experience, but also to expose and break down illegitimate prejudices; we want to listen carefully to experience rather than simply reassert our cultural values and beliefs.

When we attempt this in the investigation of 'suffering' and have a broad look at etymology in many systems, the first big finding is 'diversity.' Every language addresses the idea of suffering by a local metaphor – but very often even in the same language many different ideas appear – making a survey even of a few languages offers the inquirer a very large collection of metaphors that serve to express the idea of suffering. This finding of diversity brings us to the idea that there is never only one way, *the* way, of seeing suffering. Listening to world language – envisioning all the images that help convey the meaning of suffering – becoming more familiar with the diversity of world conceptualization of suffering, becomes a powerful argument against dogmatism.

The finding of diversity also supports the claim that, whatever we have come to, there is more – there is still more for us to see. The finding emerging out of a review of the world's vast vocabulary for the expression of suffering is the understanding that we have *not* seen everything relevant to the case; the idea that each of us is an ocean and a drop in an ocean; i.e., the lesson of variety is vastness.

Suffering and Culture

Suffering, seen through the filter of culture, seems like an incongruous jumble or hodgepodge.

Suffering occurs in every culture, religion, social world, but it can disappear for an outsider, or reappear under a new perspective. We can lose our objectivity or regain our focus in the throes of suffering. This makes it easier for suffering to appear like a jumbled up incongruous bunch of responses.

This thing that we are taking on and must bear, the theme of myth-making, is variously the lot, portion, share, doom, fate, fortune, kismet, chance, luck or destiny of man – determined by the Moirae, the Parcae, by the Norns, by Bhaga, by Quetzlcoatl, by Sudz, by Meskhenet, by Gad – many tribes have a tale that speaks to this idea. In a success-culture, such as ancient Greece or Japan, the issue is not what a person *feels* under this weight, but what he shows publically, i.e. how he saves face. In a guilt-culture, such as ancient Judea or medieval France, the actor has to contend with a divided conscience, i.e. with how he *feels*, so that the struggle goes on 'inside.'

Suffering in Irish families – Jewish families – Chinese families – Russian families – Hopi families – Kikuyu families – Kansas families – Egyptian families – Thai families ... in every case suffering takes a special cast, e.g. out of a sense of personal guilt, suffering is felt to be a punishment; or suffering is something shared by an entire people – suffering is a common heritage; or suffering becomes a magical, protective shield – suffering is a mystical power; or suffering is a gift or a chance or a test; or in suffering you offer up your pain – you become holy; or you are called to bear witness; or you are called to bear in silence; or suffering is something that you wear on your sleeve – a pride.

The contemporary Israeli writer Avraham Burg makes the point that the shared experience of suffering in Jewish culture has become pathological in recent Israeli history and even appears to wipe out all recognition of suffering. To make a too-frequent reference to mind-numbing suffering threatens one's ability to appreciate suffering in the present. Thus the constant reference point becomes the slaughter of six million Jews in the nineteen-forties – the Holocaust – but we end up cheapening the Holocaust by referring to it too easily.

"'Occupation? You call this occupation? This is nothing compared to the absolute evil of the Holocaust!' And if it is nothing compared to the Holocaust, then you can continue. And since nothing, thank God, is comparable to the ultimate trauma, nearly everything becomes legitimate." Burg writes that "we lose the ability to be sensitive to what happens to others and in many ways we become indifferent to the suffering of others." "We confiscated, we monopolized, world suffering. We did not allow anybody else to call what happens to them *suffering* –

no one can have a 'holocaust' or a 'genocide' – no one, be it Armenians, be it Kosovo, be it Darfur – save us" (*Defeating Hitler*, 2007).

Burg tries to document how the extremity of the Holocaust creates a pathology decades later. Instead of improving, things get worse over time. He tries to make the point that suffering puts our *objectivity* at risk. In many cases *our* suffering makes us blind to *everyone else's* suffering. Suffering looks less like an opportunity and more like a trauma. Suffering is less like an opportunity for moral growth and more like an injury that brings about moral degradation. It knocks the mind off kilter and makes it sick – physically, mentally and morally ill.

Freud makes a related point about culture as such, losing its moral objectivity, especially focused on religious culture – "the religions of humanity must be classified as mass-delusions" – this is because "(religions) try to obtain assurance of happiness and protection from suffering by a delusional transformation of reality" – i.e., the suffering is explained away in the further elaboration of religious doctrine (e.g., God permits suffering to exist because He wishes to save man's freedom of the will; or, evil no longer counts as evil but serves the cause of good in the broader context of a humanly-incomprehensible, divinely-ordered purpose; or, suffering is a test of the faithful, and how we bear up under suffering informs God's verdict about us at the Last Judgment) (*Civilization and Its Discontents*, 1929).

Greek religious culture makes a good counterexample to Freud's case – i.e. a religious culture that faces suffering but does not lose its objectivity. In this case (in Greek religious culture) suffering does not make believers partisan but equalizes all humankind as sharing the same fate.

Homer stands out among the poets for his truth-seeking. Chronicles of ancient times, and mostly more recent accounts, do not see a human being in the national enemy. As the critic Northrop Frye puts it: "it is hardly possible to overestimate the importance for Western civilization of the *Iliad's* demonstration that the fall of an enemy, no less than that of a friend or leader, is tragic." Frye claims that poetry without objectivity is propaganda; that is, nearly all poetry is propaganda; but in exceptional cases, saving the quality of objectivity, poetry acquires an authority like that of science, "a vision of nature as an impersonal order" (*Anatomy of Criticism,* 1957).

Thus we can portray suffering as carrying the weight of holiness – offering up our worship or bearing witness to our truth – or, in a very different life-pattern, we can show the depth of our commitment to truth by resisting the temptations of hate – we can even give up the idea that we have any special truth to uphold. Everyone wrestles with suffering. This is why there are myriad responses to it. But getting to something like an *objective* perspective – recognizing suffering not just close to home, but in many different life-patterns – in every world of feeling and belief that a person encounters – this has not been the norm, but has been a rare achievement in history.

It has been rare, but it is possible to travel from our own reactions to a large context in which we see 'suffering humanity' sharing much more than differing – sharing the same fate – more united than at war.

//

One conclusion emerging from this study is that spirit or moral being can be bigger than suffering. Another is that this overcoming or transcendence has the character of a decision. Another is that in some cases the agent is *not* able to come back against suffering and make this decision. Thus in some cases suffering results in weakening or mental illness or moral degradation and in other cases suffering makes a person stronger, healthier and better. Another result is that suffering appears to be at work in social life and that societies respond to crises by becoming less or more. Culture can respond to suffering by losing objectivity or by opening to the world. It is also important to note that when one person makes this decision, he does so in a world in which many other people do not; and this is also true for cultures.

The Axial Age

Karl Jaspers made what is perhaps his greatest contribution to intellectual history in his idea of the *Axial Age*, a period between 900 and 200 BC, in which the spiritual foundations of humanity were laid down simultaneously and independently in China, India, Israel and Greece. This is the period of the Buddha, Socrates, Confucius and Jeremiah; the Upanishads, Sophocles, Mo Tzu and Zarathustra. This is "The Great Transformation" in which ancient spiritual traditions turn earthward and teach justice – the origin of the idea that spiritual consciousness shows itself in moral action. The Axial Age works through the change from competitive virtues (strength, courage, cleverness) to cooperative virtues (hospitality, justice, mercy) – from honor to dignity – from shame to guilt – from social standing to strength of character.

Jaspers thought that the Axial Age represented a kind of atemporal disjunction. "The Axial Age can be called an interregnum between two ages of great empire, a pause for liberty, a deep breath bringing the most lucid consciousness." A human being can also become a special site of consciousness – what Jaspers calls a "paradigmatic personality" – someone who exemplifies what a human being can be – a pause between empires. Jaspers tried to be such a person.

The defining challenge throughout the "Axial" period is the encounter with *suffering*, which Jaspers also calls the universal theme of myth. He defines the theme of myth as follows: "existence is suffering, action brings suffering, and suffering comes to an end in death." Thus the problem of how to overcome suffering is at the same time the question about how human beings fit into the scheme of things. Suffering defines the fundamental human situation and suffering directs us to the fundamental human task.

An initial 'Axial' principle is something like *humanitas* – just pointing out the human in the midst of things – especially by defining the human realm in between the extremes of animal life and the gods. The anthropologist Paul Radin used to argue that the history of human civilization is largely the account of man's attempts to forget his transformation from an animal into a human being. Becoming a conscious being must have been a terrifying, traumatizing, wildly confusing experience. The step in between is dizzying. Probably the most important support human beings give one another to keep their balance at this dizzying height is to create another chasm, just as staggering, on the other side. Man is infinitely more than an animal and also infinitely less than a god. He walks the razor's edge in between – the narrow path, the high mountain road, the way. This is the first step in the mythology of the journey.

Another 'Axial' principle is the idea of suffering *as a story* – what happens to man along the way – the idea of suffering as theatre for the gods. The gods seem to love suffering – they are drawn to our plight – this means that our demise is something more than the death of an animal. A bit of light shines on us in our moment on the stage. The sages, too, appear to love suffering:

"The sages are drawn to the sickroom and the jail, they strike a match to bring some light, they cook rice and feed us, they bring medicine and doctor us, they show what *jen* (humaneness, human-heartedness, compassion) can do" (K'ang Yu Wei, *Universal Principles of Mankind /One World Philosophy*, 1902).

Suffering offers the sages an opportunity to think harder and discover something of value. The thing they offer – wisdom – is itself the fruit of suffering – suffering lies at the core of wisdom traditions.

The 'Axial' principle of wisdom is stated variously but always includes the 'transformation.' Suffering teaches us the meaning of life – suffering leads to happiness – God speaks to us in our suffering, he is teaching us, the evil we endure is overturned, it becomes good – we suffer, but the gain of it is wisdom – "pain that we cannot forget even in our sleep falls drop by drop on our heart and in our despair, against our will, wisdom comes to us" (Aeschylus). Learning from pain, teaching ourselves at the call of pain, we begin to see that *everything depends on us* – the important thing is to take responsibility for ourselves, to discover our own strength, but also to see its limit – to stay focused within our own world of concern, to find some peace about things that are out of our control – "happiness is a choice that requires effort at all times" (Aeschylus).

This is only a slight shift of emphasis, making some things less, and other things more important, but makes the huge difference of bringing 'big mind' (a framework that tries to capture the grandeur of the universe and the drama of existence itself) into 'little mind' (a framework that tries to hone in on everyday life and the comedy of human interaction) – bringing spirit to earth and metaphysics into ethics. Thus we keep the flame alive but also control the beast.

The idea of the *transformation* – the response to suffering by making a slight shift in emphasis, assuming responsibility, bringing a large frame of mind earthward, and making an explicit choice of happiness – is a theme in 'Axial' sources from China, India, Persia, Greece and Judea.

The existentialist thinker Albert Camus appears to restate this 'Axial' principle in our own epoch: "in the depth of winter, I finally learned that within me was an invincible summer."

It is presumptuous to claim to possess wisdom; it even seems a part of wisdom to disown wisdom; this is another important 'Axial' principle and is variously stated by Pythagoras ("I cannot call myself wise, but only a philosopher – someone in search of wisdom – since God alone is wise") and Solomon (Solomon may excel in wisdom, but even he must die and leave everything behind him; nothing brings him any peace but instead "All is vanity and a striving after wind" – "all is vanity and a vexation of spirit" – "what happens to the fool also happens to me; what then is my wisdom? Then I said in my heart, this also is vanity") and Confucius ("How dare I claim to be a sage or a benevolent man?—No one can say this and still tread the path"). Most famously, Socrates held this principle ("I know very well that I am not wise, even in the smallest degree").

The disowning of wisdom includes the idea of *weariness*, i.e. the idea that through enduring suffering, we outlast suffering, i.e. suffering burns itself out; desire burns itself out, because so much of it is frustrated; craving conquers craving through long acquaintance with bitterness. It makes sense to disown 'wisdom' both because we know so little and also because so many chances have to conspire to keep us alive long enough to see. The disowning wisdom also includes the idea that we become harder, stronger, deeper – we become more – by enduring hardship. This inward turn includes the idea of self-responsibility – of becoming our own refuge – the idea that we have to rely on ourselves to make the important change – standing up for ourselves but also not taking credit for it. Arguably, the principle of disowning wisdom is connected to the fact that for every victory over suffering, there are countless defeats; *because* so many chances have to conspire to support coming back against suffering with something like resilience, there is more truth in self-effacing wisdom than in self-assertion.

The 'Axial' principles are *humanitas*, suffering as story, as journey, as theater for a divine audience, the 'transformation' and explicit choice of happiness, and wisdom-disowning wisdom.

We are trying to discover some themes in the consideration of suffering that cut across culture – ideas that appear in many if not in all cultures – making a beginning in the 'Axial Age' and the important cultural changes that take place during it.

One theme in particular, emerging from the confrontation with suffering, seems to jump out from the study of cultural paradigms across the entire geographic area stretching between China and Europe. This is an idea that scholars refer to variously as 'doing for nothing,' 'selfless action,' 'intrinsic value' – the yoga, practice, way *for its own sake*, and not as a means.

A place to begin in developing this idea is the *Bhagavad Gita* – the 'Song of God,' 'Krishna's Song,' 'Song of the Divine One' (*Bhagavan*) – the heart of the Indian epic the *Mahabharata*, 'Great Tale of the Bhartas' (the origin of the ancient name of India, *Bharat*, or *Bharatavarsha*, King Bharata's Realm). By tradition the author of this work is the immortal scribe Vyasa.

By current opinion, the work dates from between the eighth and fifth century BCE.

The *Gita* recounts a conversation between the god, Krishna, and the hero, Arjuna, taking place on a battlefield just before the start of the Kurukshetra War, a conflict for Hindu society analogous to the Trojan War for the Greeks. The war pits the rival clans, the Pandavas and Kauravas, against one another. These are sibling clans, pitting relative against relative. Arjuna hesitates before rushing into the battle, debating with himself, not wishing to fail in his duty, but also not wanting to attack members of his own family. He peers over the battleline and sees his relatives facing him. Krishna appears at his side to advise him and steer his chariot. The god explains the *Nishkam Karma Yoga* ("the Yoga of Selfless Action") as the path to truth and answer to Arjuna's dilemma.

Arjuna hesitates because he cannot see the end of his action – he feels secure in his intention but is uncertain where his actions may lead – whether to victory or defeat, but also between moral right and wrong. He cannot see the later consequences of the simple things he is proposing to do right now. Krishna explains that "you have a right to action, but not to its fruits." The determinative principle for action should not be that it will have a certain effect, but instead that it is the right thing to do. This makes the difference between *doing for something* (in order to accomplish a purpose, or 'desiring action') and *doing for nothing* (duty for duty's sake – 'detached action' or 'mindful action'). Krishna concludes his discourse with the verses: "abandon attachment, with an even mind in success and failure" and "abandon the fruit of action and attain steady peace."

Krishna, the god, tells the human being, Arjuna, that human beings cannot know very much – and perhaps we need a god to tell us this. He says, whatever you are is created in the present in which you live it, and its later consequences, like every future, are uncertain. All you have is the present moment in which to perfect your practice (what you do, your action). Therefore: practice your aim, archer, and let your arrow fly.

The Confucian *Analects* conceive the similar idea of "knowing *ming*" (fate, destiny, decree, mandate), i.e., acting without regard to the results of one's actions – "always mindful of fate's capriciousness" – virtue in search of itself and taken as its own reward. "The Confucianists developed the idea of 'doing for nothing' from the idea of righteousness…to *know ming* means to acknowledge the inevitability of the world just as it exists, and so to disregard one's external success or failure" (Fung Yu Lan, *History of Chinese Philosophy*, 1948). Confucius was ridiculed in his own time as someone who knew that he could not possibly succeed, but who kept on trying anyway. Confucius answered this criticism by noting that the point of action is not whether your principle will prevail. Nothing external to moral compulsion is important. The point is simply to do what you ought to do, to do what is right (*Analects* XIV, 38, 41; XVIII, 7).

Interestingly, the same theme comes out in the counterpart tradition, Taoism, in the Taoist idea of *wu-wei*, "without action," or "having no action" – non-action – the idea of acting without artificiality or arbitrariness – variously translated with phrases such as "effortless action," "flowing action," "natural action" and "doing for nothing."

In some contexts this idea suggests "completed in the moment," in others "not over-doing" – hitting the mark – not too much or too little.

Sometimes it suggests simplicity, i.e. not to have too many desires or to know too much, thus to be like a child. Sometimes it means, "getting yourself out of it."

The Indian tale directs us to intention, the will, human purposes, and to giving up anxiety about the results of our choices – the Chinese sources intimate ideas about a finished or perfected quality in action itself, and the irrelevancies of everything that follows – both to putting away the future, both to creating 'mastered moments' in the present – to perfect practice.

This same idea appears in the *Gathas*, an ancient text written in the Avestan language and by tradition a composition of Zarathustra himself, dating from somewhere between 1200 and 900 BCE. The state of mind that enables a person to accomplish his duty is named *vohu manah* ("good purpose"); the ethical goals of Zoroastrianism are said to be "good thoughts, good words, good deeds." But it is not in man's power to see the consequences of what he does; this comes at the end of time, after the world-devouring Fire, which also brings an end to suffering (*Yasna* 33.14).

A further ancient source for this notion is *Ecclesiastes* 11:1, "Cast thy bread upon the waters," i.e., act despite the uncertainties of life. The satisfaction of work cannot be in its results (2:24). "He who observes the wind will not sow; and he who regards the clouds will not reap" (11:3-4). Man cannot wait for certainty if he is to live. Thus "remove vexation from your mind, and put away pain from your body" – i.e. choose happiness, bear your suffering and do what you can "while the almond tree blossoms" – act quickly "before the dust returns to the earth" (12:5-8).

Perhaps the clearest modern exposition of the idea of 'doing for nothing' is set down by Camus in his 1954 work *The Myth of Sisyphus*. Sisyphus is set an absurd task: ceaselessly rolling up a rock to the top of a hill, whence the stone would fall back of its own weight. But Camus imagines him satisfied, "saying yes," "superior to his fate," "stronger than his rock," with "no fate unsurmounted" by human creativity. He "takes over his fate," "making fate a human matter," "settling fate among men," "settling fate among the fated," settled in the human realm, struggling in the human realm, "the struggle itself toward the heights is enough to fill a man's heart." "One must imagine Sisyphus happy." (Or as he wrote in his unfinished novel *The First Man*: "Life, so vivid and mysterious, was enough to occupy his entire being").

One response to suffering is the 'transformation' (the choice of happiness). Another is the strategy of 'doing for nothing' (the restriction to intention). Both imply aspiring, struggling, effortfulness – but also limits, humility, awareness – in Camus' words "convinced of the wholly human origin of all that is human." He says that a person who reaches to the limit, but also knows his limits, "contemplates the series of unrelated actions which become a fate" – "created by him, combined under his memory's eye, and sealed by his death."

Camus said that he could not keep from being drawn to everyday life and "toward those, whoever they may be, who are humiliated and debased." "They need to hope" but still "that does not mean we should sacrifice our artist's nature to some or other social preaching." There are many dangers and we must accept them, but we must also reject bitterness. We have to be on guard not to let suffering unbalance us – becoming insensitive to pain or, oppositely, so intent on eradicating pain that we get caught up in a cause and lose ourselves. The main task for a human being is to be human, which is neither pure sensibility, nor pure advocacy, but something in between. "We must simultaneously serve suffering and beauty."

Modern Ideas

Einstein noted that if life is meaningless for us then we are not only unhappy but even unfit for life; because life requires us to be in the struggle and look for meaning. When we are fit for looking for it, we begin to find it; and if this is wisdom, then we should try to shape up and get fit to look for it. But there is a value higher than mere survival – we might as well call this *meaning* – that thing without which, or in the absence of which, being-reality-existence (the cosmos) becomes a lesser thing, gets reduced down, and simply becomes another sheer fact.

In his *Lecture on Ethics* Wittgenstein imagines a big book that contains all the facts in the world. He notes that this book would not contain anything like an ethical judgment. He mentions Hamlet's words, "Nothing is either good or bad, but thinking makes it so," to make the point that thinking, too, is just a fact like any other. Thinking is a process, i.e. thinking takes place. The upshot is, here is another fact. Thus the thing that is missing in the big book is *us* – the reality of human sensibility and advocacy – which argues that our humanness is *not* a fact. Likewise the whole thing, the big context, the cosmos, the big book of all the facts in the world suffers – it suffers without including *us*. It becomes a dead thing – a meaningless, blank fact.

The foundation is laid in the Axial Age, in the enormous change that calls up ideas about social cooperation, human dignity, and strength of character. *Suffering* is the issue – the theme of myth – we are struggling to find our place in the world. We are trying to figure out what we should do with human sensibility. We are wrestling with suffering and trying to figure out how to live with it.

What Einstein and Wittgenstein are getting at in the passages just cited is that human beings are dealers in meaning – meaning-makers – the idea that what human beings add to the fact of the case is meaning. This is also what the Buddha is getting at when he tells us that we must all be our own refuge – that each of us must make an island for himself – each of us has to take responsibility for our focus. Each of us tries to bring something we care about into being – to make it and preserve it – to see it through. As Nietzsche says: this is your work; be proud of it.

Heidegger, writing in his 1927 work *Being and Time*, claims that the phenomenon of anxiety plays a fundamental role in understanding human reality. The experience of anxiety returns a person from everyday familiarity with things to the uncanny reality that 'here I am,' here I am in face of my death, here I am with only myself to look to in order to make sense of what I am about. "A person caught up in the mood of anxiety experiences the present moment as a moment of vision that stands *at the ready*." Yet the fact that a person experiences this feeling does not mean that he will seize the moment, determine its meaning, and do the urgent thing he feels his life is about ("authenticity"). It is just as likely that he will run from it or sink back into everyday familiarity or find some other way to avoid facing himself ("inauthenticity"). Anxiety is a kind of guide, but not an infallible one. There is more than one way to wake up – many things can wake us up – many things can lull us back to sleep again. Heidegger arrives at the same conclusion that seems to emerge from thinking about the Oedipus story – the idea that there is no explanation for human strength greater than the decision to be strong. Heidegger came under a good deal of criticism on this topic – he was called a "decisionist" – and seemed to his critics to be following a course of reason laid down by the German legal scholar Carl Schmitt. Schmitt held that the *fact* that a decision is made (e.g. by a political or legal body), rather than the *content* of the decision (e.g. as upheld by a moral tradition), determines its validity. Schmitt became an important member of the National Socialist régime and offered his thesis as a justification for the atrocities it committed. This seemed to many scholars writing after the war years to represent a kind of practical refutation of the "decisionist" idea. There is a *higher* appeal than the appeal to mere fact – higher than the fact that I decide anything or that a party is in power – there is something to respect beyond peoples' decisions or government officials. Yet the debate also brought out the point that the validity of a moral idea counts for nothing unless it is freely granted by the moral agents themselves. This paradox is another way of stating Camus' idea. In all cases "we must simultaneously serve suffering and beauty."

Looking at another emotion – grief – it is easy to see that grief comes out of something like arrogance; that is, someone who is suffering and comes to grief is claiming the *rights* of his pain. He stands on his loss. His understanding may grow, or get to a point, or evolve towards something *more* than grief, or he may even surmount grief. This takes a person some ways towards humility. There is an understanding that comes from seizing on the idea that *we have no claim* on anything, that everything is given to us and also quickly taken away. This takes us beyond the moral calculus that everything occurs because we merit it or deserve it. Looking closer, we see that the agent is nothing or almost nothing. The agent is only a bit of strength; a bit of belief or faith. A person doesn't deserve anything, but if a person wins any victory over desire, clinging, or thirst by being more thankful than wanting, more resilient than needy, then he can claim that his efforts worked. He can take credit for the quiet that overcame the noise.

Another and probably a better way of putting this idea is that people who lead lives that are so full of suffering that it would be insane to expect them to respond with humility, quiet and thankfulness do nevertheless respond to great suffering with precisely these qualities.

Gloom is another kind of secreted belief in the right to something better: a glimpse of primordial meaning-making that the agent can actually take over and explicitly shape. Gloom takes over and shapes the meaning of things, although by itself gloom cannot count as much of a creation. Not being aware of the illegitimacy of making its complaint, emerging out of ignorance, refusing whatever is right there directly opposite, and falling into despair – drifting towards making an end of things – thus (paradoxically) giving up on the human project and meaning-making – gloom is nonetheless proof of the human sway over everything human. Abraham J. Heschel talks about the "delicate grace of existence" located at the *opposite* end of gloom; this is a place where, instead of arrogantly thinking about deserving anything, the agent offers a Stoic thanks, even in hard cases. Travelling from gloom to happiness shows an elegance that trumps suffering. Heschel's version of Camus' idea of serving both suffering *and* beauty – thankful even in hard cases, and going on with the human project despite all arguments against it – shows resilience, strength of character facing suffering, and more of the psychology of acceptance.

Not thinking about Suffering

The British thinker Iris Murdoch used to argue that talking about suffering is not an exercise in realism but more like a kind of escape. She held that Romanticism transformed the idea of death into the idea of suffering, because it could not sustain the stark honesty of the Enlightenment. The Age of Reason accepted the idea of death and urged man to make his stand in the transient moment he is given. This was its 'rational' solution and prototype of a brave spirit that achieves a kind of self-conscious poignancy by accepting human limits. Romantic thinkers sought to burst these limits and to defy death and thus began speaking about suffering on the model that purgatory wins back life – that is, by entertaining the idea of "a rather exciting kind of suffering," we try to rid ourselves of the fear of death – we can forget about death because the painful and exhilarating kind of suffering we will have to endure in the afterlife will burn our sins away and open us to eternity.

Murdoch claimed that talk about suffering is just another example of the "avaricious tentacles of the self." The humble man, who sees himself as nothing, makes no bones about suffering. "He sees the pointlessness of virtue and its unique value and the endless extent of its demand." He knows that he has to face real death and real transience and real chance. He sees that he just has to get on with trying to promote the good. If we accept death, then we accept our own nothingness, and thus we get going with what is *not* ourselves, which lies right in front of us. We try to do some good while we have the chance. Thus the attempt to promote the good is a kind of consequence of humility (*The Sovereignty of Good Over Other Concepts*, 1967).

Looking more broadly in history, the ideas of suffering and death tend to get linked together, rather than set in opposition. Some thinkers advise us to think on these dark subjects, whereas others counsel us to avoid them. Different schools of Buddhism divide over this issue (Theravada vs. Mahayana); different schools of psychology divide over the issue (existential vs. cognitive-behavioral); philosophers counsel us against thinking about death (Epicurus) and also for it (Heidegger).

Some thinkers try to make the case that we will live a fuller life if we remind ourselves that life is quickly coming to an end; this will help us savor the few moments we have and try to eke out of them our driving purpose. Others argue that we will live a fuller life if we look for the sun, rather than wander through shadows. Spinoza reasons for this conclusion, as follows:

"A free man thinks of death least among all things; and his wisdom is a meditation not of death but of life. *Proof*: A free man is one who lives under the guidance of reason, who is not led by fear, but who directly desires that which is good; in other words, who strives to act, to live, and to preserve his being on the basis of seeking his own true advantage; wherefore such a one thinks of nothing less than of death, but his wisdom is a meditation of life" (*Ethics*, IV, proposition LXVII).

Spinoza's argument counts on the power of *reason* as a guiding principle of action, so that the agent does not require (and would not benefit from) any external determinant, such as the consciousness of impending death (which for Spinoza equates to a kind a *fear*), to direct or support conduct. Spinoza is accounted a 'rationalist' thinker because he equates freedom with freedom from the passions – or, since that is strictly impossible in his system, freedom has to do with restraining and moderating the passions – on his understanding, we must reason the way forward, and we cannot scare ourselves, into happiness and virtue (but reason is also a kind of 'intellectual love,' so that we can describe the process as *love*; thus the big conclusion here is that love, not fear, points the way to virtue).

Oppositely, Heidegger argues that human reality comes into its own "in an impassioned freedom towards death." Death is the "possibility of the impossibility of any further existence." The state of anxiety brought on by the awareness that one is going to die represents a focus of personal energy unlike any other. "Anxiety in the face of death is anxiety in the face of the potentiality of being which is one's ownmost." In Heidegger's argument, this experience of anxiety is a spur to self-confrontation and a healthy engagement with life; when we fix on the impending "impossibility of any further existence" we project ourselves into the future with a powerful sense of purpose. Kierkegaard originated the argument that human beings have to make their way to freedom via the "intermediate determinant" of anxiety. They have to scare themselves into the good life, and cannot reason (or love) themselves into it.

Theravada and Mahayana Buddhists argue over the same question, whether awakening depends more on thought or feeling – on insight or compassion – on detachment from worldly things or sympathy with fellow creatures.

Should we *extinguish* desire, as Schopenhauer advises, or *exalt* it, as Nietzsche teaches? Should we try to abstract more and feel less, or abstract less and feel more?

This study began with the Buddha's idea that suffering is *the* central problem of thought. Nearing the end, we reach the opposite claim, that suffering is the least of our problems.

Returning to the Buddha

"What we are today comes from our thoughts of yesterday, and what we think now builds our life of tomorrow. Our life is the creation of our mind – our focus is our reality – everything we are is made of our thoughts."

These are the beginning lines of the *Dhammapada*, a Buddhist text from India in the third century BCE. By tradition, the *Dhammapada* is a collection of verses spoken by the Buddha himself. The term *Dhammapada* could be translated as 'the basic teaching.' An important theme in the book is that little things have big consequences. In time, a few drops of water fill a water-jar; in time, they become a raging flood. Both good and evil accumulate. There are many verses about *not hiding* – there is no safe hiding place – "not in the sky, not in the ocean, not in a mountain-cave, a man cannot run from life – he cannot free himself from the evil he has done – he cannot escape the power of death." Nor is there any one path that everyone can take – there is no one place where we can all come out from hiding and show ourselves.

Little things matter. Small changes matter. But things are complicated; there is no 'right way' for everyone. Also, we cannot control much; to lead with wishing, desiring many things, is to court suffering. The more so, because we cannot quite find our 'self' and because the 'world' shifts around endlessly. The book says: we can try to find stillness; we can try to make channels for water to flow; we can try to make our arrows straight; we can try to use straight timbers and be good carpenters; we can try to take and keep control of ourselves.

By the principle that *our focus is our reality*, whatever arises in the mind is also present to the individual as a choice – human reality is not shaped by accident but by choice – the *beginning* of what happens to us or a part of it is "fate," but this is *a kind of fate which we can take over* – we can become its authors – a process that the *Dhammapada* calls "reigning within."

Thus the mind is the place where impulses, moods, hopes and projects appear on the stage. Life-instants as we think and feel them show themselves as fragile and arbitrary constructions. Gradually we begin to see that *we* give them life. In themselves they are empty. Thus the mind is the place where we have a real chance to take hold of things. We can take ownership of meaning-making.

Thus what seems like necessity gradually weakens, fate becomes something one can choose, through the process of getting to know oneself – via introspection – which is said to be the beginning of *moksha* (release, freedom, happiness, fulfillment).

The thoughtpath of the *Dhammapada* seems adapted to the division of opinion about extinguishing or exalting desire, leading with insight or compassion, or making suffering the *most* or the *least* important among our thoughts, since it resists claiming any special absolute and also refuses to call out one way above all others as *the* path, *the* place to come out and show oneself – the true way or the right way or the way of ways. It appears to recognize that at the outset it appears that we are powerless and cannot come back against suffering but are simply its hapless victims.

But it argues that what at the beginning of the process looks to be an inexorable mechanism and a fate over which we have no power, is later at the end of a process something that we hold in our own hands and which is completely our own creation.

The text also offers some vocabulary to support the opposite ideas that a person takes ownership of meaning-making by an inward turn or (contrariwise) by turning outwards. Consider:

Mano-sancetan-ahara. This means something like "mental volition as nutrient." I think the idea is that by diving into ourselves and overcoming the patterns we are born into, we give ourselves strength and help ourselves to grow and be more; and the practice of trying to overcome and be more makes it easier to continue to overcome and be more; it becomes (as it were) a nutrient (perhaps 'vitamin'). There are patterns that will drive our life if we don't change them (as in Nietzsche's analysis of the human condition and what the "higher type of man" does to overcome this pre-existing script for his life). One way to help ourselves get over this script is through sheer will – the core idea in Stoicism, for example. You grow because you dig into yourself – you do this for yourself – making this effort strengthens something in us and emboldens the power of choice.

Phass-ahara. This means something like "contact of the internal sense-faculties with the external world as a nutrient." It's a parallel with the concept of volition-as-nutrient, but in this case the idea is that we take a step in overcoming our prior determination, and becoming our own meaning-author, not through will but through *experience* – via getting out into the world and allowing ourselves to feel all sorts of things. This idea addresses the power of experience to take a person out of himself and become a changed person. You grow because you get out into the world – first you take this step on your own – then the world does something to you.

The Search for Wisdom

The discussion has called up some ideas from history and brought them to the focus on suffering, including the *dukkha nirodha gamini patipada*, "the way leading to the cessation of suffering," but also "overcoming the will to live" and "asserting the will to power"; also the heroic ethic and the figure of the prophet; also *satyagraha*, "holding on to truth"; also 'Axial' principles, such as *humanitas*, choosing happiness, and doing for nothing; and 'Modern' terms, such as fact, meaning, meaning-refusing and meaning-making, contrasting anxiety, grief and gloom with grace.

The reflection about suffering offers up the idea that human prospect achieves its goal of fulfilling the meaning-potential of life situations by *disregarding* suffering, *defining* an ideal, *realizing* this ideal in concrete action, but also by *relinquishing* any claim to this achievement.

Relinquishing the claim to any special achievement makes it possible to stand against dogmatism and also keep faith with a perception of vastness – the idea that suffering is immeasurable – the idea that we never see everything relevant to the case. Humility makes us reject narrow thinking and also invites to see ourselves as part of something much larger than ourselves.

Further, we define the concept of 'the transformation' as pointing to a small change in emphasis. This is the simple and familiar idea that the same circumstance might be regarded many different ways, e.g. as an obstacle or as help; as a battlefield or a playground.

Lastly, we note that suffering may be the least or most important among our thoughts; we note that we give life to the thoughts stirring in us; that we make choices; that we "reign within" or abdicate this reign; that we make decisions and also change our minds in various ways.

Question: is it just talk? We are transcribing this-or-that vocabulary – this is how people speak, these are some ways that people have talked about suffering – but is any of this *wisdom*? Where can I say *I know* without any reservation? Answer: nowhere. My own argument has brought me to the conclusion that if I have gotten anywhere at all on this question, I will forego saying 'I know.' Paradoxically, there appears to be more wisdom in self-effacing wisdom than in self-asserting wisdom. At best we can follow Socrates and say: "I know very well that I am not wise, even in the smallest degree" (*Apology* 21 b4-5).

It is presumptuous to call any of the preceding *wisdom* (since it is part of wisdom to disown wisdom), but perhaps I can say that this is a thimble full of wisdom or, if not this, then perhaps there is suffering but still no wisdom – instead only the search for it.

A Thimble of Wisdom

When you dig into the problem of suffering and try to fill up a thimble full of wisdom about suffering, you begin to see a great many things, the ages begin to speak to you, every language, every culture, and in unison many voices say that everything in this thimble was put there by human beings. You see the human origin of everything human. And at length you see that without us, without human beings, there would be no suffering and the thimble would be empty. Something makes us try us to fill up the thimble and also to empty it – to see that we fill it up and we empty it – and there is a kind of peace in this.

Hope

"The future belongs to those who offer the next generation new reasons for hope."

Teilhard de Chardin

Philosophers have a good deal to say on the subject of hope. Some thinkers whose ideas are explored in this essay are Immanuel Kant, Karl Mannheim, Albert Camus and Ernst Bloch. The wisdom traditions of India and China offer many teachings about hope – so do the Abrahamic religions – so does Ancient Greece. The aim of this brief study is, first, to survey a few of these way-stations in the landscape of hope.

I am making the assumption that it does a person good to explore this subject – to wonder a bit about hope, to track something of its history – to make hope a companion of thought. I believe that I am a test case for this proposition. Perhaps these notes bear witness to the good effect of making a study of hope. However, if what I have to say is dull or of no use, that is surely no slight against hope.

The above quotation from Chardin suggests that discoveries in this field may play an important role in times to come. Coming at the problem from another direction – from the past rather than the future – the Russian thinker Nadezha Mandelstam makes the point that we have seen the triumph of evil over the values of humanism many times over. Our thinking about hope has often been too naïve. As she writes in her work *Hope Against Hope*, "I think now we may find a better foundation for our values, because of the lessons we have drawn from experience."

I cannot claim to have made any shocking discovery about hope or to have reached unheard of depths in my analysis. I think I have reached a clear view of the idea of hope. My intention is to try to see things clearly in order to make out the difference between true and false hope. Clear-sighted hope helps to lay out the path ahead and, as the theologian Jürgen Moltmann writes in his work *The Theology of Hope*, "to set everything in motion and keep it in a state of change."

Hope and Human Action

Regarding matters of fact, statements are either true or false, but hope never enters into the question. That is: the *fact* of a case is not altered by hoping. Hope does not move mountains.

Hope and hopelessness seem to apply to problems of *action* – e.g. where talk about hope offers guidelines for conduct – and in questions like these (also e.g. in questions of value), it makes sense to worry about whether recommendations lead to hopelessness or, on the contrary, whether they offer some hope, some help and a prospect of making an advance towards a desired end.

Thus at the outset we face the question: what is human action and how should we understand it? What is the right understanding of ethics or morality or value? What is the right way to think about what people want and what they do?

The Polish philosopher Leszek Kołakowski held that there is one man – and one only – with whom every thinker on this planet identifies, even if they reject all his ideas – and that man is Socrates. So let us begin with Socrates.

Socrates notices that young people jostle each other around a great deal and try to outdo and outshine each other. He tries to get them to change the terms of the game. He suggests the idea of striving towards *arete* (virtue, excellence, human flourishing) rather than striving for public acclaim. He translates this idea as follows: we can make an ideal powerful simply by holding it out in front of ourselves and by trying to reach it.

Hegel makes an important contribution to this line of thinking. He takes a new perspective on society, on economic competition and jostling for position. He decides to take a look at human labor, human work, what people actually do and how they earn a living. He notices that every society and every organization in society seems to demonstrate the same *principle of hierarchy*, a principle of domination and submission, which he calls "the principle of master and slave." He thinks that this circumstance gives us a kind of measuring stick for progress – progress happens when the individual is less determined by the Other and more determined by himself – when he is less determined by mere power and violence and necessity and more determined by reason and discussion and choice.

Freud makes an important contribution to the same line of thinking. He takes a new look at society, at competition and striving for supremacy, by taking a look at the germ of society in its root form in the family system. He tries to describe the conflict between regressive and progressive forces in an even more primitive economy than the one that Hegel studied – i.e. not in the market economy, but in the love economy – the mental economy. He thinks that he can find a still more fundamental measuring stick for progress buried in human history and, especially, in personal history. Progress occurs when the individual gets himself *out of the position of fantasy* and wish-fulfillment (trying to escape the problems of the world by jumping into the dream-world). Progress occurs when the individual gets himself *into the position of realism*, maturity, seeing things they way they really are, making real changes (trying to deal with the problems of the world by jumping into the real world). He claims that we can measure human progress by the indices of facing and working on real problems, by effort and trying to become masterful in some arena of human experience – by "effective action." It doesn't matter if the result is limited – even if the drama occurs in a tiny space – even if we pass our lifetimes in a very small, temporary, and 'merely personal' space – what matters is *work*.

My conclusion – trying to learn from Socrates, Hegel and Freud – the upshot of my studies and what I will call the 'right understanding' of human action, value, and aspiration – is that *my own intention to hold myself responsible for my conduct is a powerful influence on that conduct.*

That is, in declaring myself to be morally responsible, I am not offering a psychological hypothesis – I am not offering a scientific theory or a philosophy of action. I am taking or making myself responsible by my own decision – by my intention, my project, by my pledge of loyalty. I make it true by being true to it.

This is what I am calling the *right understanding* of human conduct. The idea is that a person defines himself or herself by his or her project, into which he or she puts his or her energy and which he or she tries to realize. The idea is to take a prospective view, not worrying about what has happened, about the past, but focusing instead on the future and what is possible. A name for this idea is *hope*.

Greek Stories about Hope

Starting from more ancient premises – e.g. investigating the concept of hope as it comes out in the Ancient Greek story of Pandora – thereby trying to think about hope in the vocabulary of a far less hopeful time, offers some reality-testing and helpful skepticism. The point of this investigation is to rescue genuine hope from blind hope. In truth, some hopes are false hopes, whereas others ring true. The body of knowledge encoded as Greek mythology helps to sort this out.

Zeus, angry that Prometheus has stolen fire – disobeying the gods and benefiting men – decides to even the scales. He creates a lovely creature, Pandora, as foolish and mischievous as she is beautiful and desirable. Prometheus's brother, Epimetheus, woos her and wins her in marriage; as a wedding gift Zeus offers her a brightly colored box but also warns her never to open it. But (of course) immediately she opens the box – and at once every kind of horror floods out of the box – every evil that plagues mankind including bitterness, envy, disease, ignorance, deception, corruption, hunger, war, poverty, cruelty, hard labor, old age – even death. And, according to the ancient story, the last evil, the worst evil, the cruelest fate to crawl out of Pandora's box, after everything has spilled out including death, is *hope*.

Forethinker (in Greek, *prometheus*) makes a stride forward but Afterthinker (*epimetheus*) is easily led astray. The wedding gift is said to be a "beautiful evil" (*kalon kakon*), also a gift to lady Allgifts (*doran to pandoran*) – something like bringing coal to Newcastle – where the last to escape is Hope (*Elpis*).

Hope's parents are Night (*Nyx*) and Rumor (*Pheme*) – images of darkness and uncertainty – lady Hope is portrayed as a young woman, carrying flowers or a goat's horn overflowing with fruit (*cornucopia*). Her Roman equivalent is *Spes* – lady hope, lady expectation – *speranza*, *espoir*, *esperanza*.

By another account, Pandora is said to be the first *woman* in Greek myth; Zeus equates Fire with Woman; Woman is the lovely mischievous creature who makes men hope.

By another account, Pandora is the child of *Eris* – strife – which if eternal nonetheless gives birth to Hope, bright virgin holding a fresh flower, who always sees the bright side; her breast is a comfort, however bleak life becomes.

By another account, when all evils save one flew out from Pandora's box, mankind was filled with despair – *dis-espere*, hopelessness – and was near resignation to death – but then hope meekly crawls into the light; hope is there to balance all the evils of life; hope the equal of them all. On this account, hope is not a danger, a monster or an evil, but instead hope is the great rescue and release from evil.

By another account, overcome by all the Spites that escaped into the world, Man and Woman fell into despair and were on point of suicide, but then, a soothing, kind, delusive creature called Hope reached into their minds and tempted them with more life and new expectations.

Stepping back: these ancient stories portray hope as a kind of blindness or insanity, helpful or hurtful, a bulwark against pain or itself the deepest pain, the stupidity of clutching onto the vanishing future, the genius of disregarding the present and stepping forward – beautiful, pure, comforting, giving, rescuing; evil, tainted, lying, callous, damning.

The pessimism in this thinking is epitomized in the Delphic motto: *know yourself*; know what you are; know that you are dust; know that you are nothing; know that you will die. Ancient Greek misanthropy sees and accepts the elemental character of human striving, the 'reaching' character in the human constitution, but accounts it as nothing, countering with the claim that if we really see our own character and make a fair estimate of our estate, we will despise ourselves as nothing.

This ancients' wisdom, sometimes called Silenus' wisdom, named after the companion and tutor of the wine-god Dionysus, is that "the best for man is never to have been born." "Next best is to die quickly." Striving never arrives at its goal. The sooner the delusion of life is cut short and ended, the better.

Thus the 'gift' of hope and leaning forward into the future is accounted a monstrosity and dark fate – the human condition is the Sisyphus condition – delusion, followed by meaningless repetition, followed by death.

In more recent times, Camus rethought the Sisyphus condition and derived a solution very unlike the pessimism taught in these ancient stories. Camus' rejects the cynicism that *nothing matters* and that nothing we do means anything. He teaches the contrary idea that *striving is enough* and that struggle is its own fulfillment. "The struggle itself is enough to fill a man's heart." Hope, according to Camus' account, is its own completion; hope is its own reward. Hope in his conception is *doing for nothing* – i.e., simply doing, without any thought of a future – thus fulfillment in intention, commitment free of expectation, without any calculation of results.

The existentialist perspective on hope appears to have confronted the cynical idea that hope is a kind of delusion – a fantasy that lulls a person into a comforting sleep. Hope like this does a person no good and must be rejected (unless we are cowards). But the existentialist has also taken something from the ancient story to the effect that hope is a kind of superpower. We can think of hope as a kind of heroism that stands alone and is the match of any foe. This kind of hope is however like Sisyphus' hope, which is sufficient in itself, but has no opening to impact the world. Radical skepticism and superhuman autonomy are perhaps opposite terms in a continuum, into which hope falls somewhere in the middle.

Hope and Despair

Subjectively there is some truth in the idea that the tone of human experience swings between extremes of hope and despair. On this account, human sensibility shifts between poles of a basic opposition – optimism and pessimism, affirmation and negation, Yes and No – so that the picture is complete when we describe human experience as a kind of bipolar condition, disassociation or schizophrenia.

Hope on this account is half of the fated couple: Black and White, Empty and Full, Yes and No.

Misanthropy reaches a kind of summit in the Pandora story, but at the same time there is a kind of heroic ethic buried in the story, in that Elpis is the equal of all the powers of despair. Elpis gentle, small and last is enough to hold back the night – which seems a victory for the human scale and a terrific confidence – hope the equal of so many gargantuan and implacable forces.

The Christian principle of justification by faith breaks out of this dualism in an interesting way. The ancient teaching is that Sinful Man is made acceptable to Holy God by Mysterious Grace. The sinner is declared just in the sight of God, *merely by the act of believing* and living on. This principle is implicit in Catholicism (justification by works – the believer rescued in an act of contrition) and explicit in Protestantism (justification by faith – the believer rescued by belief itself).

The theology of hope in ancient times, especially in the Hellenistic age, was centered around the idea that the soul strives for eternity, aspiring to a position outside the flow of time.

Among modern writers, e.g., in Kierkegaard or in works such as Moltmann's *The Theology of Hope* (1962) and *The Experiment of Hope* (1975), the idea has to do with flourishing in "the fullness of time" rather than escaping time altogether. Hope on either principle is conceived as a triumph over change – over time itself – in a final culmination or completion. Hope is the eschatological equivalent of the transition from belief to knowledge, darkness to light, sin to grace.

Hope in a Christian context is given the interpretation of justification by faith. There are similar principles in the other Abrahamic traditions – in stories from Judaism and Islam – e.g. in the story of Job; Job believes and waits for God's answer; and also e.g. in the Sufi way: "Stain your prayer rug with wine / Yes you will fail but you are accepted / Blessed be His name" (Rumi).

These strains of thinking in Abrahamic traditions support the idea that *hope is superior to despair* (to hopelessness). Hope is not merely an equal and opposite counterpart to despair, on the model that *good* is an equal and opposite counterpart to *evil*, e.g. in dualism such as Zarathustra preaches. Instead, hope is greater than despair, just as expectation (waiting for something) is superior to indifference (just blankly passing time); on the model that positive freedom or ecstatic freedom (following an inner impulse with absolute conviction) is superior to negative freedom or mere freedom (the lack of impediments).

Subjectively, hope is half of the fated couple: Yes and No. But in teachings from around the world and in many periods of history, thinkers have thrown up the opposite idea – hope superior to despair.

Hope as Magic

Following another course of thinking: consider the idea that hope may not be the *name* of anything, but instead an incantation. Hope is a magic spell or magic word or magic rite. That is, the meaning of hope comes out in what hope *does* or by what is *done* in its name. Saying 'abracadabra' opens the secret gates; the magician says 'abracadabra' and pulls a rabbit out of a hat; an amulet with the word 'abracadabra' wards off fevers and disease.

Perhaps the meaning of the concept *hope* comes out in the ways in which this concept is enacted. Thus 'hope' may be defined recursively as 'the right of appeal in the name of 'hope.''

Hope on this understanding is self-defined, self-directed, self-constructed, self-fulfilling (hope is shorthand for the idea of self-responsibility: *my intention to hold myself responsible for X wields great power over X)*. Hope is a kind of supercompetence that is always able to come back from harm with self-responsible activism.

Hope on this understanding is a commitment to action; a search ahead; a leap of faith; a jump into the future. Hope is simple courage and no guarantees. To have hope is to go on, to have no final stage, to have no end.

Hope pursues an ideal goal that cannot be defined in advance in any other way than as the *limit* on which the potentially infinite process of hoping converges.

By one metaphor, the sought-for, hoped-for ideal is already in existence somewhere, so that the fulfillment of hope seems more like a discovery than an invention; by another metaphor, every renewal of hope refashions the ideal of hope; by another, hope seeks itself (or hope preserves itself) through the medium of human expectations. Perhaps 'progress' is a metaphor, or the significance of advancing towards a goal; there is also the metaphor of *always trying to return back to the beginning*; or of the sun rising up behind the clouds; hope is a wellspring or a gentle breast or a song or a heartbeat.

These are images or metaphors or messengers of hope, a small sample from a potential infinity: magic spells, incantations, invocations, enchantments in which or with which or under which we take this step; where potentially anything or any circumstance can take on or convey the meaning of hope. This is, roughly, *an open construction* – a positive, confident step forward – making the pledge and going on.

Subjectively – just as much as we see the polarity of hope and despair – interior experience also supports the constant of human striving, impulse, love, desire, care, longing, going on...

The objective counterpart of endless striving is the endless falling apart of being into the moments of time.

Thus in brief and for the whole: the sensory apparatus is aroused continually, the intellect must order continually, and the heart must strive continually.

The import of hope comes out in the word 'continually' – hope understood as magic equates to *persistence* – going on, without seeing the end, without knowing. Pope, *Essay On Man*, Epistle 1: "Hope springs eternal in the human breast: / Man never is, but always to be blest: / The soul, uneasy and confined from home, / Rests and expatiates in a life to come."

Hope often Stumbles

Hope (thus far) is the positive construction, the bright side, opening outwards rather than closing inwards – uncaused, unmotivated, unfounded – the upsurge of life against lifelessness – inexplicable or its own explanation, unrewarded or its own reward, meaningless or its own meaning. Since it has no foundation but is 'baseless hope,' hope lives in the dark; hope is a free step in empty space. No wonder that it stumbles around so much.

Consider Hope the Pollyanna. Hope is sometimes the dupe, the fool, poor innocent, the victim; hope with the wool pulled over his eyes, ingenuous hope, hope laid low – artless, naïve hope. Hope can become Pollyannaish – derogatory for a kind of cheerful blindness; hope can be insistently optimistic without a reason, or gleefully optimistic even when given cause not to be. The analysis of hope must fail if we refuse to look at blind hope.

If we think about hope in terms of its object – what hope hopes *for* – then hope is allegiance to the cause, advocacy, commitment; but every 'good' cause may become a 'mere' cause; as everything we care about may in time show itself in a different light and disappoint us, be less than we hoped.

The fact that hope can be dashed is not an argument against hope but a part of its definition; hoping is not hoping if the hoped-for outcome is already certain. Hope hopes for and against uncertainties – hope assesses chances and is therefore an appreciation of reality. Thus we cannot aim hope at the past, and hope lives (as it were) in the objective world of fact. I can wish for anything, but I cannot hope for the impossible. Hope is constrained by the limits of human will. Hope often stumbles – this is a good start at a definition of human willing, human being.

Hope like will may outlive itself – hope may outlive its temporary resting-places and forms – the quality of hope may outlive the episodes of hope – hope can become a history, or many histories, hope that has suffered, hope that has flourished, hope that meets the unhoped-for.

Hope therefore is not vain when it is deceived; hope becomes vain when it ceases to hope; hope is fruitful as long as it outlives itself in new hopes; hope is hope so long as there is no last hope.

Moral Hope

Kant calls his work *Perpetual Peace* an exercise in "moral hope." "We may expect Providence to produce the circumstances required for peace." We may *expect* – although we cannot *know* – if we can find it in ourselves, we can take the step of making the *choice* to hope. This will be the free choice to believe that what we hope for is still possible – the choice to go on – the choice to take up a positive construction. Kant thinks that this choice makes practical sense and can even be said to be the result of *rational* reflection. Hope is the result of philosophical inquiry.

Kant argues that hope is rational on the ground that most of our impulses draw us into moral error, but we have a great many of them; we have so many that our impulses act upon each other. "It is precisely because these propensities counteract one another that reason is given free play to subdue them; and the reign of hope, once it is present, is self-maintaining."

What does this mean – "The reign of hope, once it is present, is self-maintaining"? – I think that this is a way of saying that hope allows hope to hope; hope is a kind of self-constructing performance; hope is permission to hope and hope obeys its own law, at least in this measure. Hope assesses chances, appreciates reality, is constrained by physical limits, but its persistent character, its loyalty to the cause (until this is dashed), somehow trumps natural necessity.

Kant argues that there would never be any chance for peace if natural necessity were all we had to rely on; we cannot achieve peace by any calculation. But natural necessity "comes to the aid" of moral hope in the variety, and subsequent conflict, of the most powerful forces in our lives – human desires. Conflict among these "forces of nature" (i.e., the natural forces that express themselves as our impulses) makes an opening for moral will. Thus hope lives in a medium in which emotion is at a standstill; hope has its roots in instinctual conflict, which produces a kind of numbness and a moment of quiet. This quiet is like a void that reason fills with hope.

Kant says that this hopeful kind of thinking is also a modest kind of thinking that does not claim to know. But (he notes) this is a strange kind of modesty that is also a towering pride. There is a standard in the human heart. The moral law is inscribed in us, in our hearts, in our being – we *know* some moral truths, we know what is right – and this standard would still be valid even if all our hopes should fail (*fiat justitia, ruat coelum* – "let justice be done, though the heavens fall").

Kant is arguing that there are high principles, set apart somewhere, that always live on and are valid, whatever the course of events. But he also argues that a kind of opposite principle is also at work, according to which the principle of reason (which should and must rule) is given the chance to rule (as it were, to be itself) by accident. That is, "the forces of nature" in the form of human impulses get pitted against one another, and cancel each other out; the balance of these irrational forces is what makes it possible for reason to enter the game and conjure up hope.

"Kant teaches us to live by, and to act upon, opportunities which may founder in life. The situation and the task of man is to live with the possibility of total failure in the world – to be ready for this failure, but at the same time, despite it, to build, and to keep moving towards a goal, on the strength of human rights that grow bright in the pursuit of philosophy. This is a way of thinking that knows by not knowing. It can guide us, but cannot calculate from a principle what is to be done. ... The aristocratic freedom of reason cannot stand aloof from the world, cannot set itself up as a cold and distant standard and cannot pose as a sage who teaches merely to judge; its purpose is *to enable us to enter the world* with clear sight and clear will – its purpose is to help us act" (Karl Jaspers, *Kant's Perpetual Peace*).

Finding and Losing Hope

To understand is to compare. I compare hope to courage, to doubt, to love, to hallucination. Hope is an angel, a breast, a monster, a sickness, a magic word, a recursive algorithm. Hope is right understanding. Hope is a pledge to the world and a word of encouragement to oneself – as applying to action, as choice, as leaning into the future, as a positive number – relevant to an end, promoting an end – or as having no end, being endless or unending; hope that springs eternal. Hope is perhaps too many things, a contradiction or even several contradictions.

What is there to say? – if you are going to hope, then go ahead, but don't expect to discover any great truth about it – hope or don't hope, it's up to you – sing or cry, do whatever you like.

I think there is something to say about hope. There is something to be right or wrong about. The point of talking about hope is to see an important (though likely obvious) truth: that my intention to hold myself responsible *makes* me responsible; that I am what I hold myself to. This is the idea that there is nothing more important, more fundamental, older, deeper, or higher than human beings. The main thing is human decision, human action, the human scale, the human take on things, human nature rather than capricious or indifferent forces crashing into each other.

If there is any value anywhere in the world, it is because human beings feel and grasp this value and uphold it by their own efforts. Thus we have to be our own defense against stupidity and cruelty, and cannot count on magic to fulfill our hopes. Ultimately we have to be our own defense even against ourselves; for the truth (as Solzhenitsyn expressed it) is that "the dividing line between good and evil cuts through the heart of every human being."

My intention to hope, to *wish forward* into the future with hope, with a positive number, laughing rather than crying, is merely that, i.e. *my intention*. The truth that comes out here is the human truth, that there are no final truths, that there are only temporary truths, only relative truths. Everything we cherish must be tested and proven over and over again. The human truth appears to be that there is no foundation but what you make. The deep thing, the underlying truth, the thing you can count on, is *yourself*; the deep thing is as deep as you can make it. This fragile, changeable, vanishing thing that is our strength – what we call *will* or *heart* or *courage* – has to be its own basis. It is exactly what it wills itself to be.

Thus it doesn't make much sense to talk about hope and look at it and try to see into it or discover its secrets. It's empty, there's nothing there, every one of us has to fill it ourselves. It's what we make it. There is nothing more fundamental than human purposes and human efforts and human actions: the things we do, their consequences and (after falling down and losing the track) picking things up again and going on.

Thus the truth about hope truth is that I have to rely on myself. If I'm hopeless, then I have only myself to blame; if I'm hopeful, it's only because I'm standing on my own two feet. I have to be my own hope, my best hope and last hope. Without hope, I have nowhere to go to look for it. There is nowhere I can go, and no one can stand in my place; no one can give me hope or take it away; I have to begin it and keep it; and when I lose hope, I must find it again on my own.

Ancient and Modern Hope

Wrestling with this conclusion for a while, I saw that it had to be wrong – wildly wrong – since the whole point of hope is that you *don't* rely on yourself – hope does not rely on anything.

Hope cannot be understood as a philosophy of renunciation, of self-reliance or self-sufficiency. Hope has a kind of innocence, whereas stoicism is a worldly outlook and comes out of experiences of suffering. Self-denial and self-command are not the kind of things people associate with hope. Hope is not a philosophy of the will. Hope does not appear to spring from depths of self-examination, but from good will, openness, trust, faith. Unaccountably, hope takes up a positive construction – *not* protecting or fortifying the self with principles or convictions or powers – not defending but welcoming.

Modern people often praise the hopeful person for going positive, for his welcoming gesture, crediting him with confidence, optimism, courage, and counting hope a strength, a virtue, a bit of progress towards an ideal. Among the ancients there is good consensus that hope is admirable *only when it has been tried and found true.* On this latter account, the hopeful person *sometimes* earns our admiration, first taking account of basic truths, especially on the condition that the hopeful person has suffered. Innocent hope is enviable but not admirable.

The modern argument turns on the idea that people who see things as 'half full' and who generally take a positive outlook are demonstrating an important strength of character – and since it is so easy to do the opposite, we can and do credit them with making this choice.

The ancient argument turns on the different idea that we should never claim credit for something that is not in our power. For them, real hope is hope that seems like courage and earns our praise, on the understanding that there is nothing to praise in mere fantasy or in denying an obvious reality; they held that there is no value in illusion or wishful thinking that runs away from pain and hard reality. Hope that seems like courage (real hope and not blind hope) is praised by the ancients as great-heartedness in face of *nemesis* (courage in facing Olympian power leveled against human arrogance). They considered this kind of courage rare.

Ancient hope and modern hope appear to be two very different phenomena. Yet both involve choice – in the modern sense, because hope is a free act chosen despite the opportunity to 'go negative'; in the ancient sense, because hope is a free act chosen despite the precedent of suffering.

Thus the paradox: hope is not a philosophy of the will; hope is a welcoming gesture rather than an act of self-preservation; hope leaps from the self undefended and joins the world; nonetheless, hope counts for nothing in its first innocence, before the actor has experienced defeat. Hope that earns our praise is awake to suffering or may even be a response to suffering.

The paradox is that hope is not an effort of will, but at the same time hope is an explicit choice.

The Axial Age thinkers direct us to this paradox – in the *Bhagavad-Gita*, to the "Nishkam Karma Yoga" (the Yoga of Selfless Action); in the Confucian *Analects,* to "knowing *ming*" (to act for virtue and entrust the results of action to fate); in the *Tao Te Ching* (Book of the Way and the Power), to the concept of *wu-wei* (acting without artificiality or arbitrariness) – a kind of emptying of the self that is (simultaneosuly) an ethical commitment and program for action.

Self-sufficiency, selflessness, emptiness, transcending worry, inner quiet and simplicity, not willing but (at the same time) choosing, making a commitment to a cherished value, acting: these are different formulations for the pardoxical conception of hope we are examining. Research finds this idea in the East and in the West. It is a theme in recent philosophy, both in existentialist writings and analytic philosophy. This is a new hope and also a very old one.

The Projective Character of Hope

Hope seems to lean into the future with a definite project and thereby seems more like *action* than standing still. 'Doing for nothing' is therefore not simply 'doing nothing' but expressly does *work*. Hope accomplishes a peculiar kind of work, even if this is difficult to pin down.

The theologian Jürgen Moltmann denies that hope is "merely a transfiguring glow superimposed upon a greyed existence" or any merely epiphenomenal ornament to finished reality. He argues that hopes are "real perceptions at the horizon of real possibility." However, this perspective forces him to distinguish between *kinds* of hope. Moltmann does not distinguish between true hope and false hope but instead between practical hope and naïve hope – hope that works towards some real option and hope that escapes into a pleasing fantasy. This distinction is somewhat a strain on his argument, in that the central idea with which his work is concerned is the hope of life after death. Moltmann picks up the ancient theme that innocent hope is enviable but not admirable, and he reasons that hope that has suffered no loss is still naïve whereas hope that knows reverses is hope adapted to reality. Thus the distinction between fantasy and practicality. As it were: Moltmann is arguing that hope's work sifts through fantasies and real options and, culling mere dream from practical truth, sets its sights on the practical outcomes. This is an interesting argument and merits thinking about. But it does not capture the Axial principle that hope is *doing for nothing*; that is, it does not capture the idea that hope is a positive focus – a commitment to action – unconcerned with consequences. Hope does seem adapted to reality – it cannot look at the past; it assesses chances; it cannot set itself on the impossible – I can *wish* that I had wings and could fly, but I cannot hope for this. Moltmann I think has tailored hope to fit his wish for a Christian afterlife. But at least part of his argument is correct. Hope is not merely a transfiguring glow. Hopes are perceptions. Hope does work – the question is, what kind.

Camus' hope was welcomed in its time as a candle in darkness and a word of encouragement. But in the present state of things, talking about the power of hope seems an unlikely theme. It is a campaign theme, already tarnished some, and makes us wonder whether we are being taken in. It may make more sense to talk about the weakness of hope – the stupidity of hope, the stupidity of trust, the stupidity of faith, the laughable way in which people are taken in by charisma, the damage wrought by fear of authority and uncritical acceptance, the complacency that leads fools into darkness. Hope is too easily simply a slogan. The dire situation of worldwide suffering calls for skepticism, for careful analysis, for an explicit 'doing for something', not simply trusting or believing or hoping for results, but *demanding* them.

In the present state of things, hope may look more like a distraction than an incitement to action. Recent experience shows what hope looks like as an agent of control or as a ploy to silence dissent. Hope sometimes seems a fool's errand and a useful tool for tyrants.

However: Moltmann is right; hope is not simply a useless fantasy; hope expressly does work; the fact that tyrants try to use hope is very direct proof of its power. Hoping, expecting, waiting for something, getting ready for something, summoning up all the psychic power we can muster to lead forward – this is work. I think Moltmann is right also that hope is a perception of the possible. That is, hope is an appreciation of reality, but especially of that part of reality which is possible; since part of reality is what is possible (and everything that is impossible is unreal).

The work of hope is directed to, focused on, zeroing in on the future – on something that is still possible, but not yet actual. Hope acts on the future, changes the future. *Expecting* changes the future, as surely as not caring about anything changes the future. We can also see this in psychological states such as anxiety and boredom, both of which act upon the future, change the future, lay out the future in characteristic ways. Hope and despair are change-agents.

There may be a neuroanatomical variability of hope; or a hope gene; or a peculiar brain chemistry, or serotonin recipe for hope; or hope may depend on conditions with a different kind of contingent status, e.g. as in Kant's discussion about the psychological standstill that leaves an opening for hope. There may a related point in the hypothesis that the conditions that render human cognition hopeful (native hope, native optimism, intuitive confidence) also dispose it to systematic error (overconfidence that has to be burned away through recalcitrant experience). Thus hope rises in youth and falls in old age; or hope rises with good luck and falls with bad.

According to this kind of analysis, the optimistic mind will become the pessimistic mind by a kind of natural development. We swing from one extreme to another, without any power to change the terms of our lives. This result directs the argument back to the fated couple: Yes and No – also to attempts to break free. If this is right, hope may be a change-agent, but it isn't chosen.

Do I choose to hope? Or am I hopeful simply by chance? We are trying to examine hope and look into its etiology – its cause, its origination, the reason for it, why it occurs – and it does seem clear that hope stands on many sorts of contingencies; e.g., hope often varies with age.

As a way of getting at this question, we look again at the two forms of hope that appear in every literature about hope – rookie hope and veteran hope – also the two judgments that go with them: that hope is a pretty little flower; and that hope is the very breath of life. Thus hope is not a virtue without further qualification. We shouldn't praise people simply for being hopeful; we may even pity them or merely count them lucky; pity them for the idiocy of still hoping or count them lucky for never having had their hopes ripped apart. But oppositely a person who has given up on hope – discouraged, despairing – seems to be actively undermining his own will. The important thing is to see that the hopeful perspective jumps out of the present with a kind of counterfactual conviction – a counterfactual claim that, despite everything that has happened up to now, the future will be X – and in every case the question is, *what kind of claim are we making?* – is this innocent hope still untested? – or is this greathearted hope, phoenix hope, hope that has suffered? Answering this question helps us sort out the difference between silliness and resolve, fanaticism and reason, psychosis and sanity. It also shows the difference between random emotions and the choice to determine for oneself what one's outlook will be.

The Axial principle of hope, and Camus' approach, which is 'hoping for nothing,' that is, breaking free of the cycle of mania and depression and unaccountably *taking* up *a positive perspective* – is an explicitly considered, chosen and owned perspective, taken up in the face of its alternative. This is something like strength to continue, being chastened but not despairing, facing sorrow and coming back against it. This attitude surmounts the merely existent. It projects forward into the future. But at the same time the hopeful person is still right here in the present.

Imagine that you are swimming in a kind of alphabet soup or walking over a landscape of symbols and icons, struggling to make your way and gain some understanding of your experience. Camus advises us that the struggle is reason enough, is *sufficient to itself*, even if you never decipher what is going on around you or accomplish anything at all. All your effort is taken up in the struggle. Camus' hope – 'existential' hope – seems therefore like a grim hope and, to many observers, cannot really count as *hope* at all. But if we examine existential hope we soon discover Arjuna's hope and Confucius' hope and Zeno's hope. It is a vision of being lifted up by the quality of one's own thinking, without regard to the worldly fate of one's cause.

Wrestling with the idea of self-sufficient hope for a while, I saw that it had to be wrong, because hope is undefended. Hope is not a hardened willing or impassiveness or indifference to pleasure and pan. Yet I came back to the idea of self-sufficient hope and even found it confirmed in the literature and wisdom traditions of many cultures. I saw hope become a political weapon, I saw that my epoch of history is out of joint for hope, but I came back to hope anyway. I saw that even if I have to do *much more than hope*, I have to hope too. My hope cannot be innocent and blind. It must be chastened and perceptive. In a word: my hope will be worth as much as I am, no more and no less, since it is exactly *my* intention come alive.

Karl Mannheim, writing in Weimar days, heir to the disaster of WWI and awake to the threat of WWII, defined "the present situation of thought" in terms of hope, hope especially in the sense of bright ideals just escaping our reach. Mannheim was alive to many problems about hope such as appear in this essay: thinking about the work it does, whether it is a distraction, whether it jumps up by accident, whether it is merely one mood among others, whether it is innocent or experienced, blind or perceptive, and how much work we have to do in order to keep it alive. As an historian, Mannheim was wary about ideals, and he worried about the power of hope as an agent of control. But as a philosopher, Mannheim saw ideals at the core of everything human, and he set himself the task of understanding how they operate. Some of his principles are: that those who proclaim an absolute also tend to assert their superiority over everyone else; that the absolute is a spur towards the future, but also becomes a tool for lording over the present; that sobriety makes us skeptics of ideals, yet without ideals we would quickly devolve into lesser beings.

"The complete elimination of reality-transcending elements from the human world equates to a kind of 'matter-of-fact' mentality which ultimately leads to the decay of the will. ... The disappearance of utopia brings about a static state of affairs in which man himself becomes no more than a thing. Left without any ideals, man becomes a creature of impulses."

The main argument of Mannheim's work *Ideology and Utopia* leads to the thesis that the hopeful, projective, future-oriented character of thinking underlies the human capacity to shape history, but (even more) the capacity to *understand* it. Mannheim contrasts the 'matter-of-fact' mentality that registers phenomena with the 'utopian' mentality that connects phenomena. Mind as he describes it draws incoming messages into a vast network of precedents, alternatives, analogies, potentialities, tests and stories and lines of argument. *Registering* phenomena in the sensorium of consciousness is a step in the process – a subroutine from a vastly more complex system. The telling characteristic of this system is projective connectivity.

Mannheim is looking at the mind as a collection of functions – motivation, sociality, cognition. The motivational system sweeps the environment as the agent of for impulse, emotion, affect. Affect programs include 'surprise' and 'fear' – reactions human beings share with reptiles – as well as 'guilt' and 'grief,' which may be unique to human beings. Like echolocation or an active sonar device, we send out bursts of affect to test the environment, trying to fine-tune and speed up basic decisions such as fight or flight. We make our way through an environment by means of an emotionally charged positioning system. Social constructs work on projects like 'detecting predators,' 'seeking protectors,' and 'reciprocating in kind' – which appear to reach back very far in evolutionary time – as well as very new patterns such as 'welcoming strangers' or even 'showing mercy.' Part of the social interaction function has to do with detecting *agents* versus mere objects; as it were, this function is a human-specifying and human-defining function; likewise it has to do with establishing and maintaining relationships with agents beyond their physical presence; e.g., social hierarchies that include temporarily absent members. These same networks form the background for something like 'group feeling' or 'coalitional psychology' or 'principles of social cohesion' – e.g., detection of kin or in-group members and feelings such as loyalty (thought to have evolved from cross-group or sub-group competition); inclusion functions based on kin-detection that motivate trust and cooperation and lending of aid; also submission patterns, behavior signaling respect and feelings such as respect and awe relative to leaders (thought to have evolved from primate hierarchies). Cognitive modules include something like a 'causal operator' (a function that searches for causes and effects) and a 'holistic operator' (a function that searches for wholeness in the midst of diversity). These functions represent a kind of hard-wired metaphysics: they test for 'reality' and define patterns of explanation. All of these functions are *prospective.* The environment appears on the screen of consciousness as a result of their interplay – the mind is a kind of laboratory for testing affective, social and cognitive hypotheses – mental functions are future-oriented, projective, trial connections that we send out, cross, extend and trim back continually in order to way our way through a landscape.

Mannheim concludes that "the utopian mentality" does not represent an escape from reality or unscientific idealism but instead is *the core thinking function* of asserting a project and setting it loose in the world.

Thinking (on this way of looking at it) is a kind of creative experimentalism that continually makes connections and proposes hypotheses; an idea is like a lifeform that emerges from its environment and must adapt to changes in it as they occur. Failure to thrive is one kind of outcome. In another case the idea takes hold and becomes a new model for adaptation.

Hope, Idealism, utopia on this reading is the basis of understanding *what is directly in front of us*, even more fundamentally than wishing for anything, expecting, or trying to change anything. Human beings cannot understand their experience except by contextualizing it within an imaginary framework – a context that does not yet exist – a fabric of hopes, ideals and dreams.

Dangerous Hope

The Marxist utopian thinker Ernst Bloch (1885 - 1977), native of Germany, sometime American resident, social philosopher and atheist theologian, is the author of *Das Prinzip Hoffnung*, 1959 – "The Principle of Hope" – in three volumes – divided according to Hegel's three worlds of spirit (*Geist*), taking a human life.

Part of the problem is a 'Big Belief' (like the one that took hold of Bloch) that overwhelms a person's human responses. Our hope – our utopia – our ideal can get away from itself. Ideology can become enormously powerful. Dogmatism of one kind or another, tribal connections or some or other religious or national faith, all these sorts of 'Big Belief' can become so big that nothing can stand up to it. Neither our human responses nor our appreciation for the obvious can stand up to it. It pushes everything out of its way and drives ahead. There is a difference between trying to determine what is real by offering hypotheses and determining what is real by issuing edicts.

Bloch accepted Marx's and Lenin's idea that philosophy should not seek objective truth but instead should advocate on behalf of a cause. Philosophy should be a form of action and should be judged by its practical effects. Lenin established a policy of political murder that he himself called "mass terror." By this measure, by the practical effects of this philosophy, Bloch's ideas must surely be accounted false.

Perhaps there is some remainder of truth in Bloch's researches still discoverable – truth we can also find in Kant's researches – also in Mannheim and Camus and Moltmann – the idea that *nothing can succeed without hope*. Hope is inscribed in everything we do. We live by hope. Hope guides every step we take. Our power of understanding is energized by hope. Hope empowers the lies that keep us down. We save ourselves by reclaiming the hope and exposing the lie. In every case each of us must seize hold of hope and make it our own.

Part of this message is the ancient idea of self-reliance. *Spes sibi quisque:* Let each man's hope be in himself; let each of us put trust in our own resources.

Seen from a different perspective, the same idea of self-constructing hope points to something that takes form by the efforts of many people working together. Robert F. Kennedy's speech in South Africa in June 1966 at the University of Capetown makes this point very briefly and clearly. "Each time a man stands up for an ideal, or acts to improve the lot of others, or strikes out against injustice, he sends forth a tiny ripple of hope, and crossing each other from a million different centers of energy and daring these ripples build a current which can sweep down the mightiest walls of oppression and resistance."

What makes hope dangerous (perhaps) is not its translation into collective action or practical effects, but instead the problem of 'Big Belief' that overwhelms a person's human responses. Bloch is right that culture is saturated with utopian content and that nothing can succeed without hope. But he is wildly wrong in thinking that 'mere understanding' is of no account, and especially in his conviction that an Ideal of Hope, or Big Truth of Hope, is more important than a human life. He did not see how quickly idealism can get out of hand. Grand solutions, even from noble intentions, quickly become nightmares.

True and False Hope

Philosophy approaches hope as the core interpretative and affective/social/cognitive positioning system by which human beings navigate their environment. Hopelessness on this account is almost an oxymoron. We can no more cease hoping than we can cease feeling or thinking.

Hope is also a powerful antidote to despair that emerges from suffering. The instillation of hope is an important therapeutic goal, as signaling strength, adaptive capacity and openness to the future. The lack of hope also seems to be a kind of oxymoron in this context as well.

To see this, let us study hope among the hopeless, with the hopeless and as one among them. Let us look for hope in Pandora's box. Let us see if we can find hope in the evils that plague mankind – e.g. in poverty, ignorance, crime, war, fanaticism, disease, trauma and despair.

If we make this study we see immediately that in every such case there is a kind of hidden wish. It is the desire for a witness – the desire to be seen – a desire that is persistent and which shows itself as the compulsion to repeat, to undo and redo, as often as need be, until it is finally done. Freud refers to this phenomenon as the "repetition-compulsion" – also as the "destiny neurosis" – which is the desire to master the sensation of loss by reliving suffering in a new context. Repeating the trauma is a way of gaining belated mastery over it via a corrective emotional experience. Thus the purpose underlying the destiny neurosis, and making the same mistake over and over again, is the hope that, by going through the material again and again, we will finally get to the bottom of the unresolved conflict and arrive at a successful solution.

The British pediatrician and psychoanalyst D.W. Winnicott, an important figure in "object relations theory," is known for his work on the role of play in the development of personality and insights such as the "good enough mother," the "holding environment," the true (creative) self and the false (compliant) self, the "transitional object," and the inherent "sense of being." Winnicott also focused on the instilling of hope in therapy as the reparation following suffering. This comes out particularly in his concept of the "anti-social" tendency. The "anti-social" tendency is not a diagnosis, but a normal component in human psychology. Winnicott regards it as a cry for help, a search for "holding" that the family could not provide, a measure of suffering. Winnicott argues that in extrapolating from cases, e.g. of childhood abuse or working with people in locked wards or prisons, people who have suffered enormous misfortune, people who have been subjected to unheard-of cruelty, but also people who have perpetrated these crimes, you come to see at last that the "anti-social" tendency is characterized by the agent's attempt to get *someone else* to pay attention to him (since the "false self" is a defense, this 'someone else' may one's own "true self," capable of experiencing feelings, including extremely painful ones). That is: this tendency is a kind of buried hope. The basic feature of deprivation is "lack of hope." As a result of deprivation, the agent "gets into the mode of regression." Regression becomes useful because "it carries with it the hope of a new opportunity for unfreezing the frozen situation." Thus "hope underlies the compulsion to steal," for example, and in general "the anti-social tendency *always implies hope*" (*Through Pediatrics to Psychoanalysis*, 1975).

Another way of getting to this idea is to ask the question, *can we hope for something sick?* The answer here is that we can *be* sick and in such a case our hopes will show our sickness. Hope can be twisted by sickness. Thus it is not always other people who twist us around and use our hopes against us (e.g. the kind of cases imagined by Marx and Bloch, in which would-be leaders manipulate us by attaching their aim to our hope). There is also the case in which we do this to ourselves.

At the end of the chain, the condition of being deprived – suffering – is what motivates compulsiveness in the first place. Yet it is *not* a universal truth that those to whom evil is done always do evil in return. Winnicott takes an initially deterministic stance on this issue and offers the distinction between the "good-enough" parent, who creates a successful "holding environment" and instills an illusion of "omnipotence" in the infant, and the parent who is not "good enough," who creates a chaotic early environment, and who instills fear and insecurity. Winnicott argues that the sense of power underlies the infant's curiosity and ability to learn. But even in the case of the "false self," created in the matrix of the chaotic holding environment, there is still an opportunity to break out of the frozen situation and to begin living authentically.

Self-creation is limited, and some of our responses are out of our control. Existentialist voluntarism, or the idea that we can create ourselves from scratch, is an exaggeration, in that human nature is very evidently not a blank slate. We can't solve the problem of compulsiveness by denying straightforward facts. Hope in this sense is a challenge. It is an initiative we are trying to take up, make our own and carry through. It is a way of talking about the attempt to take responsibility for oneself. The "destiny neurosis" is a starting-point. Human fate is a kind of fate that we can take over. This is true even if we often fail in this attempt and have to pick things up and start again over and over. Hope 'springs eternal' because the belated mastery we are looking for is available just as long as we believe in it – as long as we keep trying.

If we assume responsibility for our hopes, then we cannot evade the problem of protecting them. Hope in this sense does not rely on anything, but we have to rely on ourselves. God cannot protect us, but instead we must protect God. That is: we have to protect our ideals and keep them safe. We even have to protect them from overgrowing themselves and crushing simple human responses such as compassion and kindness. Probably this is why our hopes are so ragged, since we are so weak and prey to so much nonsense.

True hope experiences real fears and represents a kind of courage in facing them. False hope has no fear and wins nothing in its advance against despair. To offer false hope is to try to *manage* a person to become *less* responsible for himself, less an agent and more a thing. To offer true hope is to try to *lead* a person to become *more* responsible for himself, more an agent and less a thing. True hope rouses us to action by making the case for the cause. To offer true hope is to learn from experience, to cite evidence and appeal to reason, to model resilience by one's own example, and thus to strengthen in us the powers of deliberation and choice.

Sane hope

I conclude this reflection about hope with some notes from my studies of the works of the late Polish philosopher Leszek Kołakowski (1927 – 2009). Some titles from Kołakowski are *Husserl and the Search for Certitude* (1975), *Metaphysical Horror* (1988) and *My Correct Views on Everything* (2005). Kołakowski was a Marxist and an anti-Marxist; a positivist and an anti-positivist; a student of Kant, Husserl, Heidegger and Wittgenstein, and a critic of all of them; a storyteller, freedom fighter, teacher and scholar. Kołakowski brought a sense of humor to the study of philosophy. He thought that self-doubt was an important quality that helped a person to reach real depth in his thinking. He spent his life working on political and philosophical problems. He often wrote about hope.

Kołakowski's generation lived through the Nazi invasion of Poland, the Warsaw uprising, the horrors of Auschwitz, liberation by the Allies at the close of WWII, the Soviet invasion, Stalinism, the Solidarity movement and the end of the Cold War, the introduction of market capitalism into Poland and even the beginnings of contentious party politics.

Kołakowski directs us to Socrates to find a perspective capable of taking in so much suffering. Socrates adopted the standpoint of questioning all manner of beliefs and subjecting them to a kind of cross-examination, as if the belief were on trial and had to testify and endure the prosecution.

Kołakowski directs us to Descartes, who decided to pursue a method of universal doubt in order to purge his mind of all opinions held merely on trust and open it to genuine knowledge.

He directs us to Kant, who held that reason perverts itself if it limits its powers of criticism, skepticism, or doubt, by censoring itself or prohibiting any line of inquiry or search: "Nothing is so important through its usefulness, nothing so sacred, that it may be exempted from this searching examination, which knows no respect for persons or traditions. Reason depends on this freedom for its very existence" (*Critique of Pure Reason*, A 738).

He directs us to Bertrand Russell, who extended the method of doubt from problems of knowledge to problems of action and even considered doubt to be the key to human happiness, since doubt easily shows furious and intolerant believers that they have no reason to hold their creeds. "Dogmatism, in the present age as in former times, is the greatest of mental obstacles to human happiness."

Kołakowski often uses the term *skepticism* and tries very hard to dig into this idea and grasp its power. The term *skepticism* originates in the Greek term *skepsis*, which means to look. The skeptic is literally the inquirer, someone who wishes to know more than he already knows, a person who looks or searches or seeks. There is a beautiful passage in Hesse's novel

Siddhartha that expresses this idea: "Seeking means: to have a goal. But finding means: to come to the end, to have no goal." Socrates is perhaps the quintessential seeker in the Western tradition. He seeks and freely admits that he does not find. He says that he knows enough to know that he is ignorant. This puts him in an odd position, from which he draws his famous *eironeia* or 'irony.' He has the humility to admit that he doesn't have the answers, or understand his own experience, or grasp much even about the things he cares about most, such as courage, justice, beauty and wisdom. He tries to find out if anyone else knows. He discovers that they don't.

Here is one way of putting Socrates' skeptical and ironic project of inquiry: You believe in and trust the power of intellect; you constantly remind yourself that you do not know; you believe that knowledge is possible, that truth is attainable, and that you are bound to seek it, even though the evidence is overwhelmingly against your finding it. Thus in a sense skepticism itself is a kind of buried hope that, by engaging in the search, we may cure our sickness and know.

"I would be happy to cross-examine you, provided that you are the same sort of human being as I am. By this I mean the sort of person who is pleased to be refuted if he says something untrue, and pleased to refute someone else if that person says something untrue, but more pleased to be refuted that to refute. It is better to rid oneself of the greatest evil than it is to rid someone else of this evil; and I do not believe that anything could be more evil for a human being than to harbor false beliefs" (*Gorgias*, 458ab).

Kołakowski considered hope and skepticism to be equal partners in building the spirit of truth by carrying on the project of inquiry. This partnership cleans our minds of prejudices and prevents us from being carried away by wishful thinking; but it also trusts in the search and the project of continuing to dig deeper towards unseen foundations. He held that philosophy cannot pierce the mystery and that philosophy is a hopeless quest; oppositely, he held that philosophy shows its strength by its determination to go on, and that going on is precisely what makes us human.

This strain of thinking returns us to the emotional pendulum and the fated couple Yes and No. Hope is a part of our experience. So is suffering.

Kołakowski writes: "there is no voice of God in the world" – "if there were, it would be irresistible" – but further: "German thinkers have been telling us for quite a long time now that the human race has a natural 'hermeneutic' tendency – in all its experiences it searches instinctively for meaning." Much of Kołakowski's writing is about this search for meaning and the quarrel between thinkers who burn with a claim to have discovered the secret code and other thinkers who keep their cool and are still at work in reading the book of the world.

Some people simply *become* their hopes; ultimately this is all they see. Others have hope and reach for hope, but for them hope is mainly an idea, a chance, something to work on.

In the search for meaning, experience often shows us 'more' – love is 'more' than sex; home is 'more' than a roof; knowledge is 'more' than power. Hope is 'more' than just being positive, in the same sense that human beings are 'more' than just bits of living matter. Kołakowski tried many times to capture the gist of this 'more,' but he confesses that he never quite got there.

Kołakowski returns to a theme from the Pandora story and also an idea that comes out in Kant's thinking about hope: the idea that hope does so much with so little. There is a staggering power in holding myself responsible for something; in expecting something; in getting up after falling; in living with the possibility of total failure; so great a power that we end up protecting God, rather than God protecting us. This truth is so striking that we might even want to reverse our earlier conclusion about hope and mountains. It may be nearer to the truth to strike the saying that hope does not move mountains. Hope moves mountains.

Striving

> The love of truth (*philalethes*) is a desirable mean state between the defect of irony or self-deprecation and the excess of arrogance or boastfulness. Aristotle, *Nicomachean Ethics* 1127b3.

> The love of truth is the never entertaining of any proposition with greater assurance than the proofs it is built upon will warrant. John Locke, *An Essay Concerning Human Understanding*, IV, xix, § 1.

> Reverence is the supreme test of integrity: but in the entire history of philosophy there *is* no intellectual integrity – rather only 'love of the good.' Friedrich Nietzsche, *The Will to Power*, § 460.

Suffering incites philosophy and philosophy emboldens hope. Between suffering and hope is the work of philosophy itself. According to my conception, the work of philosophy is therapy. Philosophy confronts suffering and tries to appropriate it as human reality. Marx encapsulates this idea in his saying that "suffering humanly considered is an enjoyment of the self for man." Philosophy is a way of taking suffering, taking it in, working with it and moving beyond it. But if suffering is the starting-point, and philosophy is therapy, then different philosophies represent different interventions. Philosophies address different clinical problems and offer different kinds of treatment. And if hope is the ending point, and philosophy leads to hope, then different philosophies encourage different hopes.

When we are practicing philosophy, we are demonstrating what we care about, what we love and what we are pursuing, and we have formed unawares or explicitly an idea of truth emerging from our confrontation with suffering and truth that gives us hope. *Philosophia* demonstrates *philalethes* – how we practice philosophy demonstrates how we love truth – how we look demonstrates what we are looking for.

Aristotle conceives this truth as something we have to discover in ourselves. The real problem in pursuing philosophy is our own character. We cannot say that we love truth if we puff ourselves up, but equally we cannot say that we love truth if we drag ourselves down. We must find a way to face ourselves squarely, without adding or subtracting anything. We are looking for balance. But the opposites we trying to juggle are varieties of self-deception. The goal is self-respect.

Locke thinks that the problem is not about how we look at ourselves (and whether we can avoid self-hatred and self-love) but how we go about believing (and whether we can avoid believing too little or too much). Thus the real problem in pursuing philosophy is sticking to the facts. Sometimes we get our facts wrong, and sometimes we make mistakes of reasoning. We are juggling bits of information and processes for interpreting information. The goal is science.

Nietzsche thinks that moral ideas trump everything else. Thus the real problem in pursuing philosophy is prejudice – what people call 'confirmation bias' today – the tendency to exempt favored ideas from scrutiny. Biased search and the overconfidence that results from it effectively blind us. They prevent us from ever having an honest look at things – they shield us from reality – we become lesser creatures. For Nietzsche honesty trumps everything else. He doesn't want to be spared anything, or have things cut down to size. He wants to live life to the full.

Nietzsche is telling us that love of truth is fearlessness at the risk of our most cherished ideas.

The Nietzsche cure, therefore, tries to attack prejudice and replace it with honesty; he tries to pry loose very old ideas and free up curiosity, creativity and an experimental attitude; then he digs deeper and proposes to treat the underlying condition that instilled fear in the first place.

The Nietzsche cure is a cure for "enfeebled instinct," exhaustion, weariness, surrender, and is meant to instil energy, well-being, hunger, "tempting courage," and soaring aspiration.

The Nietzsche cure is for going on. The therapy never terminates. We are never entirely cured.

The Socratic cure is also for going on. It is meant to help us live. Socrates prescribes philosophy, which he defines as practice of death. We have to keep practicing while we live. When we're dead, we don't need to practice anymore. We're done, the therapy terminates, we're cured.

The Nietzsche cure prescribes a number of strong medicines including philology, introspection, experimental thinking, metacognition and the critique of values. It prescribes conversation. It must be talked about, talked over, talked through. It is a kind of dialogue therapy, reality therapy, psychodrama – a kind of group therapy. Nietzsche also wants us to get up and walk. We have to walk some things out, walk through some thoughts, as the Peripatetics prescribed.

Nietzsche is sick – he has the sickness that he is trying to cure – he is both patient and doctor. He first noticed the disease when he was a child. He sensed that it would catch hold in his society and that it would spread to every corner of the globe. He calls the sickness "nihilism." This is new – it emerges in very recent history – he sees it as the defining problem of his epoch. Nihilism is a kind of existential crisis. The old values are crumbling away, old ideas lose their authority, the new situation is misunderstood and resisted. The time is suffering. Buddha set out to solve the problem of suffering, and Nietzsche in his way wants to solve this problem too.

Nietzsche calls nihilism a "hatred of life," an infection that saps all the vital energy out of life. Buddha wants to help us achieve a transcendent calm in face of suffering and his cure works on overcoming suffering, overcoming desire, but Nietzsche argues that Buddha was wrong to want to abolish suffering, or back away from life, or end striving. Nietzsche strives for all he is worth.

Plato was also trying to solve a problem like this and redefined the ancient word 'therapy' –*therapeia*, 'service to the gods', 'attending to the gods' – to get at this problem. The problem is ignorance – living in darkness – not knowing who we are. It is personal, in the sense that every one of us feels it. Different as we are, we are all subjected to the same condition. We are chained inside the cave. We play a game with shadows – many games

– we are oblivious to our slavery and know nothing about ourselves. We have stopped aspiring, reaching, striving for excellence. This is a social disease, a social problem, and Plato thinks that we may have to construct an ideal society – the *Republic* – as *therapeia*, 'service to man', 'attending to the patient,' in order to treat and cure this sickness. The *Republic* is meant to reverse the order of things in normal society, which is upside down. No one knows what virtue is and few people take the time to search. The lower is set above the higher. Good men cannot pass on their goodness to their sons. The Right is inverted. Vulgarity, war and confusion reign unchallenged. This is the frenzy Plato thought had overtaken his society and drove it to execute Socrates.

In Plato's *Republic* the cure for society's ills is philosophy – the very thing that Athens tried to stamp out by executing Socrates – which Plato conceives as a long process of education beginning with mathematics and ending with dialectic, or pure philosophical inquiry. He also compares learning to walking – getting up, moving, setting a course – walking into the light. Philosophy answers a need in society and offers to teach society and become its guide. The "Guardians" or founders of the *Republic* will know truth and build a society on its foundation, telling a "big lie" or "noble lie" (a kind of religion) to the common people. Wise "philosopher-kings" will steer society and devise its educational plan. Philosopher-kings will throw off their chains, exit the cave, see the light, and return to bring light into darkness.

Plato did not consider that people who have seen the light might become dangerous.

His insight is: society is wrong because men are wrong, and men are wrong because their wills are contorted – their hearts and desires are twisted and sick – thus the will, the principle of action, has to change before everything else. Philosophy has to begin by changing the way people desire. "Truth cannot be discovered unless the main stream of desire be directed towards it" (G.M.H. Grube, *Plato's Thought*, 1935). Make people better than they presently are, if you want them to see the truth. And how do you make people better? – You construct an entirely new society – i.e. you educate young people to guard the "big truth" that you think will free them.

Plato counted on painting a dazzling image to distract the people and, for the *aristos* or the 'best' people in society, the power of tradition to cheer the heart with the precedent of noble deeds. Because your ancestors climbed up ahead, you have to climb up too and surpass them. Plato's 'therapy' consists in getting a person outside his usual prison, into the light, then introducing dialectic to make him self-aware. When a person becomes self-aware, he will wonder-question-philosophize and, as Socrates taught, start getting ready for death. This is the change Plato is counting on and wants to see. He wants to clarify striving, not abolish it.

Plato did not consider that constructing a society on the model of a "big truth," which is simultaneously a "big lie" – divided between the people and the aristocrats – might become a nightmare that envelops the Guardians as well as the people they are lying to.

Plato was right about the psychological root – desire is the principle of action – but desire is *personal*; the problem is different in each case; and there are no social solutions to personal problems.

Buddha respects the idea that liberation has to be personal, that there is no social solution to human ills. He aims at the individual and at helping the individual achieve realization. He does not propose to reorganize government founded on Buddhist principles, but instead proposes to found a small, separate society, a society in retreat and at the side of "householder" society, the *sangha* or monastic order. This is an assembly of people possessing some high degree of realization, but is not intended to replace existing society.

Buddha confined himself (like a physician) to the relief of suffering. A doctor heals rather than founding cities. Buddha's political ideas for the *sangha* define an idea of tolerance and uphold the social ideal of a small egalitarian republic governed under the rule of direct democracy.

Nietzsche is like Buddha in not proposing a *social* solution to the problem of human life. The Nietzsche cure is not social, not aimed at the group, but personal. It is true that Nietzsche is speaking to everyone and has a passion to communicate – a mission to help others; but mainly he praises solitude, and he requires isolation in order to give birth to his powerful thoughts.

Nietzsche says that he "is so close to Socrates that he is thinking about him at all times." He also calls himself an antidote to Plato and to the huge mistake that he thought Plato had made – the mistake of not seeing the damage done to earthliness when we portray our "big truth" in the sky – when we fall victim to the delusion of teachable philosophical knowledge. He also calls himself an opponent of Buddhism, which he associates with weariness, exhaustion, surrender.

Nietzsche says that the task is "to make oneself at home on earth," the place where we do not know very much and what we do know we must learn for ourselves, a terrestrial place, rather than heaven, an inquiry rather than possession of truth, striving rather than realization.

Nietzsche defends the interests of philosophy and his therapy, like Socrates', Plato's and Buddha's, is a course in philosophy. He defends the interests of philosophy from what he sees as its greatest threat: the "big lie," i.e. religion, the big story told to keep us down, which he thinks of as a kind of despising of the human condition, or hatred of the earth. This may be why he became such a hated figure. He wants people to outgrow fairy tales and "toughen up" and for society he imagines a place where someone like Socrates would be safe: someone who does not know but is trying to know. However, he does not imagine creating an ideal city or a monastic order. He imagines creating a new human being, the Overman. The Nietzsche cure is an original contribution to philosophy, an entirely new therapy for a brand new disease.

Some further medicines prescribed by the Nietzsche cure include: the project of changing 'it was' into 'thus I willed it,' or taking responsibility for one's life, or *amor fati*, or loving destiny; learning to live in the moment; accepting mortality, but not giving up or dying too soon.

In sum: here are a few episodes in the history of philosophical therapy: Socratic therapy (practice of death); Platonic therapy (lessons in exiting the cave); Aristotelian therapy (learning self-respect); Buddhist therapy (learning to disengage from craving and achieve meditative calm); Empiricist therapy (learning scientific method); and the Nietzsche cure (overcoming nihilism, appropriating human reality, learning to live on the earth, practicing striving).

With this as preface, I want to start again with Nietzsche, face the problems he faced, study his arguments, and become his patient; to take the Nietzsche cure; and thus learn about striving.

Nietzsche / Brief Biography

Friedrich Wilhelm Nietzsche was born in 1844 in Röcken, a small town in Northeastern Germany. His father was a Lutheran minister and his mother was a teacher. His father died when he was four years old; his little brother when he was six; his grandmother when he was twelve. At fourteen he was awarded a scholarship to attend the prestigious boarding school in Pforta. At twenty he began his university studies, first in theology, then in classical philology, beginning his studies in Bonn and graduating in Leipzig. At twenty-four he was appointed as a full professor of classical philology at the university in Basel. His teacher Ritschl said about him at the time: "In thirty-nine years of teaching, I have never known a young person to become so mature so quickly and at such an early age as this Nietzsche...he is the idol of the entire world of young scholars here in Leipzig. You will say that I am describing some sort of prodigy. That he is, but he is also very amiable and humble. He will accomplish anything that he puts his mind to."

At twenty-four, as Prussia began a series of war campaigns, Nietzsche renounced his citizenship; he was an outspoken opponent of nationalism, anti-Semitism and racism, and was willing to say so publically; for the rest of his life he lived as a stateless person, shuttling mainly between Italy, Austria and Switzerland. During the Franco-Prussia War (1870-71), he volunteered as a medical orderly, but soon fell ill with diphtheria and dysentery (and, some say, syphilis); he also suffered from myopia, dyspepsia, and variously diagnosed nervous conditions; he could only eat bland food and could not smoke, drink coffee or alcohol, or take any kind of stimulant; he suffered from fits of coughing, stomach cramps, vomiting and migraines; was often confined to bed for long periods; his physicians prescribed him barbiturates, chloral hydrate and opiates.

Nietzsche was about five-foot-eight. He was very shy and reserved, but made close friendships with many of the outstanding scholars, scientists and artists of his day. Nietzsche was a talented musician and prolific composer. Nietzsche lived a very modest lifestyle in small hotels or rented rooms. His only possession was a wooden trunk, in which he kept a few shirts, a worn suit, some toiletries, a store of medicines and drugs, and mainly books and manuscripts.

Nietzsche's early writings have a Romantic character – he praises passionate feeling, aesthetic experience, the wonders of nature, ancient wisdom and ruins, and especially the creative genius, who likely is misunderstood and must suffer the fate of an outcast. For several years Nietzsche adopted another position – positivism – a point of view most associated with the French thinker Auguste Comte – emphasizing rationalism and the scientific method. Between 1882 and 1888 he wrote a series of books that soon made him world-famous – developing a completely new point of view – including five influential works from 1888, among them *Twilight of the Idols*, *The Antichrist* and *Ecce Homo*. In January 1889, at age forty-five, he suffered a complete mental and physical collapse, followed by a series of strokes that left him partially paralyzed and unable to walk or speak. Several diagnoses have been proposed for this sudden break including tertiary syphilis, manic-depressive disease, dementia and cerebral arteriopathy. He never regained his faculties and died after his long illness on August 25, 1900.

Nietzsche the Student / a few translations from some of his writings as a young person

1858 (14 years old)

(journal entry) Great revolutions are near at hand, once the masses understand that all Christianity is based on assumptions: the existence of God, the authority of the Bible, immortality and inspiration will always be problems. I have tried to deny everything. But it is much easier to tear down than to build up.

1859 (15 years old) (note: Charles Darwin, *The Origin of Species*, published 1859)

(journal entry) We do not know whether humanity itself is merely a stage, a period in the universal whole, simply another station of the process of becoming. Is there no end to this eternal becoming?

1862 (18 years old)

("Fate and History") If we could look upon Christian doctrine and church history in a free and impartial way, we should have to express several views that oppose those that are generally accepted. But confined as we are from our earliest days under the yoke of custom and prejudice and inhibited as we are in the natural development of our spirit, determined in the formation of our temperament by the impressions of our childhood, we believe ourselves compelled to view it virtually as a transgression if we adopt a freer standpoint from which to make a judgment on religion and Christianity that is impartial and appropriate to our time.

Such an attempt is not the work of a few weeks but of a lifetime.

1863 (19 years old)

("My Life") I can look back with gratitude at almost everything, whether it be joy or sorrow, that has happened to me, and all the events that have up to now led me along like a child.

Perhaps it is time to seize the reins of events myself and step out into life. Thus man outgrows everything that once embraced him; he has no need to burst the fetters, for if a god commands it, they fall away of themselves; and where is the ring that finally encloses him? Is it the world? Is it God?

1864 (20 years old)

("Moods") Moods, I salute you, marvelous variations of a tempestuous soul, as manifold as nature itself, but more magnificent than nature, since you eternally transcend yourselves and strive upwards, whereas the plant still exhales the same atmosphere it did on the day of creation. I no longer love as I loved some weeks ago; I am no longer this moment in the mood I was in when I began to write.

To the Unknown God (poem)

Once more before I draw on
And send my gaze forward
I raise my hands together
Upwards to you, to whom I flee
To whom I, in deepest depths of heart
Solemnly consecrate altars
That through all time
Bring again your voice

There grows deep inscribed the words:
To the Unknown God.
Yours am I
Though I live in an impious world
Arrows pierce and draw me down in battle
If I fear and think to run, the words hold me back
and compel me to Your service

I would know you, Unknown one.
You who reach deep into my soul
Like a storm rumbling all through my life
You – incomprehensible – my kin!
I would know you, even serve you.

1865 (21 years old)

(letter to his sister) Suppose that we had believed from childhood that all salvation came from someone other than Jesus – say, from Muhammad – would we not have experienced the same blessings? ... Faith does not offer the least support for objective truth. This is simply where people part ways. If you strive for peace of mind or pleasure, then believe; but if you wish to devote yourself to truth, then *search*...

1870 (26 years old)

("On Truth and Lies in an Extra-moral Sense") Once upon a time, in some out of the way corner of a universe dispersed into numberless twinkling solar systems, there was a star upon which clever beasts invented knowing... But what is *knowing*? We believe that we know something, for example, when we speak about trees, colors, snow and flowers; we believe that we know something about these things themselves when we speak about them; and yet we possess nothing but metaphors for things – metaphors that correspond in no way to the original entities.

What then is truth? A movable host of metaphors, figures of speech, and anthropomorphisms: in short, a sum of human relations that have been poetically and rhetorically intensified, transferred, and embellished, and which, after long usage, seem to the people who use them to be fixed, canonical, and binding. Truths are fantasies whose origins we have long forgotten.

Nietzsche / Influences

Romanticism and positivism are formative influences for Nietzsche; so is Lutheranism. Nietzsche had a religious calling from his earliest youth and began his university studies in theology. His mother was a parson's daughter; his grandfather and father were parsons; Nietzsche himself is buried beside them in the church graveyard in Röcken.

Nietzsche trained as a classicist and retained lifelong the three directive Socratic precepts: *he among you is wisest, who knows that his wisdom is* worth nothing; *the unexamined life is not worth living*; and *virtue is knowledge*. Nietzsche is focused on the problem of virtue or excellence or happiness – he holds that wisdom is the key to happiness – he is a skeptic about happiness because wisdom still eludes us. The original title of his first work was *Pessimism and Hellenism* and his writings over the years underscore a Greek sense of dark fate.

Schopenhauer's pessimism is another important influence for Nietzsche. Nietzsche was enamoured of Schopenhauer's writings and wrote a youthful work of praise to him entitled *Schopenhauer as Educator* (1865). Schopenhauer hypothesized that the "will" is an underlying force or energy that constitutes the sole and universal reality. Will is blind and unconscious until it is "objectivized" in human beings, in whom it first attains consciousness or the "power of representation." Thus the title of his work: *The World as Will and Representation*. Schopenhauer argues that the essential nature of will is to desire and strive; that perpetual desiring and striving leads to suffering; that to relieve suffering, the agent must extinguish the will, and not will at all; so that the end-goal of all life is to "overcome the will to live."

Nietzsche wrestles with Schopenhauer and ultimately rejects his whole approach as a failure of nerve. Nietzsche tries to rethink pessimism and to create "a new pessimism of the strong." This is a love for difficult, problematic things, for angry things, dreadful things, "from overflowing well-being, from living existence to the full" – "a tempting courage of the keenest sight that demands what is terrible, like an enemy – a worthy enemy – in order to test its strength."

The experience of illness is an important element in Nietzsche's worldview. As a young man Nietzsche was in good health – his teacher Ritschl calls him "strong, robust, vigorous, brave in body and soul" – at this stage he was 24 – but ten years later Nietzsche himself records "in 1879 I experienced 118 days of serious attacks; I do not count the milder ones," *Letter to Eiser, February 1880*). Nietzsche could not tolerate the idea of becoming an invalid ("the only ideas that are worth anything are those won by walking," *Twilight of the Idols*, I,34). He summoned himself out of depression, out of sickness, out of bed, and into his beloved Alpine forest (a recent scholar has published a book describing Nietzsche's favorite trails – Paul Raabe, *Spaziergänge durch Nietzsches Sils-Maria*, 1994). This may help explain why ideas like *will* and *power* are so important for him ("I took myself in hand and made myself well again. I still consider myself a basically healthy person. A typically morbid nature cannot become healthy or, even less, make itself healthy; but for a typically healthy person, even getting sick can be a powerful stimulant for life" (*Letter to Gast, April 7, 1888*).

Some writers that Nietzsche felt particularly close to include Heraclitus ("Here I feel warm and better than anywhere else. The affirmation of passing away and destroying; saying Yes to opposition and conflict; saying Yes to becoming, along with a radical repudiation of being; all this is more related to me than anything else," *Ecce Homo*, IV, 3), Thucydides ("Here is a thinker who takes the most comprehensive and impartial delight in all that is typical of men and events and believes that to each type there pertains a quantum of *good sense* – this is what he tries to discover," *Dawn*, 168), Montaigne ("this freest and mightiest of souls" who "teaches a cheerfulness that really cheers...with certainty and simplicity, courage and strength," *Schopenhauer as Educator*, 2), Spinoza ("the purest sage"), Goethe ("a genius without envy even of Shakespeare," at once "a man of science and a consummate artist") and Dostoyevsky ("one of the most beautiful strokes of fortune in my life") (*Twilight of the Idols*, IX, 45). Nietzsche often puts himself in illustrious company: "That which moved Zarathustra, Moses, Jesus, Muhammad, Plato, Brutus, Spinoza and Mirabeau is the medium in which I live" – also "When I speak of Plato, Pascal, Spinoza and Goethe, I know that their blood flows in my veins" – also "my ancestors, Heraclitus, Empedocles, Spinoza and Goethe" (see Karl Jaspers, *Nietzsche: An Introduction to the Understanding of His Philosophical Activity*, p. 35).

Romanticism, positivism, Lutheranism, classicism, pessimism – an accomplished pianist who began to compose at age ten – a child prodigy, an academic star, but personally very shy and self-effacing – a conscientious objector, volunteer medic and man without a country – someone who read very widely and passionately, drawn to authors in whom he heard echoes of his own struggles and ideas – strains of thought as different as Heraclitus, Dostoyevsky and Buddha – struck down by illness, fighting off illness, and measuring his strength against it ("what does not kill me, makes me stronger") – losing his father and brother very early in life – growing up as the only man in a house of devout women – awkward around women from youth on – his few, impetuous, overwrought marriage proposals refused (Matilda Trampedach, Frau Lou) – a passionate longing for friendship, but also a trail of broken friendships (close friends with whom he later broke include Paul Deussen, Erwin Rohde, Paul Rée, Frau Lou, and Richard Wagner) – a loner, nearly a recluse ("Philosophy is a voluntary living amid ice and mountain heights," "There is a great *emptiness* around me, and there is literally *no one* who can possibly understand my situation," "In truth, not being able to *communicate* with other people is the most terrible of all forms of loneliness – a mask that is more iron-like than any iron mask") – and perhaps most strikingly, a person of extraordinary self-awareness, whose self-analysis laid the foundation for much of contemporary psychology.

Freud's verdict about this aspect of Nietzsche's character is particularly striking: "Nietzsche knew himself better than anyone who ever lived – or is ever likely to live in the future."

At the outset, Nietzsche is a kind of compound vector, or summation of forces; a collection of talents or powers; a person of extraordinary self-awareness, a "psychologist," as he calls himself, who studies drives, affects, sublimation, projection, individuation, merging, and the art of composing oneself; aimed at his times, diagnosing his epoch, treating the crisis of modern life; offering himself as a case study in the disease; the first patient to try the Nietzsche cure.

Nietzsche / Modernism

Nietzsche is a question. In studying his works, we have a chance to ask this question – to think through what it means to live in modern times – to study his analysis, diagnosis and solution – to see what has become of his ideas and where things stand today with the dilemma of modernity.

Nietzsche is a place to do this – a site for this kind of work – but he is not the first person to see the problem. Arguably, very early figures such as Nicholas of Cusa (1401-1464) and Giordano Bruno (1548-1600) began to look at an infinite, centerless universe in which man is of no more account than a sun, a meteor, a fungus or any other natural occurrence. Immanuel Kant (1724-1804) is a pioneering figure along this line. So are Fyodor Dostoyevsky and George Eliot (Mary Ann Evans) – born in the generation before Nietzsche. Nietzsche grasped the problem at a very young age (his journal entry, cited above on page 91, written when he was fourteen years old, shows that he already sees it) – but what makes Nietzsche a central figure for modernism is not that he was first on the scene or that he grasped the problem at so young an age – the reason that he looms so large on the modernist landscape is his reaction – he didn't flinch – whereas *all* his predecessors did. He *accepted* the new situation – he *welcomed* it – he saw it as a new truth, as growth – no regrets – he was *happy* to awaken in this new universe and urged all of us to join him as "free aeronauts of the spirit." "The task: to make oneself at home on earth."

Nietzsche's general argument is very straightforward – it helps to keep it in mind in thinking through the great profusion of things he has to say – a kind of anchor in the wild Nietzsche sea. His argument has three steps:

There is a problem (dysfunctional value)
The problem has a cause (misattributed value)
The problem has a solution (reconceiving value)

The issue is modernism – modern times – the modern world. Modernism means many things, such as the end of feudalism, the end of the medieval world, the end of traditional society, the loss of certainty – the realization that a rational, absolute certainty can never be established once and for all; the shift from the country to the city, from agrarian society to industrialization; the beginnings of capitalism, the beginnings of secularism, the beginnings of the idea of progress – affirming the power of human beings to change and improve their lives. The modern period ushers in enormous change – it is disorienting and highly charged – at once resisted and defended – some responding to change with a nostalgia for the past, others rushing ahead with grand schemes for the future. Modernism is a conflict zone, a controversy, and especially a great fight about values. The problem, in brief, is that the old values don't work anymore.

Medieval values do not work in a modern world – traditional values become problematic in secular culture – "the highest values devaluate themselves" and leave us with nihilism.

There is a sickness in modern times. It shows itself in the self – in emotions such as anxiety, alienation and a fragmented sense of identity. It shows itself in society – in behavior (such as crime, addiction, random violence), social patterns (such as divorce, isolation, alienation), and social movements (such as fascism and communism – mass movements that try to replace past value systems with new ones). It shows itself in culture (the culture industry, mass-produced entertainment, trending towards dumbing-down, trivialization, conformism, depravity, sentimentality). It shows itself in the environment (urbanization, automation, pollution).

It also shows itself in history – e.g. in war – marrying a disjointed sense of value and a mechanized weapons industry – the sickness in modern times shows itself most dramatically in the body count. More than one hundred million people died in war during the 20th century.

Nietzsche was far ahead of his time in seeing that discontent with secular modernity could take form as political movements – channeled into conservative politics, back-to-traditional-values movements, or morphing into grand social experiments such as fascism and communism that explicitly try to re-engineer human nature ("manufacturing" new values).

Nietzsche asks: what kind of vermin brings us this plague? What is the origin of nihilism? Where does it come from? What has happened to value? What made it dysfunctional? His answer is: *religion*. Why? Because religion leads to the systematic devaluation of *this* world, in favor of the next. By hollowing out this world, religion becomes destructive of *all* value, including its own. Nietzsche sees himself as living in a wasteland created by otherworldliness.

"Consider the damage all human institutions sustain if a transcendent higher sphere is postulated that first permits and underwrites these institutions. By growing accustomed to seeing their value in this sanction...one has reduced their natural dignity and, in effect, denied it ... The problem is that we have measured the value of *this* world according to categories referring to a completely fictitious world ... Actual values are misconceived in their origin and, thereafter, systematically degrade into non-values" (*The Will to Power*, 12, 245).

Nietzsche proposes to explain how this happened, psychologically, socially and historically. He wants to demonstrate that large-scale political schemes for reorganizing society – such as extreme positions of the right and left – cannot resolve the problem, but only make it worse. And he wants to offer a *transvaluation of all values* – a completely new approach to moral value – to answer the dilemma of modern life. Nietzsche's new approach to morality offers itself as the solution to the disease of modernism and a return to the sanity of making oneself at home on earth. Nihilism has made it impossible for us to want anything. Healing sets us free.

Nietzsche's subject is man. His approach is complex – at once biological-scientific, experiential-psychological, sociological, ethnological, linguistic, intellectual-historical – an exploration of religion, myth, literature, the arts, music – in any given passage he seems to be addressing philosophy, ethics, the sciences, aesthetics, politics, religion, psychology, linguistics, history, culture, Wagner – all at the same time. He has an enormous curiosity, but he disavows all system – he refuses to construct an interconnected system of ideas – he refuses to become a "philosophical architect" who lays down foundations and raises a new house of conclusions.

He doesn't think we know enough to create any such system – he also thinks that people who try to create big structures for thought have no integrity – if they had any self-esteem or belief in themselves, they would not try to avoid having to develop their own judgment by referring problems to an anonymous mechanism. There is no substitute for personal engagement and thinking things through; at best there is "unquiet living" and constant search; we have to warn ourselves not to succumb to the deception of teachable philosophical knowledge; the problem is to keep thought alive in the face of enormous forces lying in wait to destroy it. The task of philosophy is to think. Thinking lives in the inspiration of the moment – it lives in the historical moment – it cannot abdicate its life-problems to authorities – it must *engage* with authority and become an authority for itself – "Every word is useless, that makes no call to action."

Nietzsche / Beginning with his Times

Many currents of political life in Nietzsche's day began in Germany: Prussian militarism, Pan-Germanism, the unification of the German 'homeland,' the creation of the German Empire. From Germany, in quick succession, every European nation was drawn into a violent contest of ideas and causes, and especially of prejudices – of class, ethnicity, geography – anti-Semitism, racism – nationalism, imperialism, fascism, socialism – in reaction, liberalism and conservatism – also feminism and independence movements. New varieties of extremism, intolerance and unquestioning patriotism grew up in Europe – colonialism transported them to every corner of the world – soon the world was set on fire. As Bismarck foresaw, the great questions of the times could not be resolved by speeches or elections, but only by "iron and blood." The contradictions of the latter decades of the nineteenth century, which are the birth-pangs of the modern world, took shape as the Franco-Prussian War, and World War I, and World War II.

Nietzsche understands his epoch in terms of the overriding theme of modernism and the problems created when a value-world originating in religious doctrine is exposed as a myth; without the support of religious conviction, the whole edifice of law and social order begins to corrode; the upheaval in belief inaugurates a new and very dangerous period in history.

"The waters of religion recede and leave behind swamps and ponds; the nations draw apart and prepare for hostilities... Scientific advances crystallize and dissolve everything that was firmly believed... Many changes work together at the precipice of an approaching barbarism. The time is marked by egoism, acquisitiveness, military despots ... an indescribable poverty and exhaustion of ideas, despite an indescribable variety of ideas – the heritage of world cultures... The mob takes hold, mediocrity becomes a danger, the rapid many-sidedness of modern times threatens to extinguish man ... The age becomes inventive in producing intoxicants... The *machine* takes hold and converts whole groups into machines and individuals into specialized tools... The press, the railroads, the telegraph are a few premises in a thousand-year conclusion that no one has yet dared to draw."

Nietzsche finds many, if not all, of these strains in himself – he is an anti-Semite and an anti-anti-Semite; he is a woman-hater and a feminist; he is a student of science but also a skeptic about science – arguing that scientific advance is often moral decline; he was raised as a devout believer (as a child his nickname was "the little pastor"), but his name is synonymous with atheism; he accuses himself of being a nihilist but also sets himself to overcome nihilism; at the same time that he is trying to resist the spirit of his age, he is also a child of it. Much of his thinking is devoted to figuring out what is going on in his epoch, but he is also trying to surmount the spirit of his age and take a step forward (for example: he started out as a German nationalist; he became a European cosmopolitan). Nietzsche sees the modern dilemma *in himself* – he investigates the modernist disease as he looks in the mirror – he is digging down into himself but at the same time he is investigating modernity.

Nietzsche's solutions have the same double quality. He says that he is trying *to awaken the time to itself*: he is addressing the entire world. He is also trying *to awaken a personal response*: he is addressing someone like himself who is wrestling with the modern spirit. He even interprets his own point of view as the result of the double-bind of his era. Christianity teaches a systematic spirit of honesty – an uncompromising devotion to truth – and, ultimately, this honesty exposes the lie at the heart of Christianity itself – its mythic origin.

Nietzsche / Genealogy of Morals

There is a sickness in modern times – value has become dysfunctional – Nietzsche proposes to explain how this occurred – he reaches back into history to trace the course of events beginning with the concept of *value* itself in order to track how this base-term in human affairs became twisted from its original sense and falsified by a long course of changes in culture.

Nietzsche made his original reputation in philology – also called historical linguistics – a field that examines the origins of languages, back to common ancestor languages. For example, Indo-European philology reaches back to something called PIE, or Proto-Indo-European, the reconstructed common ancestor language of all European languages, originating (according to various estimates) from between 10,000-5,000 BCE, and divided into unconnected 'daughter dialects' by 3000 BCE. These latter results include ancient languages such as Sanskrit, Avestan, Hittite, Tocharian, Celtic, Greek and Latin, and also modern Indo-European languages such as English, German, French, Italian, Spanish, Farsi, Hindi, Armenian and Russian.

Nietzsche's focus in philology was on the development of moral terms. As a young scholar, just beginning his study of moral terms in classical languages – Sanskrit, Greek and Latin – he made a discovery that had a profound influence on all his subsequent thinking. This discovery was largely rejected by his contemporaries, but has since turned out to be substantially correct.

He discovered that the word 'good' (and words like it) did not refer originally to qualities of objects or actions – it was not used to commend anything – but instead was a class-term. The word 'good' referred to a *station in society* (in effect, it is a synonym for 'noble,' 'high-born,' 'ruler,' 'aristocrat'). He began looking at a large group of Greek terms including *agathos* (ancestor of our term 'good'), *esthlos* (noble), *arête* (virtue), *kalon* (beautiful) and opposites such as *kakos* (bad), *deilos* (wicked), *aischron* (shameful), and tried to reconstruct the society that spoke these words. He discovered that this was a warrior aristocracy. This culture – the culture of Archaic Greece – is nowadays classified as a 'success' culture, a 'results' culture or a 'shame' culture. That is, what counts in this culture is success in war and prosperity measured in treasure and captives. Nietzsche discovered, further, that the oldest meanings of Archaic praise terms – older even than their status as class-terms, indicating nobility or high birth – indicate people of large physical stature who came to power as a result of their intimidating size.

The largest was also the best armed, the best armed was also the wealthiest; archaic society was a moneyless economy in which wealth consisted of land and chattel; i.e. wealth is tribute that one can take, defend and pass down. Archaic praise-terms have to do with *winning*, not with intentions. It is shameful to fail, whatever one's intentions; it is praiseworthy to succeed, whatever one may have done to take the prize.

The root meaning of the term 'value' is *to be strong*. It is related to the terms 'worth,' 'valiant,' 'prevail,' 'wield' (meaning to govern, to rule, to have power). Root contexts for these terms relate to combat, strength, courage, victory, wealth – honor (*timè*) won in the contest (*agon*) – close relative terms include 'will,' 'desire,' 'power' – also 'male' – thus 'good' in the sense 'I am good,' 'I am competent,' 'I can do that,' 'I have the power,' 'I am man enough,' 'My word is good' (I can make this happen). In German, the derivations are even closer (*wert*, value, *wille*, will, volition, *macht*, power – related to *macho, machismo*, masculine) – Nietzsche's phrase "will to power" (*Wille zur Macht*) is not too far from 'manpower' or 'strong male.'

This whole family of terms – the root words of much our present moral vocabulary – presuppose a definite kind of social order – a warrior clan – in which base-terms like 'good' and 'right' refer to physical prowess (in earliest prehistory) and to social position (in Archaic times). Nietzsche makes the general observation that "all of these terms are soaked in blood" (*Genealogy of Morals*, II,6).

Nietzsche teaches us to think through the next stages of the historical process that begins with the break-up of the warrior aristocracy (at the close of the Archaic period) and runs through the Classical, Hellenistic, Roman, Medieval, early Modern and, ultimately, the Modern period. The initial group of terms – such as *good, bad, right, wrong, duty, guilt, conscience* – also *praise, blame, penalty and reward* – originate in a warrior clan in which the term 'good' meant 'strong.' Gradually the evaluative term gets disassociated from physical prowess than wins the rule and attaches to the social station of the ruler instead. At this juncture 'good' means 'king' (thus the opposition 'good/bad' approximates to 'noble/base'). In classical times, evaluative terms begin to break off from social hierarchies – thus Theognis of Megara (6th century BCE) offers the comment that "many *kakoi* (bad men, commoners) are rich and many *agathoi* (good men, nobles) are poor" (cited by Nietzsche, *Genealogy of Morals*, I,5) – suggesting that nobility survives the loss of office.

Siddhartha (the Buddha) (6th century BCE) shows a similar change in his saying that "One is not a *Brahmin* (noble) because of lineage or caste, but one is a *Brahmin* because he possesses truth and is pure" – suggesting that the praise-element in calling someone 'noble' is separable from circumstances of birth, and can be thought of as a personal characteristic or accomplishment. At this stage 'good' refers to a *quality*. At a further stage in Classical times, this *quality* becomes an item of dispute, as e.g. in this passage from Thucydides (460 BCE – 395 BCE): "The meaning of words no longer has the same relation to things as it did in the past. It is changed by people as they think fit. Reckless action is held to be loyal courage; prudent delay is called cowardice; some call moderation a disguise for weakness; some say, to know everything is to do nothing" (cited in *GM* III, 82).

The first few stages of this history show that evaluative terms get divorced from physical qualities, then from hereditary titles, then from personal characteristics, and become unstable in their attachments and cognate words. They become free-floating abstract characteristics that begin to look like what we think of as 'moral' qualities today.

Nietzsche is particularly interested in a later stage in moral genealogy in which the original quality 'good' – a success-term from a warrior culture, closely linked with strong pride, competition and cruelty – becomes reinterpreted in a new context of cultural influences originating in Judea. 'Good' is reconceived as a guilt-term in which morality is associated with unselfishness, cooperation and kindness. The contrast between selfishness and altruism is completely absent from the original uses of moral terms. Yet Christianity makes it *the* central idea of morality. 'Moral' gets disconnected from pride, wealth and strength and gets connected to humility, poverty and weakness. 'Value' originally was an earthly, tangible, material quality whose power was evident in everyday life. 'Value' becomes unearthly, intangible, immaterial, hidden. The body was 'good' – the body becomes 'bad.'

Nietzsche argues that this same conceptual transformation has happened everywhere in human culture and that it accompanies the universal political transformation from a warrior aristocracy to a priest democracy – warrior-virtues replaced by priest-virtues. Value, which was initially invested here on the earth, is instead "stored up in heaven."

Nietzsche argues that this change is a transparent fraud. He argues that Christian goodness is a pretext or screen behind which the fundamental instincts – the same instincts that drove the competition for power in Archaic society – continue to play their game. The only difference is that the desire for power now hides behind pretty-sounding virtues such as 'faith' and 'charity.' These terms are a false front – their disingenuousness is obvious – everyone shares in this bad conscience –

everyone is caught up in the lie – Nietzsche thinks that this lie is a big part of the modern sickness he is trying to address. We have to rescue aspiration from this dishonesty.

We can see power conflicts everywhere we look – in family life, on the playground, in business, in politics, in churches and synagogues and temples of every kind. Our "value judgments" have become dysfunctional because of the history that underlies them – value predicates that make sense in a given social system cease to function with the dissolution of that society – therefore "nihilism is a necessary consequence of moral evolution."

Moral philosophy is sometimes written as if the history of the subject were of little importance. This position makes sense if we think that ethics is about a few principles that are timeless (eternal, unchanging), that everyone sees or knows them (moral truths), that these truths make up the content of judgment (the conscience, the superego), and that they are independent of perspective (personal, cultural, linguistic, racial, ethnic, religious, political influences). Moral philosophy of this kind is better called *preaching*, since it is decided about things and is not a form of inquiry. This is a kind of thinking that sits in judgment.

Nietzsche is taking an opposite kind of position – not sitting in judgment and not presuming that we have knowledge enough to preach – really, not presuming that we have much knowledge at all. He argues that that people, cultures and historical epochs demonstrate *incredible variety* about moral questions. He is trying to grasp the nature of moral change – to understand how behavior that starts out with branding rituals and caste systems can become selflessness and generosity – particularly to understand the *hollowness* we are left with in the modern epoch.

He argues that history should be our guide, but also notes that history can be told many ways and support opposite causes. He cites the authority of Herodotus on this question – Herodotus, 'father of history' and 'father of lies' – who held that circumstances tend to rule men, rather than men ruling circumstances. "Custom reaches into everything we do and habit is king."

"For if one were to offer men to choose out of all the customs in the world such as seemed to them the best, they would examine the whole number, and end by preferring their own; so convinced are they that their own usages far surpass those of all others" (*Histories*, Book III).

The situation calls for a critique of values – we have to call our values into question – we have to reassess the values of our values and rethink the bases of our moral judgments.

Nietzsche argues that we should begin the inquiry from the hypothesis of moral doubt and the reality of moral disagreement – also from the standpoint of religious doubt – also from a standpoint of radical psychological doubt – and, most radically still, questioning the vey idea of objectivity – for our critique counts for nothing if we are afraid to direct it to itself.

Too Dangerous to Read! --- The Genealogy of Morals – First Essay

Nietzsche writes on the assumption that his readers are familiar with texts and ideas that he is spending his entire life thinking about.

This explains part of the problem with Nietzsche. Most of his readers, and especially new readers, come to his writings without the benefit of a lifetime of intense study of the same subjects that fascinated him – art, language, history, philosophy and culture. Thus they fall much more easily into misunderstandings – of Nietzsche or themselves in trying to understand him. Yet even very sophisticated readers, who come to his writings with backgrounds of great learning, have badly misunderstood Nietzsche's writings. His writings have been denounced at both ends of the political spectrum. Equally so, his admirers praise him in conflicting ways.

It appears that there are a great many Nietzsches and that they contradict one another.

Because his writings are so difficult and because people disagree so fiercely about him, Nietzsche may not be a good subject for study – perhaps he is simply too dangerous to read – too dangerous an influence – too easily misunderstood and too misleading in the way he talks.

I am recommending to myself and to all of us who are working through this study together that we begin from the idea that Nietzsche is asking questions and not making any big claims. The main thing we want to follow in his thinking is his path of asking, exploring, and wondering.

Nietzsche has something powerful to teach us about inquiry and uncovering hidden bias.

Let us explore some of the ideas in his work *On the Genealogy of Morals* (1887) in this spirit.

He tells us that his big subject is value. He wants to look underneath value and try to figure out what is going on with value. He says – perhaps for the first time in human history – that he wants to try a *critique of values* – he wants to try to look critically at value, he wants to try to take a hard look at the very idea that we value something, that we consider it important, that we consider it to have worth or significance or meaning. He even says, let's have a look at analysis and science and even truth – in other words: let's look into the subject of value, but let's also look at the tools we are using to explore value – if we are taking stock of value and measuring it, then let us also take stock of taking stock – let's measure our measures – let's see if the weights we use to weigh things make any sense – let's see if we can dig down to the deepest levels in order to try to understand how our minds work and what we are up to.

The main subject of the first essay in the *Genealogy* is the idea of "good" and the questions that Nietzsche is trying to get us to ask are – where do our moral ideas come from?, and how do the origins of moral terms relate to the way we think about morality today? and what are some next steps in thought following our study of the origins of moral thinking and the course of moral history? He points us in the direction of seeing that moral terms derive from titles, stations, castes, hierarchies – from social and political structures. The prince is good and the pauper is bad – the noble is good and the peasant is bad – the master is good and the slave is bad – the strong is good and the weak is bad. This is the starting-point of his thinking about morality. He is saying: if we go back far enough, what we see is war. One group wins and calls itself 'good' – it lords over some other group and calls that group 'bad.'

This fact gets him thinking about power – in his terminology, about "the will to power" – the idea of which is very straightforward. If something is to count as a truth, there has to be a human being. Someone has to believe this truth, uphold it, plead its cause, try to make it powerful. This is probably his most important idea – the thing that he keeps coming back to.

Nietzsche thinks that in some cases this process gets turned inside out – this is what he is getting at when he talks about resentment, revenge, the slave revolt in ethics. The process goes like this: The value X is asserted and upheld by group A and becomes dominant in a society. Part of the force of the value X asserted by group A is a social world constructed on its basis. Some classes rise, others sink – the masters call themselves 'good' and they call their slaves 'bad' – this is how moral ideas get started. Group B is oppressed in this society – it begins to assert the countervalue Y. Everything that group A calls 'good' is called 'bad' by group B – and so on. Historically, group B later becomes the dominant class – they become the rulers. Then the countervalue Y becomes important and the original value X recedes.

Nietzsche wants to say that the countervalue Y asserted by group B only makes sense in the context of rejected group A and its value X. The whole process is a kind of ricochet effect – this is why he talks about it as a kind of revenge, resentment, payback – the slaves become the masters. The general point seem to be: if group C wants to assert its big value Z without falling into this trap, it has to exit the ricochet cycle that begins with group A and its value X. For example: The Pagan world asserts the value of heroism and winner takes all. The Christian world asserts the value of humility and equal shares for all. This is the original position and the ricochet effect.

At the end of Essay 1 in the *Genealogy* Nietzsche is saying: if you make a serious study of historical linguistics and especially of the etymology of moral terms, you will see the history of morality right before you – the history that begins in war and ends with judgments – the transition from political titles to free-floating ethical qualities. As soon as you see this history, you will be forced to ask the completely new question – given that our moral ideas have been shaped and perverted by war and political jockeying – *where do we go from here?* How should we think about moral ideas today? Suppose that we try to get away from the past and begin thinking about morals from scratch. "The task is the solution to the problem of value – to determine anew the order of rank among values" – whatever was obvious before has to be questioned and "every thou shalt requires an investigation."

Pregnant with Future --- The Genealogy of Morals – Second Essay

The first step in Nietzsche's ethical inquiry begins from the starting-point of praise terms like *good, noble, worthy, high, first, fine, excellent, superior* and compares these to their opposite blame terms such as *bad, low, base, least, inferior, poor.* Just listing these words side by side demonstrates exactly the point that Nietzsche wants to make: that the words we use to commend also refer to high station in society, wealth and power; and that the words we use to condemn also refer to low station, poverty and subjection.

The second step in this inquiry is to look at moral emotions or feelings such as shame, guilt, sin, disgust, embarrassment, humiliation – felt in pangs, twinges, spasms, paroxysms, tremors, shocks – waves of conscience, regret, envy, rage – also feelings of duty, obligation, debt, responsibility, sympathy, compassion – thus to take in every kind of feeling registered on the moral scale; every anxious or painful feeling and ultimately the experience of suffering itself.

Nietzsche sees human beings as emotional creatures who both send out emotional sonar in every direction – as instincts search across the environment – and also receive emotional signals constantly – always searching, always feeling, trying to discharge and take in energy. His basic principle here is that any instinct that cannot discharge itself in action turns inward and becomes poisonous. He also holds that any creature incapable of reading emotion is effectively blind in its environment and tends to become a *victim*.

Social life puts a frame around instinctual life and contains, channels and tames instinctual energy – sexuality is transfigured and no longer enters into consciousness as such – it becomes motive power in all the things that people do. But society is not simply a neutral framework. It is a hierarchy in which wealthy and powerful people lord over people who are weak and poor.

Nietzsche thinks that one of the most important steps in this process is when masters create a religion for slaves. The religion makes it seem as if the valuable things in life are actually not in life at all, but lie in wait for us after death. The religion teaches us to be ashamed of our instincts and to feel guilt about our low station – to accept our humble station and fit ourselves to it – to feel indebted every moment of our lives and subject to frightening powers that may lash out against us without warning. The more spirituality and otherworldliness and the more God there is, the more ashamed and guilty and indebted we feel. Thus we are taught to have an "evil eye" for our natural instincts. We are taught that earthliness, animal instincts and human feelings are the antithesis of heaven, spirit and holiness. Religion gives us a bad conscience about our terrestrial, earthly, animal nature and, in so doing, prepares us to submit to power.

Nietzsche wants to focus in on the creature that has been manipulated and twisted by this kind of socialization and religious indoctrination. He wants to see what becomes of such a creature after many generations of training. Long ago human beings began to live in cities, worship gods and serve kings; as a result people today are quite different than their ancient ancestors.

Nietzsche has two fundamental reactions to this training, indoctrination and slow change in human nature. He is offended by it, he sees it as a hideous distortion of our nature, he condemns it and wants to expose it as a lie: "For too long the earth has been turned into a madhouse!" At the same time he sees it as a powerful transformation of human existence that creates a completely new situation for us. The animal that rages against itself, the animal trained to be hostile to life, to slander the world and all its own instincts, the animal who interprets his innermost feelings as a kind of guilt before God, the animal trained to approach a maximum feeling of guilty indebtedness on earth: this animal is "pregnant with future" (II, 16). Human being, under the yoke of taming socialization and self-despising religious indoctrination, has become "a way, an episode, a bridge, a great promise" – "something new, profound, unheard of, enigmatic," "a lively contradiction." History has given man an illness that makes it possible for man to overflow into an unprecedented health. The training he has received in guilt prepares him to experience an unprecedented "second innocence."

Nietzsche thinks there are several unmistakable signs of these changes in the human condition. The first is that man becomes "a creature who can make promises."

That is: he can place himself in a relationship with time and hold himself accountable for things he has not done yet. Before we can become a "creature of time," we have to gain a degree of control over the future, to think causally and anticipate the future. In a word, this is training in self-control, in will, in becoming powerful, in directing the flow of attention and action.

A second sign of this change is that human beings become "the creatures who remember."

Nietzsche is struck by the fact that human beings can become the victims of their own memories. We rummage through the bowels of our past to fashion weapons against ourselves; we rip open old wounds; we become intoxicated with our own poisonous wickedness; memories invade our consciousness and render us helpless. Memory in these examples is a descent into our own private hell. Nietzsche's point is not simply to bear witness to the power of self-defeating forces within the human constitution. His point is that the same creature who has been trained to become the victim of its own memory is also the creature who creates itself through the control of its memory. Nietzsche reasons that human beings control memory through *forgetting*. "Forgetting is no mere inertia, but an active and (in the strictest sense) positive faculty of repression – the human power of limiting itself" – it is a "doorkeeper," a way of giving us a moment of "quiet," a way of "making room" – forgetting is a kind of "memory of the will" and power of self-determination (without which we would never be done with anything and thus would become inert). Overlooking creates the present (eliminating enough of memory and the sensorium to create a manageable whole) as well as the future (and thus the possibility of seizing one project, one responsibility, one course of action, among myriad others).

Forgetfulness is the key to powerful, healthy, ongoing and progressive individual self-creation.

The Ascetic Planet --- The Genealogy of Morals – Third Essay

The third step in Nietzsche's path of questioning about moral issues focuses on asceticism. This is a self-denying way of life; the idea that a person can attain a high spiritual and moral state by practices of self-denial, by extreme abstinence and austerity; a life of renunciation, especially of sexual pleasure, material pleasures and comforts, and all worldly goods; a quiet life of fasting, poverty, mortification, of self-imposed hardship, sacrifice and consecration to some higher purpose; long thought to be a kind of training of the soul for virtuous and holy living.

The term 'asceticism' comes from the Greek *askesis* meaning exercise or training in the sense of athletic training: making sacrifices and training hard for an upcoming event or more generally to practice strength and stay fit. In the first century this term was imported into Christian writings to indicate 'spiritual exercise' and training that might include flagellation and scourging – i.e. whipping and beating oneself as a way of fighting against temptations and making the body submit. Part of the idea of asceticism is that by denying oneself either to take in or to expend a quantity of energy, one begins to store up energy or 'spiritual power' – thus the greatest feats of bodily self-denial create the greatest concentrations and reservoirs of soul power – for example, such as the Buddha's feat of going for long periods without eating or drinking anything, save perhaps a single leaf or a tiny nut each day.

Nietzsche is awestruck by the universality of asceticism – by its huge role in every culture and period of history – he wonders if the earth itself might better be called "the ascetic planet":

"Read from a distant star, the big print script of our earthy existence might well suggest the conclusion that our planet was devoted to asceticism – a nook of disgruntled, arrogant and unpleasant creatures, mainly preoccupied with a profound disgust about themselves, about the earth, and about all life, who inflict as much pain on themselves as they can muster – out of the pleasure of inflicting pain – which may well be the only pleasure they can feel" (III, 11).

Thus he proposes to investigate "the meaning of ascetic ideals" and to solve the puzzle presented by the long, convoluted history and global phenomenon of human self-hatred.

Nietzsche learned some of his insights about asceticism from Schopenhauer, who saw life as a miserable thing and happiness as impossible – the best that a man can attain is a heroic life – heroism takes us out of the frenzy of pointless human activity into a self-created world of austerity and calm. The point is to get into a state where nothing can alarm or move us anymore. Cut off from life, a person looks back calmly "on the phantasmagoria of a world that now stands before him indifferently" (*The World as Will and Representation*, 1, § 68). The idea is to become remote and inaccessible and gradually put a stop to willing anything at all.

Schopenhauer's asceticism makes him regard social life with an intense cynicism. He says, if you maintain silence about anything important, it is your prisoner; but if you let it slip from your tongue, you become its prisoner. Love and be wounded in love – or not – in either case you will regret it – in both, if you try both – therefore learn to take yourself, as much as possible, out of life. Nietzsche simultaneously follows and objects to these dark themes. He is equally jaded about human relationships as his master Schopenhauer and he also praises high mountain passes and a life of solitary self-discipline. But he also says: return back to life, accept the bargain, accept the terms of life – don't stop willing, but instead will more – become bigger than you were, big enough even to surmount this human fate: learn to love fate, *amor fati*. But he also says: this takes enormous strength.

What is the relation between turning inward and becoming poisonous (which he says happens to impulses that cannot find an external outlet) and turning inward and becoming strong (which he says that we must do if we are to master our fate)? Is the poison what makes us strong?

This question becomes an important theme in many of his works – the idea that self-imposed hardship and even cruelty is necessary for becoming strong – thus also that good and evil are grown together and cannot easily be pulled apart. Health feeds on illness or, in another way of looking at it, illness is the normal human state, which in some cases calls up powerfully healthy spirits.

Man has turned against himself and turned the earth into a madhouse. Memory drives us down into our own private hell, where we constantly find new ways to hate ourselves. But the inward turn also creates the possibility of self-responsibility. Introversion is a first step in training for becoming powerful. Introversion precedes self-limitation, self-determination, self-creation.

The term 'mortification' – which Nietzsche sometimes uses to talk about asceticism – is literally 'putting the flesh to death.' Fundamentally, asceticism is a way of getting ready for death. It is a way of dying ahead of time, in order to cheat death of its victory, thus "owning death" and taking it out of the hands of mere accident. Nietzsche is trying to capture the core idea of asceticism as fear of death and a sickness grown out of this fear, but at the same time he is talking up the strength to live in face of death and even to flourish in the brief chance of life.

The large question that Nietzsche is trying to raise in *The Genealogy of Morals* is "What is the meaning of ascetic ideals?" His answer is: man's heart is divided; everything has two meanings; these ideals are ambiguous; they record our self-hating nature and the basic human illness that we spend life trying to cure; but pain, and especially pain that we inflict against ourselves, makes us strong, and strength is exactly what we need to live human lives. We need strength and health enough to flourish in our humanity, rather than sink under it, or waste our lives fighting against it.

As a last stage in the development of the argument of the *Genealogy* Nietzsche returns to the core problem "What is value?" and his aim of laying out a "critique of values." He thinks that he has discovered the hidden essence of value in the ambiguity of the ascetic ideal. He thinks he understands "the meaning of the ascetic ideal." But he also wants to track back to his original idea of exploring the tools he is using in this investigation – taking stock of taking stock and measuring the measures – seeing what we can see about the weights we use to weigh things.

On this theme he remarks that the human spirit, which has fashioned the ascetic ideal, has both defined a supersenuous reality and also excluded itself from it, since we are merely flesh. Thus the creature who fashions otherworldly ideals tends to live in two worlds – one real, one imaginary – calling heaven above 'the real world' and this earth below a 'realm of illusion.' The creature who lives these two lives begins to see that the act of seeing involves a standpoint, a perspective, a point of view from which seeing is looking at the objects it is studying. The dual reality of the ascetic ideal forces the idea of *perspective* into consciousness. The point is: there is no "knowledge in itself" but instead only a "perspective seeing" and a "perspective knowing."

Nietzsche's ultimate conclusion here is that science itself (and the method he is using in his studies) is itself a manifestation of the ascetic ideal. Science is a manifestation of a self-denying and world-rejecting attitude that has not yet acknowledged its perspectival character. That is: science has not yet acknowledged that it cannot attain pure objectivity but instead depends on "forgetting, forcing, adjusting, shortening, omitting, filling out, inventing, even falsifying" and every other factor included in perspectival, human knowing. Nietzsche considers modern science to be fundamentally dishonest about its pursuit of knowledge – about its will to truth – as not yet capable of acknowledging the faith upon which it rests – which is, fundamentally, the familiar ascetic faith that belittles everything human and strives to exalt an otherworldly ideal.

Science appears to erase man in the same measure that it brings ever more into its sphere: Copernicus shows that the earth is not in the center of the universe; Darwin shows that man is not the center of creation; Freud shows that man is not even master of himself. Nietzsche is asserting that science's devaluing-the-human and exalting-the-inhuman is another episode in the history of the ascetic ideal.

He reasons: science falls into line as another means of dissuading man from any kind of self-respect; it is another version of human self-contempt; in this sense also unconditional honest atheism is itself a very late consequence of the basic lie involved in the belief in God.

Nietzsche wants to raise these questions and call attention to the before-now unremarked basis in assumption in science, viz. the fact that scientific work requires underlying presuppositions. This last step brings him to the idea of scientific self-consciousness in which the will to truth becomes conscious of itself as a problem and begins to acknowledge the 'perspectival' character of knowing. Seeing and acknowledging the basis in subjectivity, in value, of all scientific work, presses us to drop the idea of unfettered objective knowledge. We are pressed to take explicit responsibility for the perspective we develop on things. We cannot hide behind the pretense of neutral fact – we are responsible for the values we put forward – and Nietzsche is saying: let us put an end to all this guilt and suicidal nihilism; let us explicitly work for health, for happiness, for the will, for the human, for the earth, for life.

Nietzsche / the Death of God

There is a sickness in modern times. In developing his diagnosis, Nietzsche tries out many formulations, many ways of characterizing the disease and crisis of modern times, many ways of talking about dysfunctional value. Some examples are *loss of faith, loss of certainty, age of exhaustion, the inverted order, decadence*. Nietzsche's term *nihilism* is intended to capture the spirit of the times – "Nihilism means, that the highest values devaluate themselves" – "the rebound from 'God is truth' to the fanatical 'All is false'" – "the ricochet pathology and inference that life has no meaning at all" – "nihilism: our interpretation has collapsed; but because it was *the* interpretation, it now appears that nothing is left." Belief creates the conditions for doubt. High ideals create the conditions for rejecting ideals. Love of ideals creates the conditions for hating them.

"…This realization is a consequence of the cultivation of truthfulness – thus nihilism is itself a consequence of the faith in morality – of the religious spirit."

"…We are no longer Christians: we have grown out of Christianity, not because we dwelled too far from it, but because we dwelled too far in it – because we have *grown* from it; it is our own piety, grown more rigorous and demanding, that forbids us to be Christians today."

Nietzsche sometimes talks about the modern epoch in terms of historical conditions that have prepared the way – *the ascetic ideal, otherworldliness, the worship of purity, the priestly ideal, the puritanical conscience.* Sometimes his focus is on the variety of value systems that become obvious in modern times – *war of beliefs*, the *multifold world, relativism* – this last term is intended to capture the characteristically 'modern' problem of the intersection of cultures. Relativism signals the problem of having to confront a pluralistic cultural universe, in which many cultures and traditions exist side by side, all of them demanding attention and primacy. Nietzsche is struck by this new situation in which "idols now outnumber realities." Sometimes he talks about modernism in terms of the hollow condition left to us in the twilight of naïve idealism. We were filled up, enchanted by our myths; now we are emptied out, disenchanted from the spell. What remains is *the moral vacuum, valuelessness, the dead blank.*

There is a sickness in modern times – something is dying, something has died, something is dead. What is it? – God. – The most important thing of all – the Creator of the universe – the Supreme Judge – the measure of reality, the foundation of morality, the all-seeing eye – the highest, deepest, brightest, clearest – the best, the apotheosis of everything true and good.

Nietzsche's ability to create evocative and thought-provoking language to describe the modern dilemma reaches a kind of dramatic crescendo in his famous expression that *God is dead*. Nietzsche worked on this idea for many years. In some early notes on the theme, he begins with some hints. "Either we die of this religion, or the religion dies of us" – "There is something in the old Germanic idea that 'all the gods must die'"(journal entries, 1872). Ten years later he is still wrestling with the idea, uncertain whether to emphasize its tragedy or comedy: the tragedy of loss and being left alone in the universe, the comedy of having tripped ourselves up and concocted an illness for ourselves, from which we now suffer miserably (journal entries, 1882). He announces the idea for the first time in *The Gay Science* (1882), coming at it from several different angles (108, 125, 153, 343). "An ancient and profound trust has turned into doubt."

This is "the greatest and most significant of all recent events," but for the most part, *no one has noticed it*. People do not see it yet. Pointing it out today, it falls on deaf ears. It came as a surprise, a shock, before people were ready for it. People look at you as if you are a madman if you say it! Strangely, also, even though the event has taken place – "the transcendent has become null and void" – the *shadow* of the old ideal is left behind "and will remain here for thousands of years … and human beings will have to fight and vanquish this shadow, too."

Thus Spoke Zarathustra dates from 1883 and continues the theme. It appears in five separate passages in this work and suggests a number of new ideas: if God is dead, so is sin; worshipping a statue turned a human being into a statue, but now God is dead, so now we are free to change, to search and grow; God is dead, God died of his pity for man, thus if you have a suffering friend, be a resting place for him, but make it a hard bed, a field cot, give him work to do, for if you make it too soft a place, your friend will grow weaker still and his weakness will destroy both of you; lastly, some people doubt God, but the time is long past for such doubts, God is dead, so let us laugh this off and discover our joy (*prologue, 2; I, gift-giving virtue; II, pity; III, apostates; IV, retired*).

Arguably, the death of God is also the main theme of two of Nietzsche's last works – both from 1888 – *Twilight of the Idols* (*or, How One Philosophizes with a Hammer*) and *Revaluation of All Values* (*First Book: The Antichrist / Attempt at a Critique of Christianity*). In both these works Nietzsche uses the image of the death of God to indicate the transition into modernity and to motivate a completely new way of approaching ideas about value, purpose and meaning.

Nietzsche is trying to take stock of the demise of religious belief. He is asking: what led up to it, what does it mean, where do we turn now?

He concludes: our own belief led us to this, we have done this to ourselves – "we have killed God" – we could no longer bear to have a witness like this. We outgrew our child's dream of the world.

There is also a kind of rearguard action and resistance. This is why the shadow still looms over us. We have a powerful instinct to make gods for ourselves – "to hollow out our own value and paint the horizon with our soul-stuff" – this thought or instinct works in us on many levels. It is "an error in the interpretation of natural events, a failure of the intellect," an imputation of "an imaginary cause," but also "a most enduring lie." It works in us as an emotional reality, a powerful need – "an affliction of the brain," "an instinct," "an addiction." "This article of faith can be refuted a thousand times, but if we 'need' it, we will consider it true again and again."

He seems to be saying two things. In our time, this change is *accomplished*. The transition to modernity has taken place. But also: the old lie is deeply inscribed in us and it is no easy matter to overturn it. We are undergoing a huge transformation and we are deeply divided about it.

Talking about the "death of God" is a way of talking about contemporary civilization. The "death of God" is the advent of modernism. That is, we are not talking about a metaphysical claim, e.g. arguing for an atheistic standpoint. Nietzsche is not even interested in this idea; he considers it ludicrous. His focus is on human experience and in particular the huge change it is undergoing. Ideals, principles, rules, laws, goals and values that had been set on high and gave life purpose, order and meaning, are now cast down and have no worth and power. The "death of God" is the arrival of nihilism, "the devaluation of highest values." The "death of God" is a kind of news headline, a report about a change in culture, the clock-strike of a new era.

Nietzsche is trying to resist the impulse to make new gods. He is trying to teach himself new feelings instead. He talks about beginning "to experience what has been revered as God, no longer as godlike, but as miserable, as absurd, as harmful, as an error, as a crime against life." "This was our greatest *reproach* against life, a belief that turns life into a monstrosity." "I want to affirm life, to naturalize humanity, to de-deify the world … to make myself a home on the earth" (*The Gay Science* 109, *The*

Antichrist 47, *The Will to Power* 707). Thus in his proposed "revaluation of all values," Nietzsche is offering at least two new directives for changing the situation created by the ancient and worldwide inheritance from asceticism. The first is to isolate the god-making impulse ("intuitive theism") and learn new feelings about it (on the model that society teaches man new feelings about his aggressive instincts). The second is to learn to appreciate the new situation ("the disenchanted universe"). What we experienced as emptiness, pointlessness, the meaninglessness of a world without God, has to be taken up explicitly as freedom, an open horizon, fending for oneself, a chance to test our strength.

Nietzsche / Principles of Psychology

Nietzsche's portrait of the human psyche is unlike anything that precedes it. He is also unique in calling upon man to become an entirely new kind of creature. He is moving from something like the heliocentric system to polycentricity – the self as multiplicity – offering new ideas of psychic development, disease and health, new ideas for therapy, and a new understanding of striving.

Nietzsche tracks what he considers a family of toxic ideas that have taken hold in recent times and have since swelled to an epidemic – our immune systems of belief and thought have thus far been unable to fight off the disease – a swarm of parasites, a series of infections has spread in us, hijacking our thinking and overturning our natural resistance.

To begin with, we are swamped by the number of elements that we have to contend with. The problem of integrating everything we experience is gradually overwhelming us ("we moderns have no culture of our own – we have no 'own' – what it is like for us today is an explosion of customs, arts, philosophies, religions, sciences – we are wandering encyclopedias").

"People are nowadays so complex and many-sided that they are inevitably insincere whenever they talk, make assertions or try to act on their real principles." Part of the modern problem is simply this complexity – having so much to sort through – this complexity is a central part of what 'modernism' is about. Nietzsche says that we are "choking" on all this material, we simply cannot "digest" it, there is too much information, we are reaching a state of "nausea."

But the problem is more severe – it's not just that there is a great deal to sift through – Nietzsche backs up a step and asks himself *who* or *what* is doing this searching and sorting – who is choking on all this material, who is struggling to put the pieces together, who is this person or self or identity that is doing all this work?

"When I analyze the process that is expressed in the sentence, 'I think,' I find a whole series of daring assertions that would be difficult, perhaps impossible, to prove (that the *essence* of thinking is already known, that thinking is *caused*, that there must be *something* that thinks, that there is an *ego*, that it is *I* who thinks)" (*Beyond Good and Evil*, 16).

If there is no *I* in this brain of mine, then as Nietzsche says it will make no sense to talk about sincerity – instead of my being one being and expressing this unitary self of mine sincerely as who I am (or being insincere – not expressing who I am – but instead expressing a false self) – If there is no *I* or *self* or *identity*, then what is going on, what is true, how can language work?

Nietzsche thinks that he can separate the act of thought from the hypothesis that there is some kind of substrate underlying the act of thought. He thinks that "the deed" is real – the act of thought is real – more accurately, he says that "there are thoughts." What evidence do we have that there is something real (Nietzsche calls this the "ego") that is somehow *behind* our thoughts and is the *cause* of thoughts? – Nietzsche says, we have no such evidence. The belief in the ego is "a crude fetishism." This crude belief "construes the ego as a subject." This subject is further construed as a "cause." Thus an outcome of this study, looking closely at the evidence and not jumping to mythology, is the finding that "the doer is a *fiction* added to the deed."

Nietzsche tries to start fresh and begin to sketch a more accurate portrait of thinking in action. He tries to limit himself to what he can verify about thinking from the *experience* of thinking, but also notes to himself that he has to be skeptical about what he can discover from the 'inside' – he wonders if it might even be possible that his way of looking at the world depended on *not* seeing the truth – mythology gets in the way, but even careful introspection might be unreliable because of other forces working in the system. Some of these forces are: the role of *not* knowing, of one part of the self hiding from another; the role of editing, rewriting, invention, revising, which seems to go on without end; taking on roles and shedding them; and mysteries of neurology just beginning to come into view in the science of his day. The evidence seemed to him also to point to some kind of impulse-energy that takes many forms, e.g. an under-passion animating a religious point of view, a scientific view, a moralistic view, an artistic spirit – that is, the *same* energy of emotion that assumes these unlike forms; a protean drive and various mechanisms in which it is channelled, transformed, heightened or lessened; and subject to will.

This is the new picture that emerges:

"My hypothesis: the subject as multiplicity... The "unconscious" ...Sublimation, channelling of the sexual instinct... Continual transitoriness and fleetingness... The correct idea of the nature of our subject-unity comes to this: we are something like regents at the head of a communality (not 'souls' or 'life-forces')... The regents depend on the ruled... The order of rank and the governing function are continually shifting... The 'subject' is not eternal but transitory ...The struggle expresses itself as obeying and commanding... The regent is kept in ignorance about some of the disturbances in the communality... *Not-knowing* about such things is one of the conditions of the regent's rule... The key point is that the ruler and the ruled are exactly the same kind of stuff, all feeling, all thinking, all willing..." (*The Will to Power*, 382-88; 481-493; 677).

Nietzsche begins from the standpoint of physiology – of the body – he assumes that talking about the soul is simply another way of talking about the body (*Zarathustra* I, 4). The body develops over time and gradually there is something like the adult form of the body. The soul develops over time and gradually there is something like the adult soul or the self or the I. But this apparent unity is in reality not a unity but is "tremendously complex" (*WP* 489). The soul is a concatenation, amalgam or conglomerate of experiences carried to a given point on the timeline. Some of its discernible pieces are modes, categories, or groupings of like experiences, which may be 'adult' but are not 'final' versions, but instead hold together as developing themes such as inner witness, agent of control, historian or autobiographer, victim, jester, hero, child or friend or sibling. If we learn something new, then a new atom-self is created whose history is added to the sum; this piece becomes a new element in talking about oneself, revising the way one looks at oneself, a new token in the game of self-redescription. Countless discrete bits of experience – let us call them atom-selves or ego-nuclei or kernel-selves – continually form beginning in infancy. Through the course of experience, these atom-selves are popping in and out of existence. Each of these atom-selves is or has thoughts, feelings, and also something like a will. That is: ego-nuclei have different desires and are fighting for control – they argue, plead, bargain, deceive and plot against one another – they are rivals in the mental economy. At any given time, a given part-self is in the lead and is dominant; at another moment this order has broken down and a new atom-self is rising. If there is anything like a soul as such it is "the soul as subjective multiplicity" or "the soul as the social structure of competing drives and affects" or "a shifting system of relations between various passions" or "a relation of drives to each other" (*Beyond Good and Evil*, 12, 36; *The Will to Power*, 462, 490).

"The sphere of the subject is constantly growing and decreasing and the center of the system is constantly shifting: in cases where the mass of fragments cannot organize or congeal together, it breaks into parts. The subject-sphere can transform a weaker subject-part into its functionary without destroying it and may even to some extent form a new unity with it. The thing we are looking at here is not a substance but more exactly *striving* after greater strength. The desire to preserve itself is secondary. The essence is, it wants to surpass itself..." (*The Will to Power*, 488)

The self is a kind of crowd, assembly, collection or committee – its parts are forces, powers, drives, passions – each a thought, feeling, will – contesting, unifying, breaking apart – another way of saying this is that the body is a kind of battle-zone where this contest takes place – different kinds of orders or hierarchies or systems among these affects makes for different kinds, states or episodes of self. There is something like a 'normal' multiplicity of feeling, thought and desire. This can become exaggerated into something like a dissociative disorder in a given case (something like 'multiple personality disorder' or 'dissociative identity disorder'). That is: for complicated reasons, a particular individual never develops an effective hierarchy of drives that serves to put some framework around normal drive conflict. An exaggeration in the other direction is possible. In a case lie this, one part of the self has a kind of stranglehold on all the other parts, so that normal multiplicity is reduced to a kind of mental tyranny. In contemporary terms this is something like obsessive-compulsive disorder or another form of hypervigilance.

Nietzsche discovers in himself some evidence of both these kinds of exaggeration and also discovers in his own experience psychological principles that show up because one or another strong urge is not allowed to express itself but instead has been judged, muffled, censored; he sees a kind of story unfolding in himself in which the judge rules, the accused is punished, the accused rebels, the accused exacts revenge, followed by some temporary quiet. Some of his conclusions are, that *instincts that do not find a vent outwards turn inward*; that *suppressed instincts become poisonous*; that we make a huge effort to hide something, but cracks appear in the armour and *the hidden thing always leaks out*; and perhaps most famously, his doctrine that *man would rather will nothingness than not will at all*. By Nietzsche's reading, destructive impulses are a kind of protest in response to suppressed impulse. Better an outrage than nothing at all (C.G. Jung once said: "Sometimes you have to do something unforgiveable just to go on living"). Striving is the essence of life and cannot be held back indefinitely.

Freud of course is a student of Nietzsche and adopts many of these terms – ego, unconscious, sublimation – Freud also adopts a view of the ego reminiscent of Nietzsche's model – a kind of stand-in for the monarch (the "regent"), indicating a kind of office that is occupied by various characters. Freud argues that the ego is a *position* in the mental economy that is surrounded by various other players or powers – id, superego – however he adds to the concept in several interesting ways. He thinks that the ego is not simply a position but also contains in itself the *history* of everything that has been done from this position. The ego is a history of the choices that constitutes a given person. He also thinks that the ego represents the *reality* principle, where 'reality' is a balance between obsession (hypervigilance) and dissociation (dispersion). The French psychologist Jacques Lacan develops these ideas of the 'empty self' several stages further. Lacan claims that the ego is a kind of theatre or playhouse. The play consists in a series of identifications, beginning with the primary identification established in the "mirror stage," the child's first experience of recognizing itself in a mirror, forming at once an image of itself and its nascent ego, followed by an identification with the mother and with successive 'others.' Lacan claimed that a mature person develops increasingly abstract identifications until he grasps the essential "vacuity" at the core of his own identity (Freud, *The Ego and the Id*; Lacan, *Ecrits*).

At the bottom of this system, showing itself in all these atom-selves and the complex dynamism taking place between them, is the basic soul-force that Nietzsche calls *will, will to power, instinct, instinct for freedom, drive, passion, affect, urge* – every discrete atom-self in the mental economy is animated by this energy. The closest we can get to understanding this force is to see that it simply has to expend itself – so much so, that it would rather will nothingness than not will at all – it must jump out of itself and do some kind of work. Thus from the outside it appears to be a kind of projective or goal-directed energy, whose goals are not fixed but vary with physiology, life-history and wildly different circumstances (*Genealogy of Morals*, III, 1). Nietzsche's basic insight here becomes a central theme in nearly all subsequent psychology: the striving soul-force is re-examined in many different systems: Adler uses Nietzsche's term *will to power*; Freud calls it *libido*; Jung talks about *psychic energy*; Maslow uses the expression *self-actualization*; Karen Horney calls it *self-realization*; Ellis calls it *self-acceptance*; it has been called the striving for perfection, superiority, competence and mastery.

For a given individual, at a particular juncture in life-history, the mental economy instantiates a particular hierarchy. At a next juncture, the hierarchy has fallen and some new order is rising. Thus the question: *how to look at this variety*. Nietzsche adopts several different ways of talking about it, often returning to Plato's distinction between 'strong' and 'weak' wills (ἀκρασία, *akrasia*, lacking command over oneself; acting against one's better judgment; weakness of will):

"Multitude and disaggregation of impulses and the lack of any systematic order – this is a 'weak will.' Coordination under a single dominant impulse – this is a 'strong will.' In the first case there is oscillation and lack of gravity; in the second case there is precision and a clear direction" (*The Will to Power* 46).

In other passages Nietzsche emphasizes creation over discovery and argues that there is no core self that is 'always there' – an innate core or a basis formed in early infancy – the essence of a given person that is waiting to be discovered and liberated. The self, the strong will, the clear direction is (instead) completely and wholly a "fiction." It is entirely one's own creation. Much of what people say and think about the self is complete fiction – people unthinkingly accept a fetishism, a mythology, a religion, a new science or jargon or faddish way of talking about the self. Nietzsche draws the interesting conclusion from this observation that we should *proceed further along the same line* – we should take over the creative function and *become our own creations*, by conducting the experiment of belief in ourselves (*Beyond Good and Evil*, 36).

"I am speaking to people who want to become who they are – that is: people who are new, unique, incomparable, who give themselves laws, who *create* themselves" (*Genealogy of Morals*, I, 13; *The Gay Science*, 335).

Expressly taking up the role of the creator sets itself against deeply-ingrained habits from infancy, socialization and religious training. Nietzsche's way of saying this is that self-creation overturns morality. The idea is to observe, understand and to attack one's own irrational, grandiose, and perfectionistic *shoulds* and *oughts* and *musts*; to get over religious storytelling, commandments, gods and devils; to see that nothing is sacred (which does not mean that nothing is humanly important); to see that nothing is demonic (which does not mean that nothing is humanly unjust). To free oneself from the hold of these precedents is see them as one's own creations; this invites the experiment of explicitly directing one's primary strivings.

"All the beauty and sublimity we have bestowed on real and imaginary things I wish to reclaim as the property and product of man – as his fairest apology. Man as thinker, as poet, as god, as love, as power; with regal liberality he has lavished gifts upon all things and thus impoverished himself – to debase himself and make himself feel wretched. His most selfless act hitherto has been to admire and worship and know how to conceal from himself that it was he, after all, who has created what he admired" (*The Will to Power*, II, epigram)

"To humanize the world, that is, to make ourselves more and more the masters of it" (*WP*, 614).

Nietzsche understood that his new approach appears to take a giant step towards subjectivity. It appears to wrest the whole question of man's nature out of the arena of scientific or objective or neutral truth. This is exactly what he meant to do. "Everything is merely *subjective* – of course! It is also our work! Let us be proud of it!" (*WP*, 1059). The point is to take responsibility – to appropriate our own reality – not trying to avoid responsibility by telling ourselves one or another kind of fairy-tale.

"Man is an animal – the not yet fully defined animal" (*N* XIII, 276).

Freedom to create and choose introduces the concepts of value and meaning into psychology.

It is at this point that Nietzsche asks himself, "What might yet be made of man?" (*BGE* 203).

Nietzsche imagines a distant past in which man is less than human and a distant future in which man is more than human – an Underman and an Overman – a less-than creature and a more-than creature – combining science's insight about a pre-human past and art's vision of a post-human future. Nietzsche is not venturing a guess or a prediction about the next stage of biological evolution ("I am not posing the problem of what will succeed man in the sequence of beings," *Antichrist*, 3). He is trying to find a way of talking about how human beings should live in *this* life. His premise is: human beings have a pre-rational, instinctual, aspirational drive – strivings that have a foundation in biology – strivings that take shape as unfolding projects – yet *satisfying* this drive has a paradoxical effect – rather than bringing about a happy completion, the experience of satisfaction brings the system to a null point experienced as frustration. Adversity stokes fulfilment, but fulfilment is debilitating; the solution is to stoke adversity. Nietzsche's way of saying this is to talk about "seeking out enemies" and "unquiet living."

Nietzsche does not seem to think that striving has any goal in itself. "Becoming does not aim at a final state, or flow into Being" (*The Will to Power* 708). Striving is relative – it wants to surpass, go on, be more, overcome, transform – striving is oriented towards overcoming but not at arriving. "Our goal is…goallessness as such…this is the principle of our new faith" (*WP* 25).

Nietzsche / Principles of Interpretation

Nietzsche says that he does not believe in anything fixed or final; but it has come to him that people get caught in a picture, a 'truth' that has gotten stuck, become frozen, solidified, that has stopped living, growing or evolving; a single moment gets mistaken as an eternal reality. This means that *truth itself* becomes the problem. Truth becomes sacred truth, truth we cannot question, truth as the hypostatization of "frozen thinking," eternal truth. The point is that the world keeps changing, whereas "truth is unconditional on one point" (*Genealogy of Morals*, III, 24).

Nietzsche proposes to "get unstuck" and get himself out of "frozen thinking" and stop being "unconditional on one point." This means abandoning the ideal of attempting to understand phenomena from a standpoint that eliminates the person who is struggling to understand. Nietzsche wants to reinsert the human being into this equation. Objectivity is a delusion and a masked form of asceticism, i.e. hatred of the earth. Thinking, feeling and willing are elements of the same experience; part-selves formed in experience think, feel and will and in so doing stake out a position; this position is located in a space of alternatives for the individual thinker (who thinks, feels and wills rival complexes of thought/feeling/will through the timeline); it is located in a still wider framework among human thinking, feeling, willing – personal and social – in the present epoch, and in recorded history. The new kind of sensibility that Nietzsche is talking about is a "perspective" sensibility – every little jumble of thinking-feeling-willing is a thought on the issue, a feeling on the issue, a plan, a way of seeing. A "perspective" sensibility tries to capture as much of this diversity as it can. The idea of the self as a multiplicity suggests the idea of truth as an agglomeration. The idea of the self as a dynamism suggests the idea of truth as a variable. The immediate problem is to escape exclusivity and permanence and to accept multiplicity and transience. The point is to *get unstuck* – to *go on* – to become a sensibility that takes in as much as possible and changes as much as possible. Truth has been "unconditional on one point," but truth reimagined will become "unconditional on every point" (*GM* III, 12).

Nietzsche calls his new approach "perspectivism" and proposes it as a critique of the way belief gets exalted into fixed truth. We have to get a handle on this belief/exaltation cycle and replace it with something else –

a perspective sensibility – instead of getting stuck we go on – a process of always moving forward, never stopping, of "endlessly bountiful creativity" – something he also calls "juggling" and "dancing" and "improvising one's life." It is an experimental sensibility – something like "'Let's try it!' – otherwise courage loses its rights" (*Human, All too Human* 51).

Perspectivism denies that truths are 'true' because they describe anything. It asserts that truths are 'true' within a context, a set of values, or from a certain perspective. Truths are 'true' *in* that perspective. And perspectives are conditioned by special facts and contingent circumstances. Objectivity, if this is understood as "contemplation without interest," or dispassionately seeing something and stating what is seen, is a nonsensical absurdity. There are no "facts in themselves." No one possesses "knowledge" *per se*. But there are facts *from* a perspective. People can indeed know something *from* a perspective. Truth therefore is not the opposite of falsehood. It may even be a *kind* of falsehood – the kind we can't live without. Nietzsche's criterion is that "the value for *life* decides." He also says that *art is worth more than truth* and that truth is a kind of lie that we need in order to live. True is a lie that has somehow caught on, taken hold, and become powerful (*Genealogy of Morals*, III, 12; *Will to Power* 853).

Now it has occurred to many people reading Nietzsche that these ideas are literally self- contradictory, since telling the truth about truth cannot be a radically different kind of enterprise than telling the truth about anything else. If telling the truth about truth is itself a matter of perspective, or a kind of lie, or a kind of error, then this account too is only a perspective, or a lie, or an error. Ultimately, we will have to exempt at least *one* truth from all this talk about perspective and error and lies, in order to explain the difference between truth in the normal sense and truth in this odd new meaning that Nietzsche has decided to give it. We have to uphold at least one truth in order to make the claim that there are no others.

But let us try to understand what Nietzsche is saying before we reject it too quickly as nonsense.

Nietzsche says: in order for something to be true, it must be held to be true; in order for me to hold something true, I have to believe it. "The estimation of value 'I believe that such and such is true' is the essence of truth" (*Will to Power* 507). When I believe something and hold it to be true, I am taking it as fixed and secure. I can hang onto it and not worry about it anymore. It becomes one of the things I depend on and becomes part of my way of looking at the world, or my 'perspective.' It becomes one of the conditions of my life. Because I believe it and hang onto it, my life begins to take shape. I can't have much of a life if nothing is fixed and secure. This is part of what Nietzsche is up to in saying that truth in essence is an estimation of value.

Nietzsche thinks of human beings as believing and holding on to ideas and not worrying about some things and taking some things as settled *against the background of the flux of experience* that he calls "chaos." Belief takes place against the background of the primordial flux. This interprets 'holding onto ideas' and 'taking them as settled' and 'accounting them as knowledge' into a form of "schematizing." "To schematize is to impose upon chaos as much regularity and as much security as our practical needs require" (*Will to Power* 515). The flux is rushing by and we make the best attempts we can to slow things down, to get a handle on things, so that we can act. In a word, this is "knowing." "The urge for security and penchant for truth derives from fear engendered by uncertainty" – and at the root it is "the longing for an enduring world."

"'Truth' is not something simply there, that might be found or discovered, but something that must be created and that gives a name to a process, or rather to a will to overcome that has in itself no end – introducing truth, as a *processus in infinitum*, an active determining – it is not a becoming-conscious of something that is in itself firm and determined" (*Will to Power* 552).

Truth has to be believed, held, determined, and preserved – it has to be held by someone – thus he says "there are many kinds of eyes and therefore many kinds of truth." He thinks that it is important to try to see as much as possible – not to insist on one point but on every point – and by this much-expanded, comprehensive vision, we begin to draw closer to what our ancestors thought of as truth. There is a higher standard for truth: *the value for life decides*. But not every life can or should be borne. "Only insofar as a truthful man is categorically determined to be *just* is there anything great about his striving for truth." But justice is a question, a problem, something to strive after. "What is justice and how is it possible? If it is not possible, how is life to be borne? I am constantly asking myself these things." "Be things as they may, we wish to be just and to go as far as is possible towards justice." "Justice is a function of a panoramic power that looks beyond narrow estimations of good and evil and has a far broader horizon of advantage. It is the intention to preserve something that is *more* than just this person or that person. Justice is the supreme representative of life itself" (*Nachlass*, XIII, 42).

Nietzsche's teaching is that truth is more than an arbitrary swindle that is simply taken to be true because it has had the luck to be believed in and made powerful in the world. Truth turns out to be more than this, because truth and people who make beliefs powerful as truths must take on a panoramic, active-determining, all-comprehending, constantly-changing perspective. That is, the thing that keeps this process honest, the guarantor of truth, is not an abstract standard of neutrality or objective cognition, but the active engagement of a thinker who develops virtues such as self-criticism, curiosity and flexibility, changeability and openness.

His method is to jump into a subject, take it whole, jump out again – not to create a ponderous *explanation* for anything but more simply to keep the flame of thinking alive. "I want to praise skepticism and inquiry… Great spirits are skeptics… Convictions are prisons" (*Antichrist* 54).

But how can this work in practice? Where is the standard? How can we insist on every point?

Consider an example case – the problem of understanding Nietzsche and Nietzsche's books.

Nietzsche's books have notoriously meant whatever his readers have wanted them to mean.

There appears to be a large crowd of Nietzsches, differently interpreted, including this dozen:

→ Nietzsche the firebrand, hothead, champion of the individual will against the compromises of society – rebel, free man, self-creating artist;

→ Nietzsche the megalomaniac, would-be God, Christ, Saviour, Zoroaster – wild man afflicted by a persecution complex and driven to towering delusions of grandeur;

→ Fascist Nietzsche, war-monger, poet of the blond beast, The Master Race, prophet of will and Germany, racist and bloodthirsty – speaking in the voice of an ancient tribal chief and conqueror – author whose book was issued to more than 100,000 German soldiers in the first days of World War I; Nietzsche imagined by his sister, Elisabeth Förster-Nietzsche, and by the pioneers of the National Socialist movement; Nietzsche admired by Hitler and Mussolini;

→ Humanist Nietzsche, cultured European, liberal in the mould of Voltaire and Goethe, who sought to define a new global philosophy of man; Nietzsche the aesthete, stylist, literary man, champion of art for art's sake, romantic scholar, musician, composer – an artist whose main study was to create great art out of himself; seer who recast the humanist ideal as the flame of thought in the eternity of the chase;

→ Nietzsche the classicist, philologist, student of Attic tragedy and its prehistoric origins; Nietzsche the critic, the Socratic, upholding honesty as the supreme virtue – philosopher of human excellence – lover of truth, intellectual conscience, justice, who tried to bring about the good by clearing away false idols;

→ Nietzsche the atheist, godless visionary, philosopher of the future, happy to cut free of man's self-enclosed ignorance and fear of the unknown – symbol of courage in the face of danger – drawn to chilly heights where he sought to challenge himself and grow his powers; pied piper of fearless secularity;

→ French Nietzsche, Postmodern Nietzsche, anti-principle of the Enlightenment, prophet of irrationalism, acceptance of fundamental Chaos;

➡ Heidegger's Nietzsche, Nietzsche the metaphysician, one among the few great thinkers of all time, anti-principle to Plato, reversing the value system emerging from the union of Athens and Jerusalem, discovering the answer to the problem of modernism by living the fate of questioning;

➡ Realist Nietzsche, in the school of Machiavelli, Hobbes, Clausewitz – the thinker as journalist who tries to deflate idealism on behalf of ruthless criticism – someone who elevates practical knowledge over hazy abstractions; someone who looks for sound principles for conduct that no longer depend on hazy thinking or absurd fantasies about man's basic goodness;

➡ Nietzsche the earthling, asserting the natural dignity of human beings without recourse to theologies, metaphysics or political ideologies;

➡ Nietzsche the first serious student of the history of ethics;

➡ Nietzsche the first psychologist in the modern sense; Nietzsche the precursor of Freud.

Perhaps we can add several other viable Nietzsches such as Nietzsche the pamphleteer, provocateur, *bon vivant*, witty commentator, urbane conversationalist; Nietzsche the raving syphilitic; also Nietzsche the muddle: the awkward, bumbling, pompous bombast, who contradicts himself in virtually everything he has to say, e.g. preaching to each of us to recreate ourselves out of our own willpower, yet also announcing from on high, against all preaching, that the cosmic cycle of recurrence is impervious to human meddling.

Likely there are other Nietzsches as well and, in some inexplicable way, Nietzsche foresaw that he would be misinterpreted, reinterpreted, expropriated, stolen, and put to every sort of good or evil purpose. He seems to have invited this fate. All this makes sense given his overarching idea. If we *insist on every point* then there is something to see from every perspective. The cure for the demise of traditional values and the inauguration of secular modernism is not the return of a Big Truth to dislodge all the others – making them lesser – but the new venture of small truths. The cure is the pluralistic universe of small truths, each championing different cause.

This theory holds that mental toughness – working hard to get things right – has nothing to do with 'sticking to the facts.' The Stoics were wrong in thinking that we have to inure ourselves to hard truths. There is nothing hard and final in the world that is pressing down on us. Just the opposite. The world is pliable, incomplete, infinite, disjointed – not a system – not a whole, not 'monolithic.' The self-respecting mind faces the problem of overwhelming input. A vast array of experiences, of vast kinds, unfolds in every waking moment. Mental toughness has to do with the mind disciplining itself for the flux. The problem is to find the strength to withstand the chaos of "affects," not shutting down in the face of influx, but staying open and welcoming.

In last works like *Twilight of the Idols* and *The Antichrist* and the unfinished *Will to Power*, Nietzsche returns to the project of directing the "will to truth" to itself, an idea he first proposed to himself in early works like *The Gay Science* and also explored in middle works like *The Genealogy of Morals.* This is as close as he can get to looking over his own shoulder. He tries to figure out how intellectual *dishonesty* works, e.g. as manifested in characteristic errors: ascribing substance or real existence to mental constructs; ascribing timeless significance to transient events; or ascribing moral characteristics to natural processes. Ultimately he thinks that the root cause of intellectual dishonesty is moral. Thinkers sacrifice their devotion to truth because they love good better than truth. His conclusion about this is plausible. In effect he is arguing that human beings do not know enough to throw out evidence in order to save a valued principle. History seems to teach the opposite lesson, i.e., that discounting evidence to save morality nullifies morality; and since prejudice masquerades as righteousness, discounting evidence serves tyranny. The solution is to take in *everything* and keep questioning, keep looking, keep the flame of thinking alive. The revaluation of all values, in the arena of truth and knowledge, is "perspectivism" – a world of provisional assumptions, tests, trials – possible valuations – thought-experiments – an idea comes to light, defines a history, has an impact or not, persists or not – is merely a *force*, is merely what becomes *powerful* – is as much *as we can make it*, or does as little harm *as we make certain* –

'good' is what we promote or prevent. By asserting that "the value for life decides," he is arguing against presumption, against permanent values exempted from criticism, against eternity. Thus we can offer as many false Nietzsches as we like. If we go on, take in everything, spare nothing, and keep questioning, the truth will out.

The Nietzsche Cure

Nietzsche's most important research project was the introduction of the concept of value into philosophy. Nietzsche however conceived philosophy as a form of critique. The point of bringing the concept of value to philosophy was not merely to define this concept, or to provide a more extensive inventory of existing values distributed through societies around the world, or to work towards a bigger and better moral consensus. Nietzsche would no doubt see all these tasks as new versions of conformism and submission. The Nietzsche cure is electroconvulsive.

Nietzsche explicitly sets himself the goal of "overcoming morality" (note from 1883). We have to reinsert Nietzsche into his epoch to give this project some context. Nietzsche sees himself as living in a time of disease. His first problem is to document the moral degradation of his age – simply to record the main currents of thought in his time – to bring his passion for honesty to the task of laying bare the society of his times with all its contradictions – e.g. imperialism, colonialism, anti-Semitism, race prejudice, misogyny, child labor, industrial blight; scientific advance, belief in progress, secularism, the march of democracy, increasing freedom of speech. His second task is revolutionary. He wants to liberate humanity from the sickness of the times. He wants to destroy the disease – destroy the old things standing in the way – this means destroying morality, 'goodness' and every other pretty-sounding idol to which we pay lip service but secretly despise. His diagnosis ultimately comes to religion as the root cause of decadence. So he attacks religion too – not just *Beyond Good and Evil* but *The Antichrist* – all for the cause of liberating humanity from superstition and all the consequences of worshipping ascetic ideals. His last task is creative. This is the creative transformation of the mind-heart-will that built monuments to ethereal, otherworldly Power, afterwards disowning its creations and debasing itself. The transvaluation of all values will create a new kind of value, free from mistakes such as hatred of the body, exaltation of suffering, and worship of an alien god. The new set of values will be centered around the artist, the artist's process, trying out new colors, not getting stuck, going on – we have to overcome pity and every other emotion that debases us and draws us down; we have to liberate ourselves from a life-diminishing eternity and celebrate the here-and-now.

Socrates defined an ideal of wisdom, a composure and emotional acceptance of the transience of human existence. He conceived wisdom to be a consequence of *understanding* that divines a reality lying beneath appearance. Historically, the reality underlying appearance is reconceived as God. Thus the reality lying beneath appearance is more-than-real and the reality right in front of us is less-than-real. In the long run this opposition hollows out transient existence and leads to nihilism. Nietzsche proposes to replace the Socratic ideal of wisdom with an ideal of art – of endlessly bountiful creativity – the electroconvulsive therapy of questioning ascetic ideals.

The observer discovers, whereas the artist creates a truth. Nietzsche criticizes discovery as passive and praises art as activity. Finding stands for getting stuck in a place, whereas inventing stands for going on, telling stories, juggling and improvising – "Art, in which precisely the *lie* is sanctified, in which the will to deception has a good conscience" (*Genealogy of Morals*, III, 25).

Heidegger summarizes the upshot of Nietzsche's critique of truth at the end of his first Nietzsche lectures from 1935: "From the perspective of the essence of Being, *art* has to be conceived as the basic happening of beings, the authentically creative moment" (*Nietzsche*, 1961).

Nietzsche asserts the supremacy of art-speech over objective logic. He holds that the driving question is whether human beings are strong enough to be artists – whether they have strength enough *to become their own creations* – willpower enough to subject themselves to the rule of their own creativity. He talks about the human capacity to *endure* the creative transformation – the transvaluation of value – as a kind of "spiritualization of cruelty" "Almost everything we call 'higher culture' is based on the spiritualization of *cruelty*, on cruelty becoming more profound." Thus creativity is a sublimated form of cruelty:

"The will to appearance...is *countered* by the sublime inclination of the seeker after knowledge who insists on profundity, multiplicity, and thoroughness, with a *will* which is a kind of cruelty of the intellectual conscience...All courageous thinkers will recognize this in themselves...They will say: 'There is something cruel in the inclination of my spirit'" (*The Gay Science*, 110).

This is an important source for the idea that creativity is bound up with passionate, violent emotions that break through social conventions; that forces deep in the soul shove themselves forward and upend morals; that *the power of will* can harness the creative process by recognizing the impersonations one has already undergone in countless episodes of social life; taking on roles in social life offers a precedent for creating a persona for oneself and acting it out; so that by conscious intention one may transform oneself into one's own explicit creation. Creative work emerges out of a place where good and evil are still indistinct, but not because self-creation is amoral; instead because art tries to wrestle raw, rude drive energy into form.

Nietzsche first gained public acclaim through a series of public lectures given in 1888 by the Danish critic George Brandes (1842-1927). Brandes interpreted Nietzsche's philosophy as "aristocratic radicalism." He explained that Nietzsche was primarily interested in moral questions, and that Nietzsche had set himself up as the opponent of the egalitarian premise in modern morals, viz., the idea of the equal worth of each person. Nietzsche, he explained, cares nothing for the "herd" or for people who have no fire of questioning in themselves. He is interested in great human beings. Nietzsche's notebooks from 1887 contain some lines that suggest this idea. "The human beings I care about" Nietzsche says: "I wish them suffering, desolation, sickness, ill-treatment, indignities – I wish that they should know profound self-contempt, torture of self-mistrust, the wretchedness of the vanquished" (*Will to Power* 910).

The Nietzsche cure is a kind of shock therapy. Instead of electrically inducing seizures for therapeutic effect, Nietzsche rhetorically induces seizures. He invades the deepest recesses of human reality by ruthless criticism, shining a harsh and revealing light on the heart's desires. Nothing is spared, nothing is left standing, everything becomes a question, everything becomes a choice. He documents the course of the disease – "nihilism"; he treats it in hopes of breaking its hold on us – "freedom"; he offers a way forward meant to replace lost ideals – "creation." Beginning from "enfeebled instinct," exhaustion, weariness, surrender, the cure runs through *amor fati*, appropriating human reality, and shocks us into energy, celebration and hunger.

The greatest aspiration human beings have ever dreamed of is exposed as a sick delusion – a form of self-hatred – we mistook its origin and thus condemned our deepest instincts. We defined a supersensuous reality and barred ourselves from ever entering it; religion taught instinct to ensoul the sky and thus instinct de-souls the earth; but now we rescue aspiration from its problematic history, its encasement in dishonesty, and its modern shipwreck. We catch ourselves in the process of stoking adversity and thus begin to understand our real power.

Overall: striving is run through the sieve of intellectual conscience and flows out cold and fresh.

Pity

Nietzsche denounces pity in many of his works and for this reason has himself been denounced as a heartless, cruel thinker. Some writers have argued that his mistakes on this issue helped to lay the ground for fascist ideology. Others defend his attack on pity as a modern form of Stoicism and a call to all of us to toughen up and bear misfortune with strength. Asking the question about pity helps to bring more Nietzsche to Nietzsche – more criticism to the critique he began – thus completing the cure by growing, evolving, advancing beyond the therapist to stand on our own.

Nietzsche says that pity is a "contagion" (GM III, 14); "the greatest danger" (GS, 271); "poison" (BGE, 30). Nietzsche sees many different kinds of problems with pity. Pity insults the dignity of the person who is pitied; it is a way of asserting that the person we pity is weak and ignoble. "The instinct of pity ... is a way of saying 'no' to life ... it is the beginning of the end, the dead stop, a retrospective weariness, the will turning against life, tender and sorrowful signs of the last stages of the illness" (GM, preface). Nietzsche thinks that pity has to do with shame and disgust at our earthly existence. Nietzsche also thinks that pity is an acknowledgement of weakness in the person who pities – a softness instead of a proud indifference to pain. He thinks that pity is secretly an egoism and is based on fear – it is a devious means of getting rid of one's own pain. But pity increases the amount of pain in the world (rather than reducing it) and (he argues) accomplishes nothing. Instead of urging to action, it counsels us to weep. On Nietzsche's view, pity leads us in the wrong direction, since he says in many places that he is not worried about happiness or pleasure or nice feelings. "My pain and my pity – what importance do these things have? I don't care about happiness. I strive for my creative work!" (Z IV, "the sign"). "I have no pity for the strong, because I wish them the only thing that can prove today whether one is worth anything or not – that one endures" (WP 910). Nietzsche says that people associate pity with cruelty, but he thinks that just the opposite is true. When we fall victim to softness and treat pain as if it matters, instead of training ourselves for hardness, then when pain finally comes, it forces us into profound sadness and a desire to strike back, to get revenge, which is the basis of hatred and wickedness. "It is on such soil, on this swampy ground, that every weed, every poisonous plant grows ... this is where the worms of rancor and vengefulness swarm" (GM III, 14).

In a letter to Malwida von Meysenbug from 1883, Nietzsche talks about inheriting the problem of pity from his confrontation with Schopenhauer and his attempt to overcome Schopenhauer's exhaustion and self-hatred. He says that the problem of pity has been the major source of problems in his life, because it requires an enormous will to persevere in realizing his new ideal for man, but pity draws him back, and he finds it extremely difficult to hold it in check. His "first nature" feels this emotion, but he is trying to instill in himself a new "second nature" that holds it in check. He calls pity a "serious practical hazard" and reminds himself that the only way his ideas can have a creative impact is for him to be "adamant about enforcing" his new ideal not only on himself but on everyone he knows. Thus he has to become pitiless and denounce pity.

Many thinkers indebted to Nietzsche have wrestled with these teachings about pity. Nietzsche "linked physical suffering with mental triumph" – as his biographer Rüdiger Safranski expressed it – thus to grasp a real truth costs suffering and to throw off the tyranny of pain proves one's strength. Jaspers and Heidegger tried to incorporate Nietzsche's ideas about pity within his larger teaching about justice, balancing his call to Stoic virtues with his ideas about authenticity. Truth worth the name is not about making statements but proves itself in the conduct of life.

My thought is that Nietzsche felt pity and sought not to; he had human nature directly before him as his own case, but in his own words he sought to transcend his first nature and instill a second; and as it strikes me I think this breaks his own principle, that human beings do not know enough to throw out evidence in order to save a valued principle. Nietzsche threw away evidence to save principle, he looked way in order to see, but by his own principle, the problem is to include everything, to insist on every point, to take everything in and continue thinking. Feeling is not contagion, danger, poison, weakness, a swamp, a practical hazard – or anything else – unless we get stuck there. Weakness is not even weakness unless we get stuck there.

The contemporary philosopher Martha Nussbaum sees through Nietzsche's teaching about pity. Nussbaum sees that Nietzsche is trying to connect with an ancient tradition that idealizes Socrates' powerful example of calm and thoughtful self-command in the face of suffering. But she also observes that Nietzsche shares with the ancients a kind of freedom of thought tied to a privileged status in society. She argues that

Nietzsche did not ask himself how self-command might be affected by slavery, or acute hunger, or crushing poverty, or a life of interminable pointless hard physical labor. He did not know what many human misfortunes feel like, and especially what it is like to have an inquiring mind but no opportunity to learn and develop oneself.

Nussbaum rejects Nietzsche's concept of hardness and his soldierly ideal of calm nobility and even his dispassionate self-command. She does not think that these are forms of *strength* at all. She argues that, ironically, Nietzsche remained a Christian moralist in a way that he was unable to see. On her reading, Christian moral thinking and Nietzsche's moral ideas – the ideals of otherworldliness (saintliness) and hardness (soldierliness) – are fundamentally alike in being forms of *escape*. Both are forms of self-protection, both express a fear of the world, both are defensive reactions to a risky world in which the things we care about may be snatched away from us at any time, and in which we ourselves are always at risk and subject to many dangers.

"There is a different kind of strength in the willingness to form attachments that can go wrong and cause deep pain, in the willingness to invest oneself in the world, for good or for bad. There is, in short, a strength in the willingness to be porous rather than totally hard, in the willingness to be a mortal animal living in the world ... (the opposite position), by contrast, looks fearful, like a person who is determined to seal himself off from risk, even at the cost of love and value" (*Pity and Mercy*, 1994).

These are examples of bringing more Nietzsche to Nietzsche and carrying forward his project of learning to live on the earth. We have to hold him to his position of not getting stuck (and his confidence that by mustering spirit he can always find a way to get unstuck). And we have to hold him to his principle of *amor fati* (and his confidence that he is equal to, can learn from, and grow by, whatever fate puts in his path, and need not wave it off or defend himself against it).

What Use Can We Make of Nietzsche's Thinking?

The late British philosopher Bernard Williams warns us that in every Nietzsche sentence there is a booby-trap that takes the sentence apart. Nietzsche's thought refuses to be summarized, or made into a theory, or carved up into words and ideas and made to serve a cause.

There is irony in the fate of this thought, since it was carved up and enlisted to serve a cause.

Probably we should not try to make what we say as difficult as possible to understand, or try to insert as many ideas as are practical in a small space, as Nietzsche sometimes does. He is playing with us but in return he gets played – by fate, by the people in his life, by history.

We may have a better chance of communicating with people if we try to make what we want to say as easy as we can make it; but Nietzsche gives us the different model of trying to write something that has the effect of taking the reader's mind apart, in order to give him the problem of putting himself back together again. When you put yourself back together again after reading Nietzsche, you are, arguably, different. You are better or worse or perhaps both.

Nietzsche gets played by history – distorted, wounded, hated – suffering an unlucky fate.

But his idea is: *amor fati*, to love one's fate, to appropriate our transformational human power. Nietzsche (though misunderstood) has the lucky fate of contributing and living on in his thinking. And Nietzsche (problems aside) does not mind if there are problems, since his motto is, what does not kill me, makes me stronger.

There is irony here too, since Nietzsche suffered an early death, after lingering eleven years in a kind of waking coma (a condition that did not kill him – not for a long spell – and did not make him stronger – instead he was unable to walk, speak, write or even feed or relieve himself).

Of course Nietzsche rejects pity and does not want us to pity him for his sins or his fate. Pity, to him, is an insult to a proud human being. He is trying to teach a very big human pride and self-esteem, and (he reminds us) Socrates and the Stoics teach a strong calm in face of fortune.

So we cannot summarize his ideas or state any short formula that captures what this thinker wants to say, or do, to us. But it is true that he looks to ancient models and thinks he is preserving something, but also creating, and overall he takes the point of view of the artist.

Nietzsche's legacy is complex but surely Williams is right that Nietzsche is trying to teach us to question, to jump in and out of experience, not get struck, feeling strength to go on and not tire. ("Nietzsche is not trying to tell us anything, but instead is urging us to ask something." B. Williams, *Nietzsche's Minimalist Moral Psychology*, European Journal of Philosophy, 1993).

Williams says that he agrees with the French thinker Michel Foucault, another admirer of Nietzsche – Foucault called himself a "Nietzschean" and said that he was applying Nietzsche's "genealogical method" – especially regarding Foucault's statement that the main issue with Nietzsche is what use we can make of Nietzsche's thinking. Williams must have thought that Nietzsche was useful since he also said he wished he could quote him every twenty minutes.

Nietzsche is addressing the individual and aiming to be an active influence on the individual – to be an artist, to love fate, to take an inquiring position in the world – he is not addressing society as a whole and is not offering a new vision for organizing society – he is not a political thinker.

Despite Nietzsche's expressed intentions, his name was plucked out of his time, and several of his phrases were taken out of context and became slogans – "blond beast" and "will to power" and "lords of the earth" – and after he died his name was attached to right-wing political causes and now conjures up ideas about "the master race" and generally a heartless, cruel, egotistical stance in life. He meant to be a champion of individual effort and personal authenticity. But he is also a meme linked with irrationalism, fascism, the national socialist régime, tyranny and war.

The immediate problem here is that the name 'Nietzsche' gets divorced from what this thinker was trying to accomplish. It becomes a free standing unit in culture whose significances change over the generations according to the ways people use and misuse it. The meme, which is a piece of cultural software, gets plugged into narratives of different kinds, and whether the meme supports a helpful or destructive cause depends on the cultural context into which it is inserted, rather than its origin. For example: the meme 'Nietzsche' originates in the thought experiments of this provocative thinker, but historically the meme 'Nietzsche' gets plugged into a destructive cause, the cause of totalitarianism, anti-Semitism, imperialism, the Third Reich.

Is Nietzsche any help with this kind of issue? – With the issue that comes up with his own particular case, i.e. that his name became associated with ideas that he would have hated? – How do we face the enormous flood of cultural ideas, symbols and practices that people learn by belonging to a society? We are all brought up in a family and region and political order, and these realities may have become perverted long before we ever learnt about them. How are we supposed to sort it all out? What use can we make of Nietzsche's thinking in finding our way?

The problem is, how to be a critical recipient, and a critical producer, of cultural material.

The swastika, an ancient symbol from independent Hindu, Native American and Chinese sources became a German symbol – carved away from its origins and made to serve a cause – and it is hard to look at the symbol today and see anything but a shameful history. But there is nothing in this symbol itself that espouses a cause. If we make the effort to think clearly about this symbol, we will see much more than the Nazis' use of it. We will dig in historically and learn that in different cultures it has signified, among other things, Buddha's heart, well-being, auspiciousness, and the number ten thousand; we will discover that it dates from Neolithic times. Nietzsche, and Nietzsche as interpreted by Williams and Foucault, is urging us to *resist the power* of mere symbols, urging us to take a critical attitude and raise questions, developing a historical sense; thus meeting the flood of cultural ideas, symbols and practices with skepticism – going on in our thinking and not getting stuck; not walling ourselves off but instead welcoming experience – doing this on our own, by our own work, not letting anyone else do this – defying the power (from the outside) and at the same time imposing the power (from the inside).

Nietzsche begins by upholding the ideals of ancient Greece in early works like *The Birth of Tragedy*. He advances by attacking all religious, moral and political ideas, comparing himself to a little animal that digs underground tunnels that undermine the foundations of mighty structures. He works underground, in the dark, and away from all human company (*Daybreak*, preface). In *Human, All Too Human* he extends the attack to romanticism, pessimism, optimism, every kind of overarching theme for life, denying even that the goal of humankind is to make new geniuses (like all the people he admires, such as Heraclitus and Spinoza). He denies that humankind has any inherent purpose – the universe has no meaning or purpose (*Untimely Meditations*, VII; *Human, All Too Human* 157-158, 162-165, 231, 258, 635). In his next work, *The Wanderer and His Shadow*, he begins to look at everything in front of him, every cultural item, as a shadow, a phantom, a hallucination that may trick him. His response is a critical, distancing, imaginative play, intended to save his freedom and the integrity of his own thoughts. This is a theme he continues in all his subsequent works. He is not trying to resolve all the contradictions inherent in culture or even in himself: "One must have chaos in oneself to give birth to a dancing star" (*Zarathustra*). He tells us that he sees what he is doing as "a shout for joy, following long days of misery, a hymn of joy in which sing reawakened powers and a reborn faith in life. I see in front of me new adventures, new problems, free seas and new purposes that I will craft by myself and make powerful" (*The Gay Science*, preface to the second edition).

The person who felt pity and who caused an uproar in his own thoughts that had to be held in check, and the person who shouts for joy following long days of misery, who suffers the death of a loved one and also sings a hymn of joy and reborn hope in life, is the same person; Nietzsche's solution has to rely on Nietzsche, who formed the idea of never getting stuck and then had to carry this out; and Nietzsche sometimes failed to live up to Nietzsche's principles; then he died. Posthumously as he foresaw he jumped out of the grave and taught life to several generations. But Nietzsche would have to take the Nietzsche cure to live again in this generation and practice his regimen of unflinching honesty in the light of everything we have learned from him and since.

The problem is, how to be a critical recipient, and a critical producer, of cultural material, or more generally of human experience. Nietzsche's solution appears to be: to do this by oneself, by one's own efforts, by willing it, by making it real; to proceed as if it were true; thus by art.

The Kierkegaard Method

Karl Jaspers began writing about the close proximity of Kierkegaard and Nietzsche in 1919 and kept up this theme through the end of his life in 1969. Kierkegaard was a devout Christian, Nietzsche an atheist; Kierkegaard had an enormous sense of humor, Nietzsche was ponderously serious; Kierkegaard was drawn to cold northern spaces and Nietzsche was drawn to the Italian Riviera. Jaspers explained: these thinkers did not count in their own lifetimes, but become increasingly important as times goes on; today they are considered the greatest thinkers of their time. They both had a consciousness of a great calamity in which they were living and which they foresaw would get worse. They both were attuned to the spiritual situation of their times, but both broke out of it; both had a sense that limits no longer mattered. Jaspers says: "it is as if they are no longer deterred in their thinking *by anything*." Everything that exists today is sucked into a dizzying vortex. They break with convention and look for authentic truth. Their doctrines, basic arguments, and pictures of the world are quite different – Jaspers says: neither left us anything lastingly important on these themes. The chief legacy from these thinkers is an intense earnestness and "a new comprehensive thought-attitude" for human beings. This attitude is conscious of its inability to resolve itself in any definite and final form. Knowledge is interpretation and interpretation is infinite. Everything that has been done or thought is open to fresh understanding and has to be won again many times to make itself felt in everyday life. Honesty is the ultimate virtue – the demand for truthfulness is more important than any championing of a truth – earnestness above certitude – questions above answers. A human being is his or her choices, and no one can follow anyone else. Each of us must follow a solitary path. The permanent putting-into-question in which a person lives his or her life applies to the self and all its choices and all its transient life-shapes and results. The "new comprehensive thought-attitude" articulated by Kierkegaard and Nietzsche is aimed at 'transcendence' but not as eternity – instead as existence lived and felt in the here-and-now – as existential truth.

Who was Søren Kierkegaard (1813-1855)? He was a Danish theologian, philosopher, writer, psychologist – like Nietzsche he was drawn to many things and had a brief career as a teacher – like Nietzsche Kierkegaard was also introduced to the world and became well known due to the efforts of George Brandes, whose first work on Kierkegaard dates from 1879 – unlike Nietzsche the Kierkegaard treatment counts more on the sense of humor and less on intellectual purity – most of all, Kierkegaard shares the Afterlife with Nietzsche as guiding spirits of existentialism.

Kierkegaard does use this term but gets very close to it in several passages. This comes out particularly in his work *Concluding Unscientific Postscript*, from 1846. He calls this book "an existential contribution." He claims that his main goal is simply to remind people of something that they already know but have forgotten. Simply stated, this is "what it means to EXIST" (216).

"Existence" says Kierkegaard, "is the child that is born of the infinite and the finite" (85). The finite is all that is concrete and particular. It includes everything that has a definite beginning and end. It is immediate action, unhampered by reflection. The infinite is unlimited and unbounded. It is time without beginning or end. It is human action made wholly reflective and perfect in its effects. Finite and infinite are conditions of phenomena and human experience.

Not everyone who is alive on this planet "exists," at least as Kierkegaard defines the term. A person begins to exist only when the infinite part of her nature – her "infinite spirit" (75) – is awakened through reflection, which is her "infinite faculty" (102). From this moment on "the existing individual is both infinite and finite" just as "existence itself is a synthesis of the infinite and the finite" (350). Until this occurs, the person lives strictly in finite, unreflective categories. Kierkegaard calls this unreflective life "the life of aesthetic immediacy" rather than existence (310n). Like Nietzsche – perhaps on the theme that Brandes calls "aristocratic radicalism" – Kierkegaard has the sense that people who live in aesthetic immediacy are not really alive or not really human or not really awake. These are not the people he cares about – he wants to talk about being alive, human and awake. As soon as a person begins to reflect, however, she finds herself caught between the finite and the infinite – this is the unsettling part of the twilight zone called "existence" – thus from the moment that the spirit is awakened, life, now that it is become "existence," becomes a *problem*, since the spirit can only find happiness in the infinite for which it longs (376).

Existence is an incomplete and impossible synthesis of the finite and the infinite, the eternal and the temporal (85). A human being finds herself caught up in the infinite and the finite, as she *acts* her life through all its concrete moments, but also intermittently as she thinks herself into the realm of the abstract through *reflecting*. Human behavior is this bizarre cross of opposites.

The opposition between reflection and action results in a fundamental disjunction between subject and object, and between thought and being (171-172). The thought of the existing subject is infinite, and as such always thinks the universal. But the being of the objects found in existence is concrete and particular. Thought therefore "must abstract from existence" in order to think the universal. In this way thought and existence exclude one another (290). "But it does not by any means follow that existence is thoughtless," says Kierkegaard, "instead existence has brought about, and brings about, a separation between subject and object, thought and being" (112).

Conclusion to this juncture: existence is an impossible synthesis and fundamental contradiction.

Kierkegaard says that the *task* of existence is to eliminate itself, i.e., to eliminate existence. Many previous thinkers, such as his predecessor Hegel, realizing that the self is enormously complex, and even filled with contradiction, tried to think of ways in which selfhood might be harmonized or mediated or integrated. Kierkegaard rejected this approach and held that synthesizing the different parts of the self is impossible. The existing subject "is not called upon to create [a synthesis] out of the finite and the infinite; but instead, as a being who is himself composed of finite and infinite, it is his task to *become* one of the two, existentially" (376). The self has one choice: to become finite or infinite: to *become a thing* or to *become pure spirit*.

Thus at this next juncture Kierkegaard argues for

→ an all-or-nothing, black or white decision (a kind of emotional, i.e. *unscientific* logic of extremes)

and

→ the value hierarchy in which thinghood is accounted a lesser thing than existence; in the great chain of being, *thing* is lesser, *spirit* is greater.

Thus the task of the authentically existing subject is to escape from mere existence (thinghood) into genuine existence (spirituality)—from body to soul; from death to eternity; finite to infinite.

Kierkegaard says that the obvious way of accomplishing this task is to ignore every finite aspect of existence and attempt to "think" oneself into the infinite. To proceed as if it were true. Why not just throw oneself into the infinite, leave the finite world behind, and float up into the realm of pure thought?

But then he offers a surprising new step in reasoning:

We can't stay in the infinite – "we can only repeatedly arrive there" – in every case we have to start again (75). Rather than say: striving stokes adversity, he says: we get there, but we can't stay very long.

"Speculation is essentially a revocation of existence" (408), but existence does not allow itself to be "revoked" for very long. Existence doesn't let us leap into the infinite. It lets us think ourselves into the infinite, but just for a moment; then it pulls us back down again, back here where things are still divided, where things contradict each other, where we continue to exist, where we live and where we are. "As long as he remains in existence, he will never become eternal" (368). This is why, even though we can think, we can only do so "intermittently" – that is, "before and after" – that is, before we are born and after we die; we keep living and dying.

The existential task cannot be achieved by reflecting oneself once and for all *out* of existence.

Kierkegaard explains that the attempt to think oneself out of the world and into the infinite is actually a kind of "thoughtlessness" – the thoughtlessness, he says, of relying exclusively upon thought (68n).

Kierkegaard denounces this error as the particular sin of his own nineteenth century, which, he says, "has unfortunately made existence tantamount to a thinking about everything" (352). Such "abstract thought" is really no more than "thought without a thinker" (296), and as such it is fairly well useless to the existing individual, since it deals only with "a fictitious objective subject, whoever that may be" (75). "The thinker who can forget to think that he is an existing individual is going to have a difficult time explaining life. He is making the futile attempt at no longer being a human being, in order to become a book or some objective thing" (85).

Kierkegaard holds that the existential task can be achieved – the task of eliminating existence –we can actually live an authentic life – by means of "a double reflection"(68). In the double movement of thought, the existing subject

➙*first* of all reflects himself out of existence, and into the infinite, through abstract thought and passionate imagination (176). But then, rather than attempting to remain in the infinite (which is impossible anyway),

➙in the *second* place he immediately reflects himself back into the finite categories of existence, to a reference immediately in evidence, which is a concrete action; but he tries to fill this reflection as much as possible with a reference not in evidence, which he has chosen (176).

Thus the subject recognizes the limitations that existence places on him but leaps into the infinite, returns almost immediately to the finite world, where he puts his understanding (however little it may be) to work on real problems. *He leaps away to an airy and impossible place only to touch down again exactly where he left off* (327).

"The task of existence is to interpenetrate existence with consciousness, thus to be at one and the same time eternal and far removed from existence, but also present in existence and becoming many different things" (273).

"[T]o make use of the dialectic of the infinite in one's daily life, and to exist in this dialectic, is naturally the highest degree of strenuousness; and strenuous exertion is needed to prevent this exercise from deceitfully luring one away from existence, instead of providing a training in existence" (80n).

"Putting differences together is the ultimate difficulty of human existence" (449). "In existence the watchword is always *forward*" (368).

The basic task of existence is to leap out of existence in order to land back exactly where one is.

This means that a person who "really exists" will never be content or at rest, but will be "constantly in process of becoming" (79); taking things seriously means always going forward, developing, progressing, always becoming more, so that his life is a "persistent striving," because, that is,

"Striving is the only view of life that does not carry with it inevitable disillusion. Even if a man has attained to the highest – whatever this may be – he would have to repeat this feat over and over again or else fall backward or become a fantasy, and so in every case he pushes the end of things further off, moved away, postponed, deferred, living by this delaying action" (110).

Thoughts that are in process are tentative and uncertain. They are never "results" that are finished once and for all. Because the thinking is still in process, it is never certain; for there is no certainty save in the infinite; and though we can think the infinite, we cannot stay there.

Kierkegaard holds that living in the tentative and uncertain world of moral reflection is filled with passion and shifting emotions and eventually transforms a person into an *artist* who comes to the realization that "*existing* is the fundamental art" (314). The task of existence, therefore, is to escape from existence, via reflection, constantly making progress, living in passion, struggling between the finite and the infinite and becoming many things, many forms, and creating art.

Kierkegaard refers to Aristotle's idea that comedy is somehow rooted in contradiction (*Poetics* V). According to Kierkegaard, not only comedy, but tragedy also is grounded in contradiction. Tragedy differs from comedy because "*tragedy is the suffering contradiction, whereas the comical is painless*" (459). The cause of the pain in a tragic situation is (roughly) not knowing any way out of the contradiction: "Whenever there is a contradiction and the way out is unknown, wherever the contradiction is not cancelled and corrected in something higher, then the contradiction is not painless but instead painful" (464). But the comic apprehension shows the way out, which is why the contradiction (in this kind of case) is painless (462). "What lies at the root of both the comic and the tragic . . .

is the discrepancy, the contradiction, between the infinite and the finite, the eternal and that which becomes" (82-83).

Since existence is a contradiction, the subject may apprehend her existential situation either comically or tragically, depending on her perspective. That is: depending on "the relationship between the contradiction and the controlling idea" in her understanding of it. According to Kierkegaard, such an apprehension of existence will differ according to one's orientation relative to the infinite and the finite.

"When [existence is] viewed from a direction looking toward the Idea [the infinite], the apprehension of the discrepancy is pathos; when viewed with the Idea behind one, the apprehension is comic. When the subjective existing thinker turns his face toward the Idea, his apprehension of the discrepancy is pathetic; when he turns his back to the Idea and lets this throw a light from behind over the same discrepancy, the apprehension is comic." (83)

Thus existence is fundamentally comic or tragic, depending on the direction one faces when viewing it.

But the subject who apprehends existence tragically has either failed to reflect doubly or, after reflecting doubly once (on one occasion), has lost the correct perspective that ought to arise from it, that of throwing "a light from behind" over the contradictions of existence, which process is *infinite* (since it never terminates in a final form). As it were: such a person has gotten stuck, and has not figured out how to go on, or needs to run through it again, or needs to start from scratch. The more experience one has, the easier it becomes to see: "and the more thoroughly and substantially a human being exists, the more he will discover the comical" (413).

Kierkegaard holds that a comic apprehension is *justified* only when it is expressed existentially, i.e., when the subject lives her entire life in it, i.e. when a person lives this attitude in choices and acts (464). Bemused irony may be said to transcend its merely idiosyncratic status (as a private response) in positive action – otherwise it falls into itself as passive capitulation to meaninglessness – and Kierkegaard is hopeful that comic insight generally overtakes sarcasm.

Kierkegaard tries to capture the fundamental ideas of this ethic in his claim that a comic apprehension of existence has two distinct levels: "irony and humor."

Irony and humor are names of particular "boundary zones" between the aesthetic and the ethical, and the ethical and the religious stages of existence, respectively (473).

Whereas irony points out the limitation of a particular finite thing relative to the infinite (moving from the aesthetic to the ethical), humor shows the limitation of *all* finite things relative to the infinite (moving from the ethical to the religious).

Kierkegaard tries to illustrate these difficult ideas through several variants of a joke credited to Socrates in Plato's *Crito*. It is related of Socrates that a man came to him with the complaint that people slandered him in his absence. Socrates replied: "Is that anything to worry about? For all I care they may as well beat me in my absence" (491n). Kierkegaard thinks this turn of thinking illustrates the *transition from the aesthetic (perceptual) to the ethical*.

Suppose, on the other hand, that a man is persecuted by slander, and that he complains to a young girl, for example, that someone or other had spoken ill of him in his absence. Kierkegaard imagines that the young girl might reply, "Then I may count myself fortunate, for he has completely forgotten me" (491n). This is meant to illustrate the *transition from the ethical to the religious* dimension of experience. Irony keeps its focus in the original setting of the joke. But humor expands from this setting to the cosmos at large. That is: the girl's reply takes in the entirety of the universe; it is defined by "the determinant of *totality*, which (unlike irony) by its specific contrast constitutes 'the humorous'" (491n).

Kierkegaard intended to make the comical "a determination in earnestness" – i.e., a serious tool for existential progress. The tool works because it "find[s] in the jest a release from the sorriest of all tyrannies: the tyranny of moroseness, stupidity, and inflexibility of spirit" (251). The comic apprehension helps to develop something like "sanity" because it helps the thinking subject ease out of existence, and yet stay in existence, in a reflective, active, passionate and artistic way.

A person who is making some progress "places the comical between himself and the world" (450) in order to blow away all of the world's finite distractions (Kierkegaard notes that the terms 'blowing away,' 'extinguishing,' have an ancient parallel in the Sanskrit term *nirvana*).

"The humorist solves greater problems than the tragic hero precisely by means of ironic mastery over himself." Ironic mastery consists in *placing the comical between oneself and the world* and "blowing away" the world's distractions (roughly: everything that exists). The ironic master also manages to avoid creating new tragedies of his own as he wanders along his way (465).

Overall, the comic apprehension works by building resistance (a learned response) to the natural inclination "to think of oneself as finished" (79). The humorous perspective lives in a smile here and now, in a world of accidents, but also looks far ahead towards the absolute. The comic apprehension is, in effect, always sending part of one's thoughts away towards some distant horizon; thus framing and accepting the dynamism of adversity and fulfillment; accepting life.

Concluding unscientific postscript: comedy is the safeguard against blank complacency and stagnation.

Journal entry, 1835: "What I really need is to get clear about *what I must do* . . . . the crucial thing is to find a truth which is a truth *for me*, to find *the idea for which I am willing to live and die*. What use would it be to me to discover a so-called *objective* truth, to work through the philosophical systems . . . constructing a world I did not live in but merely held up for others to see? . . . . This is why I needed to lead a *completely human life* and not merely one of *knowledge*, so that I could base the development of my thought not on it – not on something called 'objective' – through something which in any case is not my own, but upon something which is bound up with the deepest roots of my existence" (5, I: 34-35).

Kierkegaard came to this very Nietzsche-like thought ten years before Nietzsche was born.

Jaspers directs us to think about these thinkers who "realized through their very being" a common historical judgment about their time. Both perceived their epoch as a period of decadence. The world verged closer to immeasurable loss – to impending nothingness. But these thinkers "personify the modern dilemma in a form that overturns itself." They experience "shipwreck," "running aground," but they pick themselves up and overcome the situation by embracing life in the new situation as a "dangerous perhaps." The "dangerous perhaps" solves nothing, but gives us room to live, and *that* is what we need (*Reason and Existence*, 1935).

The Cure for Existence

Much of philosophy proposes to solve the problem of existence by getting rid of existence, either by practicing death, by dying to the world, or by storing up treasure in heaven. Schopenhauer proposes to "overcome the will to live." Nietzsche and Kierkegaard are spirit-guides for us because they return the human project back to this world rather than flying away.

Plato does not mean to abolish striving but to clarify it and set it upon its rightful target. He is not concerned about the problem of spirit that has stopped evolving, that is frozen, hardened, become stuck; he is concerned about spirit that has become corrupted, degraded, lost, divided against itself; he argues that spirit loses itself because it sinks and becomes defiled in the earth.

Eastern and Western traditions coincide in the teaching that striving leads to inevitable suffering. This is the beginning point for Nietzsche and Kierkegaard. The question is how to respond to suffering, and what remains for us to hope. These thinkers try to look at striving itself as a basic soul-force or psychic energy that takes myriad forms, noting that philosophers have observed some of its root forms (aggression, love, the ambition of transcendence) and its paradoxical dynamism (satisfying desire is drains us, frustrating desire fortifies us). Of course we have to direct it. There is nothing great about striving unless it is aimed at justice. But even doing justice will enervate us; justice will freeze, harden and die; it will become poison, fanaticism, unless we can find a way to release what has been accomplished and happily start again. The point of running striving through the sieve of intellectual conscience is to return it to its pure form as a reservoir of energy for the human project whose innermost nature is to go forward. "The goal is goallessness" and "in existence the watchword is always *forward*" and "striving is the only view of life that does not carry with it inevitable disillusion" and "striving is striving after greater strength" and "striving, not realization" and "authentic life is persistent striving." Camus summarized this teaching from Nietzsche and Kierkegaard by asserting that striving is enough.

Returning to the starting-point of this study of striving, I retrace my thoughts back to Aristotle who defined the love of truth as a desirable mean state between the defect of irony and the excess of arrogance. We cannot say that we love truth if our arrogance gets out of hand, which is a characteristic Nietzsche mistake, and we cannot say that we love truth if we let irony get out of hand, which is a characteristic Kierkegaard mistake. Nietzsche teaches us to insert ourselves into life and make the most of our transformational human power. Kierkegaard teaches us to insert ourselves into time and bring the infinity within us to bear in finite reality. Thus we cannot make everything into a joke, we cannot make everything about us, but we do need to believe in ourselves, and we need our sense of humor. Striving is for going forward – not escaping – neither into nothing, nor into everything – we cannot reach eternity or the void.

Fundamentally, striving takes some practice. We have to learn about it and learn to release it.

Striving is a way of talking about the human project, the human equation, the problem of living a human life, whose basic elements are self-respect, the ability to take form in a definite project, the ability to let this go, and justice.

Peace

Wittgenstein made provocative statements about philosophy in every period of his long career. His ideas reach a culmination of sorts in a series of passages in the *Philosophical Investigations* (I, §109 – 133). The last of these entries is among the most dazzling of philosophical diamonds and has occasioned a great deal of controversy. The subject Wittgenstein is addressing is achieving *complete* clarity, and *stopping* doing philosophy, and so finally attaining *peace*.

Some of Wittgenstein's readers argue that he is writing a kind of epitaph for philosophy. He calls us to abandon philosophy because philosophical problems are false problems that vanish when we see them with real understanding. Some hold that the passage does not direct us to abandon philosophy, but to change ourselves. We have to take aim at our own narcissism; there is no once-and-for-all issue or final problem to set philosophy going; we should work on smaller issues, ask easier questions, and try to take some small steps forward. Some thinkers read the passage as exploding the idea that philosophy has anything to do with solving problems – they try to work out its *medical* ideas – philosophy in relation to illness, therapy, and cure – defining philosophical diagnoses and making recommendations for philosophical health. Some thinkers try to cut through the reverential attitude about Wittgenstein to explicate his underlying motivations, his odd way of expressing himself or his religious worldview. The discussion of the passage is complicated by Wittgenstein's many warnings that probably we will misunderstand what he is trying to say, or that we will only end up speaking a jargon, or that he is not making any kind of claim or offering a doctrine or theory, or that he is addressing only very small audience of like-minded thinkers; he tells us repeatedly that philosophy cannot preach, but he also appears in many instances to be preaching, as when he says that philosophy must leave everything as it is and that philosophy can only describe things and that we must do away with explanation.

Wittgenstein is asking a startling question in the *Philosophical Investigations* that perhaps no one before him ever asked. And in effect he is the first philosophical therapist ever to propose terminating the cure. The Nietzsche cure is for going on – the therapy never terminates – Socrates' cure is also like this and so is every other example of philosophical treatment. Studying Wittgenstein is a way of getting at the idea of *terminating* philosophical treatment, completing philosophy, bringing striving to a close and, after long struggles, finally achieving peace of mind.

My approach in the following pages is to come to grips with Wittgenstein's core idea that philosophical problems arise from misunderstandings concerning language. I hold that it is presumptuous to argue that philosophy arises from misunderstanding. I will argue that it is more correct to say that philosophy arises from not understanding. Philosophy is not primarily concerned with human mistakes; philosophy has much more to do with human limits. Philosophy, more than many things we do, reaches out to an encompassing horizon – what is distinctive about philosophy is not that it is misguided or insightful but that it is an explicit *thinking beyond* – philosophy is an attempt to see where we are but also to break free to a larger perspective. Thus my approach is to argue with Wittgenstein. What I think about philosophy is very different than what Wittgenstein thinks. But he has made himself my partner in conversation and together we will test his proposal to terminate the cure.

Reading Wittgenstein helps us to locate the philosophical instinct and to ask what role philosophy should play in the conduct of human life. Wittgenstein's advice on this matter – in effect, 'stop bothering yourself about philosophy' – is one part of the picture. Listening to Wittgenstein, and close reading of his many pronouncements about philosophy, suggests a different course. This investigation draws attention to the contrast between Wittgenstein the therapist and Wittgenstein the patient. I argue that Wittgenstein exemplifies the philosophical search in a way that confounds his purported cure for this illness. This result argues for the survival of philosophy despite philosophers' calls for its abandonment. It also makes us question philosophers and the rather odd things that they often say (sometimes too boastful and sometimes too ironic). Thus it may not be possible to stop doing philosophy. Philosophy may not help us achieve peace of mind.

My intention is to start from scratch with Wittgenstein and see where the argument takes us.

Where philosophy comes from and where it should be directed

Wittgenstein says that philosophy is a kind of "itch," a "mental cramp," a "vague mental uneasiness," a "torment," an "illness in need of a cure," a kind of "influenza area," even a "bubonic plague" (CV 86, PI § 111, 133; PO 173-5; NM 43, 79; M 487). It's a kind of "gloomy prospect," a "somber," "depressed" position, perhaps even a "cancer in our way of life" (NM 32, vW 216). The problem is language – "language contains the same traps for everyone" – "thus we see one person after another walking the same paths" and making the same mistakes again and again (PO, 183). Completely ordinary forms of expression exert a fascination over us and bewitch our intelligence; philosophical problems come up because we misinterpret "forms of expression" or "the uses of words" or "the workings of language" (PI § 90, 93, 109, 111, 194). An example case is drawing an analogy "between forms of expression in different regions of language" – as when we say "he was a good man" and "he was a good football player" or "his life was valuable" and "it was a valuable piece of jewelry" – expressions like "being a good man" or "having a valuable life" exert a power over us that draws us into error, because we think there must be some sort of analogy to simple cases but in fact there is none (PI § 90, paragraph 23). We use dangerous words such as "national character," "patriotism," even the word "problem" without much pause, like a hack reporter who spits out a word without any thought behind it (BB 43, NM 39). Other examples include taking something as a description that is not one, taking as a name a word that is not a name, and taking something as an item of knowledge that is not one (Ms 116, p. 216).

Wittgenstein holds that cases like these are the illness and that the philosopher should try to treat this condition (PI § 255). That is, these cases are not mere mistakes, but "they have the character of *depth*." They are "deep disquietudes," "their roots go as deep in us as the forms of our language" and "their significance is as great as the importance of our language" (PI § 111). The kind of problems we are talking about are "connected to our oldest habits of thought," "the very oldest pictures that are engraved into our language itself," so that to free people from these kind of confusions "presupposes pulling them out of the immensely manifold connections that they are caught up in" (Ts 213, p. 422). The cure has to be as deep as the problem. This requires changing one's entire way of living (CV 27). Thus philosophy is mainly directed to oneself, is a kind of work on oneself, on one's own ideas, on the way one sees things, on one's ingrained prejudices, on one's pride. This is not just a game you are playing with yourself but the test of your character – the test of one's courage – the aim of which is to see things clearly and thus (winding through many turns) to bring about "thoughts that are at peace" (CV 43, 44, 165, PO 161, Ts 213, Ms 154).

The deeper source of philosophical worries and what should be done to calm them

This inner-directed work and search for thoughts at peace begins from a tormented condition – the illness – that Wittgenstein's interpreters have painted in various ways. Von Wright suggests that Wittgenstein is fighting against thought-habits that permeate the social reality of his time, the herd-mentality, and thus the intellectual culture of very recent history. McGinn talks about philosophy taking a wrong turn because it tries to adopt an experimental method and follow the example of empirical science. Kuusela sees the problem as the contemptuous attitude towards the particular case and the overblown craving for generality that stands behind it. Rorty sees the problem as the tendency to hypostatize and eternalize some present practice, which obstructs the normal response of reforming the practice and gradually replacing it with something new; we look for commandments when we ought to be trying to work out ways of getting along. Malcolm points to the confusions that we create when we begin to think that mental phenomena are somehow mysterious; instead of looking inside ourselves, we should be looking around us at the contexts in which words live and work. Cavell argues that Wittgenstein has an enormous respect for the impulse that disturbs our peace – "skepticism" – which a kind of principled ignorance. Skepticism is a searching, questioning, doubting impulse, an unquiet unappeasable tempting and correcting guardian of honesty: "the human drive to make itself inhuman, which should not end until...the human is over."

Wittgenstein's own diagnosis of the underlying condition – the condition that produces the mental uneasiness, that sets the trap in language, that makes us draw false analogies and use dangerous words thoughtlessly – the tendency to project false and dogmatic views onto reality – in brief the 'illness' – does not locate the problem in intellectual phenomena but strictly in the *will*:

"[t]he contrast is between the understanding of the subject and what most people *want* to see. Because of this, the very things that are most obvious can become the most difficult to understand. What has to be overcome is not a difficulty of the intellect but of the will." (Ts 213, 406, 407).

By these reasonings Wittgenstein and all his interpreters follow the ancients in regarding intellectual development as dependent upon and part of moral development. Socrates held that weighing and testing our beliefs is a way of caring for the soul; Plato held that we have to make men better if we want them to see the truth; Aristotle held that no one can be intelligent who is not also good.

The sense of this is that every individual has the capacity to deliberate and make choices; so that straying from the path is something a person must own and accept, whatever else may be true. The big issue is about what we do, not about our biology or the influences to which we are subject. Wittgenstein is asserting that if a person achieves something like peace of mind, then this is because he has done real work on himself. Thus he can take credit for it. We are not powerless in face of our desires, habits, prejudices, weaknesses or (especially) our governing ideals. Instead, we have it in our power *to ignore what we want* and act instead as we choose.

Thus the deep source of philosophical worries is the *will* and what is called for in order to calm these worries is *choice*. The intellectual worry becomes a test of character. Falling prey to philosophical worries and plunging into their torment is natural. Going on with the worry and getting stuck indicates moral failure. Closing it and getting to the calm signals moral progress.

The nature of peace of mind and what should be done to achieve it

The preceding reasonings are a kind of prelude to the discussion at *Philosophical Investigations* §133, paragraph 3, which is our subject. Here is the passage (G.E.M. Anscombe's translation):

"The real discovery is the one that makes me capable of stopping doing philosophy when I want to. – The one that gives philosophy peace, so that it is no longer tormented by questions that bring *itself* in question. – Instead, we now demonstrate a method, by examples; and the series of examples can be broken off. – Problems are solved (difficulties eliminated), not a single problem."

Here are some implications of the first sentence: that there is such a thing as doing philosophy; that in the course of doing philosophy, the philosopher sometimes makes discoveries; that before he has made a certain kind of discovery, the philosopher may not be capable of stopping doing philosophy when he wants to; that the philosopher may sometimes want to stop doing philosophy.

Wittgenstein is describing a situation in which there is a human being who is a 'philosopher.' This person has desires, deliberates, and acts. Wittgenstein is interested in the case of a person who acts in a certain way, does something – in this case, philosophy – and, despite wishing, he can't stop. Then something happens and the person gets free.

Let us begin the reflection with the idea that at a certain stage in the course of life an individual human being does philosophy but cannot stop doing philosophy. Wittgenstein is not the first person to pose this problem. Callicles asks the question in Plato's *Gorgias* (484c). He says that philosophy "is a pretty thing" and that many people engage in it when they are young. He praises it as an important pursuit for young people that helps them aspire to fine and noble deeds. But he also says that philosophy becomes the ruin of a person if he engages in it for too long. For an adult to do this is ludicrous. It's as if they were asking for a beating (485d).

The words that we use to describe what this person is doing are not important. Nothing hangs on any particular phrase – the word 'philosophy' or the phrase 'does philosophy' – there must be many ways of expressing similar ideas – e.g., at a certain stage in life an individual begins to wonder about things, or begins to doubt, or begins to work out his thoughts from beginning to end, or begins to think less of particular cases and tries to see the principle inhering in them – to begin to think about life, about the big questions, the big stuff. Wittgenstein is defining philosophy as a kind of extension of thought from unproblematic cases to problematic ones, spurred on (he says) through misunderstandings of how language works. This causes the illness. The goal is to isolate it, apply the therapy, cure the illness and bring about peace of mind.

Suppose that by 'doing philosophy' is meant 'X.' Then X is something that human beings do, a human activity or practice, which in some cases may be conducted involuntarily, i.e., 'without wanting to,' or 'not because one has wished it,' or 'just naturally, without any special intention.'

Now an individual might begin to 'X' because of some special influence, or even despite an explicit conscious intention to avoid doing 'X', but more simply 'X' might come about naturally, in the usual course of maturation, at a certain stage of development, or at a certain epoch in social life. It might come about as a kind of biological imperative. In all these cases 'X' would occur involuntarily and thus not be under the express control of the individual in whom it arises – any more than, say, sexual maturity. It might even take some time before one gets any relief from it, before one gets inured to it, before one is aware of it, or before one becomes in any way master of it. Wittgenstein is trying to look at philosophy from this perspective.

It may seem odd to regard philosophy as something one *suffers*, e.g., as one suffers through puberty or as one suffers an illness. Wittgenstein's passage does not imply that philosophy must have this character, though it is consistent with this idea. It implies that philosophy (however it originates) has to advance to a certain point (the philosopher has to make this advance) in order to make unphilosophy possible (philosophy can be set aside). Perhaps one takes up philosophy by choice, yet despite this (voluntary origin) philosophy gets under one's skin and the thinker gets stuck in it. The philosopher can't stop – he can't find his way out – not until he advances to a certain point.

Wittgenstein distinguishes the real discovery (the one that makes it possible to stop doing philosophy) from its implied opposite, the counterfeit discovery (that may perhaps advance a particular inquiry but has no impact on quitting philosophy). It is as if the philosopher were a kind of addict who scores another fix and gets his high in a counterfeit discovery, but is no closer to kicking his habit with a real discovery that puts an end to it. Wittgenstein's passage does not imply that philosophy is an addiction (he prefers metaphors of disease or neurosis) – but it does imply the same kind of desperation. Why is it a *real* discovery? – Because nothing up to this point has worked. As long as the philosopher is possessed, his insights are useless. They only feed new hungers.

Thus the passage confronts us with the idea that philosophy (whatever it is, however it originates) is tied up with desperation and is a threat to peace of mind. Callicles says some similar things in the *Gorgias*. Philosophy makes us ignorant of what is going on in our communities, it makes people appear ridiculous, and might even get us dragged off to prison. It appears that there is nothing wrong with doing philosophy for a spell, especially in youth, but the desperation and threat to peace come in because we go on with it too long. It gets out of hand. We end up in the desperate place where we can't control it at all and can't stop doing it.

The idea that philosophy arises naturally in the course of development and the idea of philosophy as an illness share the basic framework of involuntary action. If philosophy never got out of the control of the philosopher (and became involuntary) then Wittgenstein would be unable to make his point, i.e., that it is possible (with a certain kind of effort) to get a grip on this problem. Wittgenstein apparently believes that the philosopher is in a tough spot, but he holds out some hope for him. The philosopher is in a dangerous position. Unless he can get to a certain point, and make a certain kind of discovery, he is stuck with going on. He's hooked.

The second sentence reads: "The one that gives philosophy peace, so that it is no longer tormented by questions that bring *itself* in question." This gives us Wittgenstein's clue about 'real' discoveries – the ones that make unphilosophy possible – the real discovery as opposed to its counterfeit. Philosophy, whatever it is, however it originates, if we go on with it for too long, gets out of our control, and becomes involuntary. This suggests the idea that are thoughts are *taken over* and get out of our control, and that we feel desperate and lose our cool – our peace of mind – which suggests that peace of mind consists in being in control of one's thoughts. The countering therapy would have to be one that returns thoughts to the control of the thinker. But Wittgenstein appears to be saying something different. He says: philosophy loses its peace and philosophy regains its peace. So, in a sense, *we* are not the problem – the philosopher is not the problem – but philosophy itself. Philosophy loses control of itself and gets into a desperate state – *this* is the problem – this is the problem we are trying to solve. Thus if we go on too long with philosophy and if it gets out of control, then philosophy itself becomes desperate and loses its peace; and Wittgenstein explains, the problem that troubles philosophy is that it becomes "tormented by questions that bring *itself* into question."

Thus the big issue is not that the thinker has lost control of his thoughts, but that this activity – 'X' – turns inward.

Now it might appear that Wittgenstein is offering an historical point here, to the effect that human activities, especially intellectual activities, tend to become involuted. Every tradition has canonical texts – the base-texts of a given civilization – and every tradition develops a heritage of preserving, interpreting and adapting the ideas in these texts. The lines of development follow a set pattern. Historians of philosophy, for example, such as Herbert Schnädelbach and Ernst Tugendhat, have defined the philosophical pattern as *Being, Consciousness, and Language*. Thus philosophy initially sights things/beings/objects in the world; thoughts/ideas/conceptions in the mind come later; and later still, the problems have to do with words/terms/expressions in the language. These three periods correspond roughly to the ancient, medieval and modern periods in philosophy. When we reach the last stage – "the linguistic turn" – self-consciousness reaches an apogee. The problem at this stage is that philosophy becomes primarily concerned with philosophy. it becomes tormented by questions about itself. It loses touch with the world.

Or it might be that Wittgenstein is reflecting on a similar problem in social, moral and legal circles – on the legitimation of bureaucracy in its later stages. And the idea here is that in the first stages of society, people set down basic laws of conduct. And at a later stage in society people begin to ask questions about demonstrations, such as "what is the origin of the law?" And at the last stage, people ask questions about the demonstration, such as "what is the proof of this origin?" Then this last question becomes our obsession and we neglect keeping the law.

My sense is that Wittgenstein may have thought about cases like these, but his main idea is that philosophy reaches a point where it torments itself; and that philosophy, after it has taken the cure he is proposing, is no longer "tormented by questions that bring itself into question."

Philosophy, pursued to a certain point, takes on the involuted character of an obsession – an addiction – a sickness. The sickness has to do with philosophy peering into itself. Wittgenstein is proposing to cure this condition.

But this seems a puzzle, and we will have trouble accepting Wittgenstein's argument, because philosophy is involuted *ex hypothesi*. If philosophy loses its self-conscious uneasiness and need to review its own methods – review and check itself – it no longer counts as philosophy, but is something like haranguing or preaching or carrying out. It becomes more like doctrine and less like inquiry – exactly the opposite of the philosophic idea.

Part of the problem here is that Wittgenstein wants to say too many things about philosophy.

Philosophy is the illness – the itch – philosophy is also what the philosopher should be up to in fighting against this illness – the test of courage that has to fight the impulse – and philosophy is also the sort of work Wittgenstein is recommending that philosophers undertake on themselves – philosophy is something I have to do myself. "A philosopher is a man who has to cure many intellectual diseases in himself before he can arrive at notions of common sense" (CV 44).

Perhaps the multiplicity of roles that philosophy is called upon to play in this argument is due to the fact that philosophical problems are deep. These are "deep disquietudes," "their roots go as deep in us as the forms of our language" and "their significance is as great as the importance of our language" (PI § 111). The kind of problems we are talking about are "connected to our oldest habits of thought," "the very oldest pictures that are engraved into our language itself." These problems are *as deep as we are* – that is, in philosophy we are looking at ourselves – in philosophy we are always looking in the mirror. The sickness is philosophy peering into itself, but in philosophy we are always peering into ourselves. Philosophy cannot do otherwise and still be itself.

Wittgenstein is proposing to alter this situation. Philosophy will cease being turned upon itself. It will no longer be anxious about itself or call itself into question. Instead it will be at peace about itself. It will achieve "complete clarity." It will see the world exactly as it is and stop worrying about itself.

The initial situation is one in which philosophy is a kind of critical review but simultaneously (and confusingly) also a critique of itself. One way to understand this paradox is to call up the traditional (Ancient Greek) picture in which philosophy projects an 'ideal' that is just beyond the limit of current understanding. This picture suggests that philosophy is in a dangerous position, since it risks falling into empty reasonings and the vacuity of an unspecifiable goal. The thing that I am looking for moves away from me, just as I move towards it. The danger inherent in philosophy has to do with starting something we can never finish. Philosophy impels an *infinite* recession of the focus of critique. The working assumption gets replaced with a better one; what bothered us gets cleared up, but then something else bothers us, and we get stuck somewhere else; the point we want to make gets made, but then there is a new point. Thus what we are up to in philosophy is always open to revision — it's transient — also, it's turned back on itself. Some traditional formulations of this idea are: the good for man is to search for the good for man; philosophy is a critical discussion about critical discussion; philosophy is the love of wisdom.

The third sentence of *Philosophical Investigations*, §133, paragraph 3 reads: "Instead, we now demonstrate a method, by examples; and the series of examples can be broken off." The alternative that Wittgenstein thinks he has come up with — the 'method' that he thinks that he is demonstrating — is devoting attention to a problem; then to another problem; then breaking off. The series is *finite*. The 'method' is 'going on with thinking' — but no longer veering to itself — instead, just *using* the method and applying it. The method is a tool applied to particular cases.

The philosopher decides to work on one problem and then on another, but he might take a break at any time. Perhaps he gets tired, or has to work on something else, or he gets into a different mood. He is not driving himself to distraction under the spell of an unrelenting obsession, but works on a problem because he decides to give it some attention, *ad libitum*. He is not addicted, obsessed, driven mad. This implies a change in the psychology. The therapy is working — we're not coerced anymore —

we're not tormenting ourselves. Philosophy is not tormenting itself by turning its critical edge back towards its own process. It's turned outward.

The last sentence reads: "Problems are solved (difficulties eliminated), not a single problem." Our discussion above shows that this change in the idea of philosophy has been given some different readings – e.g. by Von Wright, McGinn, Kuusela, Rorty, Malcolm, Cavell. It is a change from working on 'the' problem to working on 'ordinary' sort of problems (making peace with the particular case); a change from the tendency to 'eternalize' problems to one in which we see ourselves coping, dealing with things, juggling things around and managing or improvising as best we can (making peace with finitude); or a change from radical skepticism to something like healthy skepticism (making peace with limited knowledge); or the difference between applying *ideal* standards, as against workaday standards, to a given case (making peace with contingency, contingent particular differences and distinct cases, i.e. with change). Many thinkers have wrestled with this problem and defined new ways to make peace with the flux. The core insight here is that philosophy has work to do in *this* world and need not tie itself up into knots.

Wittgenstein claims that practice of his new method yields tangible results. The philosopher asks his questions and accepts some answers. A troubling issue gets investigated and the philosopher pursues the argument far enough to make some progress. This is not the same thing as answering 'the' question or discovering 'the' answer. 'The' question can never be answered and philosophy that wrestles with it can never attain any peace. Wittgenstein contrasts this with the image of taking a few steps forward and making some small progress.

Frank Ramsey said something like this to Wittgenstein twenty years before Wittgenstein wrote the *Investigations*: "We are in the ordinary position of scientists of having to be content with piecemeal improvements: we can make several things clearer, but we cannot make anything clear."

It's as if he were saying: *let us make philosophy human*. Let us accept it as a tendency that we are born with, that we catch like a cold or that we learn, and let us apply it in solving real problems. Let us stop turning it against itself and tormenting ourselves that we cannot exit the closed circle of own thinking. Let's break off the search when we get hungry or sleepy or excited about something else. When we get into a problem and direct our focus to a problem, let's bring this 'tendency' that we have down to earth – let's stick to the problem and not get hung up about the thinker – let's not get too fancy or too grandiose about things – keep it simple.

In effect, the passage we have been looking at is a plea to make philosophy like us – to humanize it – to lower its sights – to take it out of the realm of wonder and make it work.

Philosophy as unyielding radical questioning

One of the odd things about Wittgenstein's train of reasoning in our passage is that his recommendation is such a poor fit with everything we know about Wittgenstein, who he was and how he lived his life, and about philosophy as he pursued and practiced it.

There is a passage in Norman Malcolm's memoir in which Malcolm quotes a letter that Wittgenstein wrote him November 1944. Wittgenstein is talking about digging down deep into things. He says: don't just stay on the surface. He writes about how much he hates superficial talk – he says he'd rather fight with people than do small talk. He's not just 'talking' about things – in a way, what he is up to is not about language at all – it's something deeper than that – nor is it about human failings or the fact that he thinks that most of the people he bumps into misunderstand pretty much everything he says. He is hurtling himself against the normal thoughtlessness and, if nothing else, he is a *philosopher*. He lives his life asking questions.

This is exactly the kind of thing that comes out in Ray Monk's biography of Wittgenstein and glimpses of him that come out in what his teachers and colleagues and students had to say about him. Like few others, Wittgenstein exemplifies the passionate, powerfully moved, all-or-nothing, deep-diving spirit of inquiry – an uncompromising, high-minded, unsurrendering commitment to truth – however little of it we can grasp – a powerful seriousness that is unwilling to set it sights lower – pretty much an incarnation of the opposite kind of condition to the one he is describing. Ludwig Wittgenstein the philosopher is not a role model for "thoughts that are at peace." He is a role model for thoughts that are at war. He is at war with himself and at war with all the forces that pull us down from the high calling of philosophy. He exemplifies unyielding philosophical questioning and impatience with cheap understanding. This is precisely what makes him great.

A thinker like this would *not* say that the real discovery is the one that helps me to stop doing philosophy. He would say: the real discovery is the one that helps me to do philosophy as it should be done.

A thinker like this would *not* say that we should humanize philosophy or lower its sights. He would say: we should philosophize humanity, and raise its sights.

In truth, Wittgenstein was always tormenting himself with questions – he was always going back to the beginning – he was always bringing the focus of philosophy back to philosophy itself –always revising his thinking, rather than resting in a fixed concept of philosophy that he was sure of and knew how to use. In working towards his conclusions at PI §133, paragraph 3, he might have settled on a completely different reading from the same period of his life. One such is preserved as *Culture and Value*, notation from 1948, first paragraph. Here is the passage:

"When you are philosophizing you have to descend into primeval chaos and feel at home there."

The chaos is the vast ocean of thought, including all the things that Wittgenstein wants to say about philosophy, all our misunderstandings of language, all the myriad different moments of feeling, thought and reaction, everything he experienced, questioned, and sought to understand.

Descending into primeval chaos

Wittgenstein often said that he was a "disciple of Freud" and a "follower of Freud." This is odd because he also records that he disagrees with virtually everything Freud says. He said that whenever he read Freud he thought, "Here is someone who has something to say." He was impressed with Freud's willingness to throw himself into a problem and to keep digging until he reached the end. He said that he understood why Freud rejected the idea that he might only be *partly* right – Freud is another 'all-or-nothing' thinker – Freud had a passion to find the essence. Wittgenstein thought that Freud had made exactly the kind of mistake that Wittgenstein had made in his own thinking (LC, 41). He sensed a kinship with someone who became captivated by a picture, who simplified a vast array of experience under one idea, and propounded a myth. Just as Wittgenstein had ignored the variety of the uses of language and forced the phenomena into the stricture of the picture theory – the idea that language works by depicting reality – Freud ignored the multiformity of human affect and forced the phenomena to the measure of the sexual theory – the idea that all psychic life is driven by the pleasure principle. The point is to see what is directly in front of you and not cut it down to fit your assumptions and categories. The mythology defines a simple relationship but, in reality, a vast complexity is at work. This applies to our understanding of language, of thinking, of the mind generally, of identity itself.

Our search through Wittgenstein's train of reasoning in the *Investigations* brings us to the result that we pretty much have to ignore what Wittgenstein is recommending and instead pay attention to what Wittgenstein actually does – we have to stop worrying about peace of mind and jump into the bubbling, chaotic cauldron that we experience every moment of our lives.

Stanley Cavell argued that Wittgenstein was really two people – really two voices – "the voice of temptation and the voice of correction" – and that in Wittgenstein's works overall the reader has a record before him of intellectual conflict and the attempt to tidy things up. This is an interesting comment and (I believe) gets us oriented in the right direction. We are talking about philosophy and, at the same time, about examining oneself, which means that we are talking about ideas but also about psychological conflict that flares up whenever we look into ourselves.

Philosophers sometimes interpret their task as looking for a way to heal the world, or at least our understanding of it. If the philosopher succeeded in clearing things up, he surely would attain some peace. But more immediately the work of philosophy is to chart the reality of conflict, rather than the attempt to clear everything up by plying one argument or another.

Looking at the conflict itself, this has to do with 'raw experience' and meeting 'raw experience' with the materials of a particular culture – i.e., the subject is human development, language learning, socialization, directed thinking and the gradual and lifelong problem of establishing a stable identity – a process that works through becoming part of a group but also has to do with arriving at an identity that is not a straitjacket – an identity that allows for change but also has some stability. Cavell's idea that Wittgenstein is really two people goes in the right direction, but stops short. What comes out of Wittgenstein's way of looking at the mental environment is the more radical notion that a human being is a colony or community or collection or minimally just a gathering of competing selves. Wittgenstein's studies of Freud convince him that what we are looking at in psychology is a vastness that we keep trying to fit into a straightjacket. It is quite wrong to think that there is only one reason why people talk. It is quite wrong to think that all human action boils down to one motive. There are countless examples and countless reasons. *Endless variety* is what we have to face and think clearly about as we try to look into ourselves.

Wittgenstein is saying that if we want to escape from confusion and really see what is going on, we have dig down into the immensely manifold connections that each life-episode is caught up in; and that the big problem, as Freud saw, is *seeing what there is* versus *what we want to see*.

Wittgenstein continued to revise his thinking, since he developed incompatible philosophical positions serially – logical positivism, ordinary language philosophy, and constructivism – all of which have adherents today. His mind was astir with ideas. "Examining life" in his case meant changing his mind about things frequently. What he was up to was much more like "being home in primordial chaos" than worrying about stopping doing philosophy or attaining anything like "thoughts that are at peace." This is also true of Freud, who propounded the seduction hypothesis, the topographical theory, drive theory, the structural theory, ego psychology, even the germ of object relations theory, serially. The point is: these thinkers *went on thinking* – they kept wrestling with phenomena and trying out new ideas – they kept struggling with what they had already concluded and the attractions of a mythology that oversimplifies the phenomena.

A thinking that 'goes on thinking' confronts 'primeval chaos' and a vast array of phenomena. Its main finding is multiplicity – myriad isolated facts, feelings, thoughts, circumstances – myriad selves. Thus philosophy can be the disease, the cure, the fight against cheap understanding, the work I have to do on myself – philosophy can be all these things and also countless others.

Descending into primeval chaos means something like democratizing the phenomena of consciousness – seeing variety and letting it stand – also extending this idea to identity itself. Uncountable little-selves or part-selves or moment-selves form themselves beginning in infancy. Learning to tie your shoes, to laugh at a joke, to work on a puzzle, to respond to a question, to pray, sing, get angry or calm down, are all independent little ego-nuclei or candidate selves. Through the course of experience, just such element-selves are continually popping in and out of existence. They are masters of different problems. They have different desires, different wills. They fight for control – they bargain with, deceive and plot against one another – they are different 'interests' – they are rivals in the psychic economy. Their scattering and irreducible variety is precisely what Wittgenstein is trying to face by "descending into primeval chaos."

Philosophy and the will

Wittgenstein makes the point that what is at stake in philosophy is the *will*. Philosophy is bent on changing us. Doing philosophy is a test of moral character. But what does the test look like?

The test of moral character is descending into primeval chaos, working through rival desires, weighing different values, choosing, bringing focus to experience *as one person*, but perhaps changing everything the next moment. The stable sense of self (the long-term self, the sober self, the reality-oriented self) is the adult. But to be an adult is (among other things) is to fend off, work through and to nurture a child (the impulsive self, the fantasy self, the addict).

The mental landscape is variegated – the mind is sensitive and therefore continually multiplies –the mind is aware and therefore always confronts new conflict that it has to manage – so that the problem the thinker faces is the ongoing problem of separating oneself from distinct contents of experience, integrating new experience within a dynamic whole, gradually individuating into a distinct adult, and resisting the attractions of a simplifying mythology.

The test is seeing ourselves, struggling with ourselves, developing some character, becoming an adult, becoming a real person. We come through it by going on – by not getting stuck – by finding this kind of strength.

Effective behavior is *spontaneous*, adaptive, growing, learning, open. Pathological behavior is *forced*, frozen, fixated, regressed, closed. We are trying to take responsibility and go on.

A 'philosophy' is what we are doing in a given moment that helps us do this. A philosophy is a new way of looking at things, a new structure, a new leading-string. "It is as if he had invented a new way of painting; or, again, a new metre, or a new kind of song" (PI § 401). Talking about mental torment, gloom, depression, shows that Wittgenstein feels these problems deeply – personally. And "the philosopher's treatment of a question is like the treatment of an illness" (PI, 255). This means that philosophy cannot be one thing but has to be a multitude. "There is no philosophical method, but there are philosophical *methods*, like different therapies" (PI § 133). What philosophy is in a given case depends on the current problem and the person who is sick – also on the ingenuity of the people confronting these problems – also on their character. There is no pat answer or common sense response to a philosophical problem. A philosophical problem is a deep confusion. It may even be a confusion that we don't know we have (F 104). The problem, the thing we have to confront and overcome, is not an intellectual problem, but is about strength of character (Ts 213, 406, 407). Thus the therapy is not aimed at changing our minds about anything – it's not about convincing us with a powerful argument – it is aimed at changing what we *want*. Philosophy is many things because desire takes so many forms.

That is: the will, desire, heart, what we want – the itch – is what causes the confusion in the first place. Thus the temptation to say: the *real* discovery is the one that makes this desire go away.

Philosophy as therapy

In our exploration of Wittgenstein's *Philosophical Investigations* and his provocative statements about philosophy, we confront two pieces of evidence that seem out of joint with each other.

The first is Wittgenstein's claim that philosophical problems arise from misunderstandings concerning language. On this assumption, there is a kind of philosophical itch or impulse or drive that gets formed, and grows, and gets out of hand, because language sets a trap for us. Philosophy on this conception is a disease, a form of suffering, which people inflict on themselves. Philosophy is also a form of therapy, a form of healing, in a secondary, reclaimed sense, that we use to repair what we have broken – to unravel the knots that we ourselves have tied (PB 2). When we see what we have done to ourselves, and get a handle on it, and stop tormenting ourselves, the treatment is complete. At this point we are cured. Our thoughts are at peace.

The second is Wittgenstein's powerful example of restless, unyielding radical questioning. Philosophy from this perspective is unquiet living, examining life, devotion to argument wherever it may lead, impatience with pat answers, refusal to surrender or to stop thinking. Philosophy in this sense is 'love of wisdom' – will immersed in the search – love that does not tire of being love. Inquiry that pursues, but never concludes, is *never* at peace; it just goes on; it is a way of living.

After struggling for a very long time to understand how these two forms of thinking fit together, I finally 'got it' – I came back to the core insight that philosophy does its work in *this* world.

Let us say that philosophy begins by attempting to clear a space in which real thinking can begin. The first step takes a step away from whatever is accepted, believed, and established up to a certain point. The thinker takes some critical distance from the inherited background in order to check belief with explicit processes of reasoning. Thus the initial step is merely 'negative.' That is, it is not asserting any new principle, or claiming that it has reached any standpoint outside of human experience. It is suspending, for a brief moment, commonly held belief, and explicitly calls belief to account. The purpose of stepping away from the normal way in which we look at the world, to devote some effort to examining life, is to take an honest sounding of belief. We want to isolate it, have a look at it, check it, see if it can withstand our scrutiny, and try to understand it.

Socrates, for example, turns earthward after the cosmic speculations of the Pre-Socratic thinkers, redirecting the focus of philosophical inquiry from the heavens to everyday life in the city. He conceives of philosophy as practice of death, as preliminary dying, getting ready to die, even being a little bit dead already because death is already there, a fact in waiting, and is ever present. But this ever-present fact is also a complete mystery. If we look into everyday experience, we quickly grasp that we know almost nothing about even the simplest facts of our existence – particularly its uneasy perch over the chasm of death. Our most basic concepts do not bear even the most cursory scrutiny. We hardly understand enough to grasp the simple fact of our ignorance. Socrates' mission began with the pronouncement of the Oracle and he refers us to the words inscribed over the entrance to the temple – γνῶθι σεαυτόν – 'know thyself,' know that you are nothing, know that you are dust, know that you are going to die. He considered this wisdom, which he struggled to understand, our most important weapon against our ancient enemy, vanity. This is the little bit of knowledge that we have – but not even this is knowledge, this is more like taking back our mistakes. We are just undoing what we have done – in which there is a kind of peace. First there is war: the test of argument, by the force of the better argument; then there is peace; acceptance, expressly acknowledging that we are ignorant. It is presumptuous to say that we *know* anything; what we can say is that philosophy, the ethic of argument, practice of death or elenchus, as Socrates calls it, immediately shows us that even our most basic ideas cannot withstand critical review (ἔλεγχος, 'argument by refutation'). Man always puts himself in the center, but elenchus reveals this to be vanity that critical questioning gradually strips away.

Socrates is not focused on the peace that comes from clearing away the mess that we have made – on tidying things up; he is focused on the humor of the odd circumstance of mortality. There is a powerful medicine in Socrates' example, which is this same treatment via comedy. He says to us: I am completely unprepared and ignorant of even the slightest facts, yet the most powerful influence on my conduct and my thoughts is exactly what this fool, I myself, expect of myself.

This is philosophical therapy in an early form – philosophy conceived as curing suffering.

Hellenistic philosophy is practical and compassionate philosophy, and all the ancient schools expressly offered treatment of *illness*, in the form of moral argument, based on Socrates' example of reasoning from the patient's charge of himself and his own sense of better and worse. Peace of mind, *ataraxia* or *apatheia* or freedom from disturbance, is taught by all the schools. Their arguments are alike in appealing to the patient's autonomy over any other consideration; thus it is because I am in charge of myself that I have to fight for my health, wisdom and sanity. The Stoics, Epicureans, Skeptics and Cynics all argued that peace of mind lasts only as long as we practice the discipline that brings it about.

We see that philosophy that is unyielding restless questioning can also be longing for peace.

Peace is temporary – episodic; but we have to look for peace. We have to work on integration, trying to resolve every kind of conflict arising in the moment, carrying it through every moment. Oppositely, the ability to register chaos, the ability to be disturbed and outraged, guards our humanity. An entity that is dead to the world is at peace, but this is not a human being.

Doing philosophy is, in brief, the thing that keeps us human. Thus the passage (PI § 133, paragraph 3) suggests an argument nearly opposite to its literal meaning. The deep argument begins by attacking grandiosity, then offers a humbler idea of philosophy, and concludes with a return to something like philosophy's traditional ambition of comprehensive understanding.

PI § 89 reminds us that we ought to try to understand the thing that is right in front of us, and that this is the thing that we usually don't understand, e.g. ourselves. Since the philosopher is a human being, this is going to be hard to do. The philosopher wants peace of mind; if he achieved it, he would cease being a philosopher. The thing that we want would put an end to us. It also makes us what we are, so long as we can hold out.

Important Nonsense

Two of the great philosophers of the twentieth century spent most of a decade wondering whether philosophy is complete nonsense.

Some issues that come up in the conversation are: how language works; what is going on in the thought process; and what ethics is. Most of the discussion is about philosophy – where it comes from, what it is, what we should do with it – much of it questioning whether it makes any sense to keep going with philosophy, and whether philosophy is really worth all this effort.

When I first started out in philosophy, it seemed obvious to me why people ask philosophical questions, since there is so much we don't know and so much we don't even know how to know. But after pursuing philosophy for a while, I had more doubts about philosophy. The philosophical kind of longing seemed weirder – less self-evident. Kołakowski said that a thinker who never suspected himself of being a charlatan – who never considered that philosophy might be a complete fraud – must be a shallow mind whose thoughts cannot be much help to us. We have to confront the fact that the same philosophical questions have been asked for thousands of years, in every place on earth, without a single example ever being answered. We have to face the fact that children spontaneously ask all the traditional philosophical questions, yet nearly all children outgrow asking them before they reach puberty. The evidence seems to be that we cannot help asking these questions, but also that most people stop asking them.

These facts make a good argument for turning philosophy inside out and quizzing ourselves whether we should stop bothering ourselves about philosophy. Thus it may not make much sense for mathematicians to spend a decade wondering whether mathematics is nonsense, but it does make some sense for philosophers to wonder whether philosophy is nonsense.

The conversation that I want to explore in what I am writing here tries to wrestle with this idea.

It is only *one* conversation, in one school of thought, that took place in the early part of the twentieth century, but I think it is repays study, because it makes us ask good questions about all conversations, and what we can expect of ourselves when we begin to talk about philosophy.

One of the questions that we get from wondering whether philosophy is nonsense is about what philosophy does to the philosopher – what is going on in the human sphere – which Camus described as "settling fate among the fated" – i.e. deciding for ourselves what is of value and what is worth our time. Philosophy is something we do and we can look at it in how it changes us and by what kind of creatures we become by practicing it. But philosophy aspires beyond the human project, seeking to *know* and, even if it utterly fails and we remain completely ignorant, philosophy still has some significance as a powerful aspiration. Thus philosophy has a divided program – it tries to comprehend the entirety of the cosmos – it is also about the inner man.

How does this otherworldly longing relate to what is going on in the philosopher here and now? People seem to reach away from the earth and hook onto something else in all sorts of ways. Do we situate ourselves on earth and as humans by reaching away from earthly things and man? Practicing philosophy is practicing reaching, inquiring, travelling, but not at arriving or knowing.

There is a bigger context in which the conversation I have been following took place – the total context of philosophy in this same period, i.e. the first few decades of the twentieth century – questioning taking place in many cities dotted around the globe, in every kind of school of thought, in which philosophers questioned philosophy. For example, during this same period, people wondered whether philosophy was a science, and why it had not yet or would ever attain to the status of rigorous science; or whether it belongs among the human sciences, or might have to call itself *art*; and whether it comes from doubt, or wonder, or anxiety, or fear or curiosity; whether it is hard-wired or merely cultural; whether it is saying anything or simply doing something – more like a statement or more like a tool; whether it is an accident or a human universal; and what relation it has to innumerable things – religion, language, politics, mathematics, psychology, wealth, leisure, sex, humor, death and the absurd. There is also a theme that appears to run through twentieth century philosophy, according to which the endpoint of rationality is to demonstrate the limits of rationality, as with Gödel's work on the incompleteness of self-consistent systems, or Rorty's idea that philosophical methods are merely contingent vocabularies that we adopt or abandon for pragmatic reasons. The dialogue I want to look at seems to draw this same conclusion: reason exposing its contingent roots.

There is a still bigger context for philosophy – the totality of philosophy through history – which is a way of talking about the big context of *fundamental problems* or basic predicaments of human experience. There are a few fixed landmarks in ideaspace; we have discovered a few points of reference, which we can locate from any starting-point; there are a few rough surveys of this terrain. Let us call this terrain 'thoughtspace.' There are a few trouble spots in thoughtspace – a few conflict zones, a few hot spots in ideaspace or questionspace. The conversation that I want to talk about takes place in one of these disputed territories. To carry on the conversation is to live in this space for a while and begin to learn your way around.

Western philosophy, Chinese philosophy, Indian philosophy – these traditions are all exploring this same expanse of space, launching satellites and space probes and building space stations – receiving data back at home, interpreting it, trying to figure out what is going on out in space. Thus we cannot exactly *know* but we can spend some time thinking and get the lay of the land.

Perhaps this is the point. We are developing a sensibility that has a huge importance in everyday life, but we seem bent on directing it to ethereal regions where it may not mean anything at all. How does this 'otherworldly longing' relate to what we can accomplish here – how does the extreme case relate to the average case – how does drawing a limit to rationality relate to applying rationality to problems in everyday life?

All of this is a roundabout introduction to a conversation whose real import (I hold) is about motivation. I am exploring more of the precursors to the psychology of philosophy. I am trying to understand more about the basic emotional circumstance, or one such, that takes voice or takes shape or by some metamorphosis becomes philosophy. I am trying to hold onto the fundamental experience of suddenly being aware that I am alive, that I am conscious, that I see the world before me and, immediately on this awareness, that I raise innumerable questions, that I start talking about this odd condition, and try to work through some of the implications of conscious mortality. I am surveying some of this territory. And at the same time I am trying to understand philosophy by wondering whether I am a wasting my time, whether I am a charlatan, whether philosophy is a complete fraud, and whether philosophy is nonsense.

Wittgenstein/Ramsey

Ludwig Wittgenstein was born in 1889, Frank Ramsey in 1903. Wittgenstein's fascinating first essay *Logisch-Philosophische Abhandlung* (*Tractatus Logico-Philosophicus*) appeared in 1921. Ramsey assisted with the first translation of this work into English in 1922. The two met in 1923 and remained close friends until Ramsey's death, at age 26, in 1930.

Russell said that Wittgenstein was the most perfect example of genius he had ever known. Wittgenstein is arguably the most influential philosopher in the twentieth century, having created three different philosophical positions – focused on the three key ideas of picturing, ordinary language, and embedded belief – all of which have adherents today.

The British philosopher R.B. Braithwaite called Ramsey "the intellectual glory of Cambridge" and an inspiration to all of us to think about the hardest things in the world with singleness of mind. Ramsey's important accomplishments lie in widely different fields, including the theory of probability (the Dutch Book theorem), epistemology (the Redundancy Theory of Truth) and logic (the Ramsey Theorem). Russell and Whitehead sought out Ramsey (then aged 21) to resolve the problems in the second edition of the *Principia Mathematica*, which has to count as one of the more challenging intellectual projects of the century. The economist Paul Samuelson called Ramsey's three papers on economic topics (dated 1926, 1927, and 1928) "three great legacies" for the subject, whose importance was not recognized until decades after they were written.

The dialogue carried on between Wittgenstein and Ramsey during the seven years 1923 – 1930 raises fundamental questions in several different areas of philosophy. The present exploration examines only one theme in this dialogue – the use of the word 'nonsense' as a term of philosophical criticism – focused on the grounding issue of the nature of philosophy itself.

My exploration essay begins with a brief account of Wittgenstein's position in the *Tractatus*, especially as regards the use of the term 'nonsense.' It continues with Ramsey's critique of this position; Wittgenstein's initial rejection of Ramsey's criticism; Wittgenstein's later absorption of Ramsey's idea; and Wittgenstein's final account of nonsense in the *Philosophical Investigations*. My conclusion offers a restatement of Ramsey's critique of philosophy as "important nonsense."

I argue that Wittgenstein and Ramsey were both mistaken about the nature of philosophy. These thinkers share the view that doing philosophy is a problematic kind of activity that needs straightening out or, alternatively, must be abandoned. For a brief spell Wittgenstein regarded philosophy in a somewhat different light – as a 'thinking beyond' – the idea that philosophy is a kind of "running up against the boundaries of language" or "running up against the walls of our cage" – he saw philosophy in these terms as a kind of "hopeless" activity but also as a "document of a tendency in the human mind" that earned his deep respect. Ramsey argued that we should expect much more of philosophy and not trick ourselves with poetic gestures. Ramsey argued that study of philosophy must have some real use or, if it has none, we must rid ourselves of it. In his later work Wittgenstein absorbed this critique and abandoned the idea of 'thinking beyond' completely.

I argue that Wittgenstein's initial hunch was correct. The most important single result from my discussion is the idea that it is possible to admit that philosophical problems are insoluble without also dismissing them as meaningless. Neither Wittgenstein nor Ramsey drew this conclusion. Today – from a perspective emerging out of contemporary philosophical inquiry – it is possible to see the import of working on a problem that one can never solve – today we can understand the usefulness of wrestling with mystery. The value of working on a problem that generations of thinkers have left unsolved comes out as a way of trying out, enacting and renewing one's sanity. Philosophy seeks conclusions but is not one itself. Philosophy is a way of being.

Wittgenstein's Account of 'Nonsense' in the Tractatus

Avrum Stroll recounts the story that the "picture theory" occurred to Wittgenstein while he was serving on the Eastern Front in the First World War. According to the story, Wittgenstein read a report in a Parisian newspaper concerning an argument in traffic court in which an attorney presented the judge with a recounting of the events of the accident by moving little pieces around in an architectural model. It would be an understatement to say that Wittgenstein was impressed by this experience. It seems to have had a profound impact on him and may be an important source for the ideas that take shape in the *Tractatus*.

Ray Monk quotes from a note found among Wittgenstein's papers dated September 29, 1914: "In the proposition a world is as it were put together experimentally (as when in the law-court in Paris a motor-car accident is represented by means of dolls and so on)."

Wittgenstein seems to be thinking something like this: just as there are pieces in the model, positions in the model and configurations of the various pieces in various positions in the model, and the model itself, just so there are objects in the world, places in the world and configurations of objects in places in the world, and also the world itself.

Wittgenstein begins with the observation that a proposition is like a picture; this becomes the idea that significant language pictures something; this becomes the idea that language must work in a very particular way and that everything that does *not* follow the required pattern is "nonsense."

This is the view he articulates in the *Tractatus* (1921), the view that he ridicules in the *Philosophical Investigations* (1945), and the view from which he draws new conclusions in the *Zettel* (1948).

This is what the view sounds when it is first announced in the *Tractatus Logico-Philosophicus*:

Language depicts reality. Linguistic atoms (= names) name worldly atoms (= things, objects). Configurations of names depict configurations of objects (or *possible* configurations, since part of reality is what is possible) (*Tractatus* § 3.21, 3.22, 4.032, 4.04).

"The simplest kind of proposition, an elementary proposition, asserts the existence of a state of affairs." A state of affairs is a purported fact, and an elementary proposition is a string of names. And all propositions are elementary propositions or truth-functions of elementary propositions. And the totality of all propositions is language (*Tractatus* § 4.21, 4.22, 5, 4.001).

The "picture theory" offers a comprehensive account of fact (what is the case), thought (a logical picture of facts), and world (all that is the case—the totality of existing states of affairs—the totality of facts) (*Tractatus* § 1, 2, 2.06, 3, 4.001)

Wittgenstein introduces the word "sense" (*sinn*) in this context and distinguishes between "having a sense" (*sinn*), "not having a sense" (also "lacking sense" and "being senseless") (*sinnlos*), and "being nonsense" ("amounting to nonsense," "nonsensical," "just nonsense") (*unsinnig*).

A proposition with a sense makes a statement that is either true or false. It provides some information – it asserts a fact – it asserts a state of affairs – it does so even if this assertion turns out to be false. Oppositely, a tautology such as "it is either raining or not raining" does not provide us any information and as such it has no sense. The same is true of a contradiction; it does not provide us with any information. We do not learn anything about the world in being told that "it is either raining or not raining" or "it is raining and it is not raining." There is no point in looking out the window to see if these kinds of statement are true.

Wittgenstein uses the phrase "having a sense" (or "making sense") to refer to the root idea *of making a connection to the world* or by some means *depicting a situation in the world*. When we have a proposition with a sense, we want to get out into the world (as it were) to see what's happening and verify or falsify this purported state of affairs. We want to confirm the report.

The situation that comes up with a "nonsensical" statement is a different kind of problem. In a case like this, the statement does not give us any information, not even false information. The nonsensical statement does not make a connection to the world at all. It does not *depict* any kind of situation. The string of words that we have put together into a sentence does not – in nonsensical cases – stay within the limits or rules of our language – it doesn't make any sense. It appears to be a statement made by someone who does not understand the logic of our language. Wittgenstein adds the comment that if a nonsensical statement *had* any kind of sense, it would have to be a kind of sense that lies outside our world (*Tractatus* § 4.003, 4.461, 6.41).

Wittgenstein gives an example of what he means by a "nonsensical" proposition as he has defined it with the question "whether the good is more or less identical than the beautiful." This is an example of what he means by a string of words that does not have any kind of sense, that does not make any connection to the world, that cannot be verified or falsified, and that seems to be the kind of claim someone would make who is not quite sure how to speak our language (*Tractatus* § 4.003).

What sense does it make to say that one thing is more "identical" than another – or that true is more 'identical' than false – the good more than the beautiful?

When we listen to things that people say and examine our own thoughts and statements we can make the effort to determine if the statements in question are elementary propositions or truth-functions of elementary propositions. If we make this effort and grasp that these statements are *not* elementary propositions or truth-functions of elementary propositions, then we can be certain that they are *nonsense*. In Wittgenstein's scheme, asserting that a statement is nonsense is presumably a way of assessing it and (therefore) making a recommendation about its use, viz. a rebuke. The recommendation is that we stop talking nonsense.

We speak nonsense when we fail to understand the logic of our own language, as when we try to say that one thing is more identical than another, but another example comes up in the case of a category mistake, as when we say something such as "2+ 2 = 4 at precisely 3:00 PM today" (*Tractatus* § 4.003, 4.1272). Another kind of case comes up when we fail to give a meaning to one of the components of a proposition, as when we say that the beautiful is [XXX] – i.e. we are using a sign but we are not giving it any kind of meaning (*Tractatus* § 5.473). Skeptical arguments also veer into nonsense whenever they raise questions where no questions can be asked – questions that are not really questions at all – as when we raise the doubts about whether 2+2=4, given the fact that [XXX] – i.e. the problem in this case is that, whatever the expression 'XXX' is taken to mean, it cannot impact the truth that 2+2=4 (*Tractatus* § 6.51).

Wittgenstein is pleading with us to steer clear of nonsense and make the effort to speak clearly and say things that make sense. He says explicitly that the philosopher's task must be to distinguish sense from nonsense and not waste words with nonsense. Strangely, though, he seems to hold out some hope for the importance of something "mystical" that when put into words becomes nonsense (*Tractatus* § 6.44, 6.45, 6.522). His remark above, however – (*Tractatus* § 4.003) – that if nonsensical statements had any kind of sense, this would have to be the sort of sense that lies outside our world – suggests that there may be more than one way for a statement to be nonsense (*Tractatus* § 6.41). Perhaps there are several kinds of nonsense.

"Having a sense" is something we can attribute to a sentence because it has made some connection to the world. It depicts a situation in the world. Wittgenstein is suggesting that a nonsense statement has a kind of sense by making a connection with another world. Perhaps there are several kinds of nonsense that emerge through connections to several sorts of worlds.

The "mystical" also has something to do with wholeness – to view the world, to feel the world, "as a limited whole" (*Tractatus* § 6.44, 6.45), which implies that we have gotten out of this world and can now see the world we live in from outside – thus making a connection to another world.

Wittgenstein informs us that most of what we read in philosophy is nonsense and that even the *Tractatus*, which offers the present account of nonsense, is nonsense (*Tractatus* §4.003, 6.54).

So – what do we make of this? – Wittgenstein tells us that his propositions are elucidations that will appear as nonsense to anyone who understands them – he will use them as steps to climb up beyond them – afterwards he will throw the ladder away – thus understanding is a kind of arrival, transcendence, or transport to another world – but we can't talk about it – it's nonsense.

Wittgenstein appears to be explaining how patent nonsense comes about. He is recommending to us that we stop talking nonsense. But he also leaves room for a special, beautiful kind of nonsense that somehow evaporates as soon as we experience it. We learn something from it, and yet we can't quite account for it, or even talk about it, and apparently we should keep quiet about it. He argues that we should keep quiet about it out of a kind of incommunicable, mystical respect.

Wittgenstein's colleague in the Vienna Circle, the logician Rudolf Carnap wrote: "Wittgenstein seems to me inconsistent in what he does. He tells us that one cannot state philosophical propositions...and then instead of keeping silent, he writes an entire philosophical book."

Philosophy and what Wittgenstein is up to in the *Tractatus* are examples of trying to use words, whose origins must lie in humble situations such as making a report of a fact, in new, very special, and perhaps even otherworldly ways. In a way the core problem is the extrapolation from the ordinary – the abstraction or generalization itself – but also the new use of old words. We want to make words do things that they were not made to do. (Wittgenstein makes this point by mocking what he was trying to do in the *Tractatus* in his later work the *Philosophical Investigations*, § 38: "For philosophical problems arise when *language goes on a holiday*.")

The *Tractatus* uses the term "philosophy" with something like these two senses – the ordinary, unproblematic sense and the extraordinary, transcending extension into the unknown. Philosophy is the kind of thing that Wittgenstein is attacking – the chatter, the problematic way of talking, the thing he wants to stamp out – but philosophy is also the instrument he is using to see clearly and make recommendations – philosophy is a critique of language, philosophy elucidates, philosophy transcends (*Tractatus* §4.0032, 4.112). Thus philosophy is the disease and philosophy is the cure. Skepticism, too, seems to carry this double weight. He mocks skepticism but at the same time seems to hold it in awe. The "mystical" seems to have this status too. It is the vital thing, the important thing, the essence; but it is nonsense.

He concludes that propositions in philosophy do not actually express "thoughts." For the same reason "it is impossible for there to be propositions of ethics." This must also be the case since "all propositions have to be of equal value." Therefore propositions cannot express anything that is "higher." Thus philosophy and ethics and the things that seem most important to us "cannot really be put into words" – they are untouched by facts and (as it were) really belong "outside the world" – they are "transcendental" (*Tractatus* §6.13 - 6.421). *Thus when all scientific problems are solved, the problems of philosophy will remain.* Facts merely contribute to setting the problems of philosophy, not solving them. The problem is essentially that there *are* facts. The problem is that anything exists at all. There is no bridge from the world of fact to everything we wish to ask about life. "God does not reveal himself *in* the world" (§6.432).

The correct method of philosophy therefore is to restrict ourselves to what can be said – therefore to stop doing philosophy – and then, should anyone raise a philosophical question, we should respond by pointing out to the person who raises such an issue that he has not really made himself clear. He is using gestures or signs or what appear to be words in trying to make a statement, but he has not actually given these signs any objective meaning.

The *Tractatus* itself is intended to serve this double purpose (speech and silence, disease and cure) for someone who understands Wittgenstein's discussion about nonsense and uses it to climb up beyond it. Such a person has a chance to "transcend" and see things right. He can reach a kind of healthy understanding and he will show what this looks like by his actions. But he will not be able to say anything about it. He will just have to keep quiet (*Tractatus* §6.42 – 7).

Ramsey's Critique of the Tractatus

Ramsey was an eighteen-year-old undergraduate when he made the first translation of the *Tractatus* into English (winter 1921). At age nineteen he was commissioned to write a review of the book for the philosophical journal *Mind*. He did so before actually meeting Wittgenstein. He first met Wittgenstein in Vienna in September 1923.

Even six years later he is still deferential to Wittgenstein and writes that "everything that I have said is due to him," that his entire view of logic is derived from him, and that "[Wittgenstein's] conception of formal logic seems indubitably an enormous advance over that of any previous thinker." Nonetheless the review itself (1923), the paper read to the Cambridge discussion society (1925), the essay "Facts and Propositions" (1926) and the essays "General Propositions and Causality" and "Philosophy" (both from 1929) are all highly critical of Wittgenstein and especially take issue with Wittgenstein's use of the term "nonsense" and his general conception of philosophy.

Ramsey puts his objection most forcefully in the first paragraph of his 1929 essay "Philosophy."

"Philosophy must be of some use and we must take it seriously; it must clear our thoughts and so our actions. Or else it is a disposition we have to check, and inquiry to see that this is so; i.e. the chief proposition of philosophy is that philosophy is nonsense. And again we must then take seriously that it is nonsense, and not pretend, as Wittgenstein does, that it is important nonsense!"

Ramsey formulated the same critique with several other memorable expressions – e.g., referring to Wittgenstein's well-known ability to whistle complicated musical compositions from memory, Ramsey said that "what we can't say, we can't whistle either."

In response to the Cambridge discussion society's invitation to speak, Ramsey noted that, given Wittgenstein's position in the *Tractatus*, nothing remained to say. That is, "there is nothing really to know except science." We might consider talking about philosophy; however, "the conclusion of the greatest modern philosopher is that there is no such subject as philosophy."

Ramsey adds: the kinds of issues we want to talk about in philosophy might depress us or excite us, but in any case there is nothing to quarrel about. Our feelings do not correspond to any facts. The facts themselves are indifferent – they have no color. We can put any stamp on them we like.

Ramsey suggests that, since no facts weigh in the case, the thinker who is depressed by the world (presumably Wittgenstein) is someone we can pity or feel sorry for (because that is what we feel for such people) and the thinker who is thrilled by life and excited by its prospects (presumably Ramsey) is someone we can cheer and congratulate (since that is what we feel about happy people). But Ramsey says that we are *right* to pity a depressed person, "because it is pleasanter to be thrilled than to be depressed." And he adds also that it is "not merely pleasanter, but better." The point he wants to make is that Wittgenstein's argument does not do justice to our ordinary judgments about people – people we pity and people we admire – reasoning that this failure should make us suspicious of what Wittgenstein is up to.

Wittgenstein's argument seems to be that the world of facts is the only world that makes sense; therefore everything we say *about* the world is nonsense, except the stark fact that we say it. Ramsey draws several inferences: Wittgenstein's argument makes it seem as if all bets are off about what attitude to take about the world – all choices are open to us and all weigh equally – we can look at the world as a playground or a battlefield – we can fall into depression or jump with joy – but in all these cases nothing real or concrete or objective supports our choices. Ramsey thinks this conclusion is a kind of *reductio ad absurdum* of Wittgenstein's argument.

K.T. Fann, commenting on this exchange in the 1960s, argues that Ramsey has missed Wittgenstein's point entirely. Wittgenstein (says Fann) is not arguing that subjects like philosophy and aesthetics and ethics are just a muddle and have no scientific value. Fann says that the real idea here is that "the inexpressible" – the things that are really important to us, such as philosophy and ethics – "cannot be said but only shown." He spells this out by equating "cannot be said" with "cannot be said by the natural sciences" and "can only be shown" with "can only be shown by music, art, literature, religion … there are unlimited ways to show the inexpressible."

He also argues that Ramsey wrongly attributes a number of statements to Wittgenstein, and that Ramsey, "although a sympathetic interpreter of Wittgenstein, is not very reliable here." Fann claims that Wittgenstein would never have said straight out that "philosophy is nonsense" or that "philosophical propositions are illuminating nonsense" or the like.

This is quite true. Wittgenstein does come say directly "philosophy is nonsense." What he says is "we cannot quite put our ideas into words here" and "these subjects are transcendental" and "their sense must lie outside the world" and "God does not reveal himself in the world" and "anyone who understands me eventually recognizes what I am saying as nonsensical, when he has used what I am saying as steps to climb up beyond what I am saying"(*Tractatus* §6.432, 6.54). These statements are exactly the kind of thing that Ramsey is objecting to.

In a way, Fann is responding to Ramsey by saying "we cannot say the thing we want to say, but on the other hand we *can* whistle it." That is, we can express it in music or art or literature or by some other allegorical strategy. But this idea cannot be defended. We can't actually *say* anything about it.

Ramsey thought of himself as a pragmatist. Pragmatism is the idea that the meaning of a sentence should be defined by reference to the actions to which asserting it would lead. Ramsey's criticism of the *Tractatus* amounts to pressing the question, *what does this mean in terms of action?* And Ramsey answers: precisely *nothing*. We cannot make out anything important from nonsense, or get any bearing from it in life. If philosophy is nonsense, it is not important; if it is important, it is not nonsense.

Wittgenstein's Initial Reaction and Rejoinder to Ramsey's Criticism

Wittgenstein credited Ramsey with rekindling his interest in philosophy, after his experiences as a schoolteacher, an architect and a gardener, and when Wittgenstein returned to Cambridge in January 1929 after an absence of twelve years he lived at Ramsey's house. The two had most of a year to argue about philosophy. Wittgenstein was also preparing himself to get back into teaching. He gave his first lecture on January 20, 1930, the day after Ramsey died.

In November 1929 Wittgenstein delivered the "Lecture on Ethics." In this lecture Wittgenstein tries out many formulations of the same incongruous combination – nonsense and import – as in the expression that *ethics is supernatural*; that *in ethics we are looking at the world as a miracle*; that we must misuse language or speak nonsense to put into words the kind of thing that all of us are trying to express with ethical ideas; that we are forced to use similes to make out what we want to say, yet as soon as we examine the allegorical language we are using, we see that it is nonsense. At the end of the "Lecture on Ethics" Wittgenstein seems almost to be speaking to Ramsey:

"You will say: Well, if certain experiences constantly tempt us to attribute a quality to them which we call absolute or ethical value and importance, this simply shows that by these words we don't mean nonsense, that after all what we mean by saying that an experience has absolute value is just a fact like other facts and that all it comes to is that we have not yet succeeded in finding the correct logical analysis of what we mean by our ethical and religious expressions…

"I see now that these nonsensical expressions were not nonsensical because I had not yet found the correct expressions, but that their nonsensicality was their very essence. For all I wanted to do with them was just to go beyond the world and that is to say beyond significant language. My whole tendency and, I believe, the tendency of everyone who ever tried to write or talk Ethics or Religion, was to run against the boundaries of language.

"This running against the walls of our cage is perfectly, absolutely hopeless. Ethics so far as it springs from the desire to say something about the ultimate meaning of life, the absolute good, the absolute valuable, can be no science. What it says does not add to our knowledge in any sense. But it is a document of a tendency in the human mind which

I personally cannot help respecting deeply and I would not for my life ridicule it."

Ramsey's essay "Philosophy" was written around the same time that Wittgenstein delivered his "Lecture on Ethics" and represents (as it were) the other half of this conversation. Ramsey accuses Wittgenstein of "scholasticism," i.e. treating what is vague as if it were precise; fitting pieces into a scheme without looking too closely at the pieces. Ramsey's pragmatic attitude calls for us to stick with the project of trying to be clear about each thing we say, trying to take small steps, and living with the "ordinary position of scientists of having to be content with piecemeal improvements: we can make several things clearer, but we cannot make anything clear."

Wittgenstein's notes from the period reject Ramsey's criticism. He writes that Ramsey is "a bourgeois thinker" who cannot abide a mess and wants to clean things up and get them into order. "This was what he was good at and what really interested him; whereas real philosophical reflection disturbed him until he put its result (if it had one) to one side and declared it trivial." Wittgenstein thinks he can *defend* messiness and the problem of having to go on.

Wittgenstein's predicament at this point is roughly the dilemma of holding a positivistic view regarding knowledge and emotion but also upholding something akin to mysticism in matters relating to ethics or religion. He says "What is good is also divine – strange as this sounds, it sums up my ethics – only something supernatural can express the supernatural." He also says "What can be said amounts to the propositions of natural science." The closest he comes to uniting these perspectives is a brief note from 1931, preserved in the collection *Culture and Value*. This reads: "Perhaps what is inexpressible (what I find mysterious and not able to express) is the background against which whatever I could express has its meaning."

My understanding of what Wittgenstein is saying to himself here is roughly this: he is saying, I, LW, am looking at something close up and I can make out a good deal about it – this is the material of natural science – but behind this and encompassing it on every side is a boundless reality that transcends everything I am able to grasp – it dwarfs the island on which I am standing; and behind this as the ultimate frame of reference is the fact of existence itself that is completely incomprehensible to me but also evident in every waking moment of my life. While I grasp this truth I am *practicing philosophy*. Philosophy is literally a 'thinking beyond.'

Thus Wittgenstein seems to want to say two very different things. He wants to say that ethics is an attempt to say something that cannot be said. As soon as we start talking about it, we run up against the limits of language and start babbling all kinds of nonsense. Thus to his friend Moritz Schlick he said "I think it is definitely important to put an end to all the claptrap about ethics – whether intuitive knowledge exists, whether values exist, whether the good is definable." But at the same time he wants to say that the sense of the mystical, the urge to talk about ethics and all our fumbling about in philosophy are indications of something important – even *the most important thing there is* – thus he says that he understands what Heidegger is referring to when he talks about anxiety, and Being-in-the-world, and the wondering at the existence of the world. Schlick reports that Wittgenstein used to refer to Kierkegaard's talk about "this unknown something with which Reason collides whenever it is inspired by its paradoxical passion."

Wittgenstein's Later Acceptance of Ramsey's Idea

In the 'Preface' to the *Philosophical Investigations* Wittgenstein says that he has come to recognize grave mistakes in the position he staked out in the *Tractatus*. He thinks now that the way he had been thinking about things for several years is fundamentally flawed. He accuses himself of being blind. "I was helped to realize these mistakes – to a degree which I myself am hardly able to estimate – by the criticism which my ideas encountered from Frank Ramsey, with whom I discussed them in innumerable conversations during the last two years of his life."

In section 81 of the *Investigations*, Wittgenstein recalls a conversation he had with Ramsey. Ramsey had said to him that logic was a "normative science." Wittgenstein confesses that it took him quite a long time to hear what Ramsey was saying. Years after the conversation took place, it dawned on him that Ramsey was trying to point out to him that there is a difference between making a comparison (for example, a comparison between a pictorial display in a trial and the way language works) and making a sweeping claim (for example, that all significant language depicts a situation in the world). This passage was written in 1946. By 1949 Wittgenstein had moved even closer to Ramsey's position and was even ready to call himself a pragmatist.

Wittgenstein writes in the "Lecture on Ethics" that language is a cage; a year later he says explicitly that language is not a cage. He has stopped regarding language as a fixed structure to which everything had to conform (a view he expressed in terms like "logical form," "grammar," "picture") and he has started regarding language as dynamic behavior that makes varying senses in varying contexts (a view expressed with new terms such as "language games," "practices," "circumstances"). His thinking takes a turn from the conception of meaning as representation to the conception of meaning as use ("the meaning of a word is its use in the language").

Ramsey notes in his essay "Philosophy" that part of pragmatism as he understands it is the effort to bring more self-consciousness to our thinking in philosophy and to pay more attention to what occurs subjectively and to try to learn from it. Wittgenstein seems to have this idea in mind when he writes that "the philosopher is the man who has to cure many sicknesses of the understanding in himself before he can arrive at notions of the sound human understanding."

An important part of pragmatism is the empirical approach – making the effort to suspend our preconceptions and instead make a careful observation – not beginning the search with an *a priori* conception or a requirement or a theory or a big truth about an underlying generality – instead "don't think, but look!" Ramsey also talks about staying close to the material and not making judgments that jump too far from the cases we are looking at.

Wittgenstein takes a cue from Ramsey towards pragmatism – he stops talking about "the unknown something," the "mystical" and "thinking beyond" – but something in his psychology overtakes this prosaic step. Wittgenstein is arguably not a pragmatist in his tendency to press his insights to extreme positions. Thus his pragmatism becomes zealous or even fanatical – it becomes the extreme kind of position he staked out in the picture theory – it becomes a requirement. Thus what begins as an attempt to stick to the facts, veers towards a new kind of dogmatism. "We must do away with explanation, and description alone must take its place."

Wittgenstein's Account of 'Nonsense' in the Philosophical Investigations

Wittgenstein's decision to continue talking about "nonsense" in his later work, even though he had abandoned the 'picture theory' that had anchored his pronouncements about this subject – including his claim that the task of philosophy is to make out the difference between sense and nonsense – is surprising. He might have chosen a completely different vocabulary to carry on the project of philosophical criticism. That he did not is thought-provoking and invites some interpretation.

In the first place, we have to try to figure out what role the term "nonsense" plays in the later work – especially in the *Philosophical Investigations* – since formerly the use of the term came out of the contrast between statement-making in the natural sciences and nonsense-talk in areas such as ethics and religion. There is an interesting duality in his early use of the term, carrying both the sense that 'this is not proper speech' and 'this is what we really want to talk about.' The early use of the term is derogatory, but also a reminder of an aspirational tendency that Wittgenstein tried to honor. This latter idea was the target at which Ramsey aimed his arrow. He wanted us to think carefully about the oddity of "important nonsense."

Wittgenstein uses the term "nonsense" a dozen or so times in the *Investigations*. In some of these passages, he is using the word to disparage his earlier views regarding meaning and its supposed relation to depicting reality. He shows that it is possible for a word to continue to have a significance for us even though the thing that it names no longer exists – we can no longer identify 'meaning' with a thing out in the world that corresponds to it. If we pay close attention to linguistic behavior, we see that we often use words without their having any fixed meaning. But, he says, this does not mean that we are talking nonsense. In fact there are many kinds of nonsense, such as the babbling of a child, nonsense in a nonsense-poem and nonsense in nonsense-happenings in fairy tales (*Philosophical Investigations* § 40, 41, 79, 282). In these example cases Wittgenstein is not using the term "nonsense" as a tool of philosophical criticism.

In other passages, the term does carry this kind of weight. An example is the idea of nonsense in section 119:

"The results of philosophy are the results of the uncovering of one or another piece of plain nonsense and of bumps that the understanding has got by running its head up against the limits of language. These bumps make us see the value of the discovery."

This use of the term is consistent with the use to which it is put in section 464 ("My aim is: to teach you to pass from a piece of disguised nonsense to something that is patent nonsense"). These passages are Wittgenstein's rebukes to himself for the arrogance of his presentation of the 'picture theory' and his wild overestimation of its value (e.g. from the Preface to the *Tractatus* – "The truth of the thoughts that are here communicated seems to me unassailable and definitive"). Thus his new way of looking at things comes out of his experience of being seduced by a picture, overdrawing conclusions about it, setting up a kind of superexperiential standard to which episodes of experience must conform, then being called on this mistake by Ramsey and having the problem of going back over the material and figuring out his mistake.

This is one of the most striking parts of the story about Wittgenstein and Ramsey and their decade of wondering together whether philosophy is nonsense or still has some use. Wittgenstein's position in the *Tractatus* is that philosophy arises from misunderstandings concerning language. This is the view that Ramsey took up, and Ramsey thought he was applying this view in criticizing Wittgenstein's fanaticism about language depicting reality. Wittgenstein subsequently drops the idea that language depicts anything and takes the more pragmatic approach of looking at what speakers do as they interact with one another in ordinary life. This is the view he develops in the *Investigations* that identifies meaning with use. Yet the *Investigations* restates the idea that philosophy arises from misunderstanding language.

Tractatus § 4.003: "Most of the propositions and questions to be found in philosophical works are not false but nonsensical. Consequently we cannot give any answers to questions of this kind, but can only point out that they are nonsensical. Most of the propositions and questions of philosophers arise from our failure to understand the logic of our language. (They belong to the same class as the question whether the good is more identical than the beautiful.) And it is not surprising that the deepest problems are in fact not problems at all."

Philosophical Investigations § 109, 111, 119, 126, 255: "Philosophy is a battle against the bewitchment of our intelligence by means of language." "The problems arising through a misunderstanding of our forms of language have the character of depth." "The results of philosophy are the uncovering of one or another piece of plain nonsense and the bumps that the understanding has got by running its head up against the limits of language." "One might also give the name 'philosophy' to what is possible before there are discoveries." "The philosopher's treatment of a question is like the treatment of an illness."

Wittgenstein seems to have taken the view, pretty much life-long throughout his varied career, that philosophical problems are pseudoproblems; that these false problems are, nonetheless, very deep;

that language is the culprit; that language sets a trap for us, and the trap has to do with generalizing and extrapolating from ordinary cases to extraordinary cases; and that philosophy can be thought of both as the disease (confusion caused by misunderstanding language) and as the cure (clarity brought on by an elucidation that returns words to their ordinary uses). Thus Wittgenstein changed his mind about language, but *not* about philosophy.

There is a slightly different tone in the later work. Philosophy is still a kind of nonsense – the diseased condition caused by wayward language – language on holiday – that causes us to say all sorts of ridiculous things. But he no longer feels that philosophy is *important* nonsense.

"Where does our investigation get its importance from, since it seems only to destroy everything interesting, that is, all that is great and important? (As it were only the buildings, leaving behind only bits of stone and rubble.) What we are destroying is nothing but houses of cards and we are clearing up the ground on which they stand" (§ 117). The value, the importance is measured by the bumps we get. We are attempting to get ourselves out of a fix that we ourselves have created. "The fundamental fact here is that we lay down rules, a technique, for a game, and that when we follow the rules, things do not turn out as we assumed. That we are therefore as it were entangled in our own rules" (§ 125).

Thus the thing we are trying to isolate and understand is our entanglement in our own rules. Thus in philosophy we are working on ourselves. "A philosopher is a man who has to cure many intellectual diseases in himself before he can arrive at notions of common sense." We are not working on the universe. We are working on a part of ourselves that we are trying to stamp out. We are not talking about a tendency of the human mind that earns our deep respect – we are talking about a tendency of the human mind to get lost in its own rules – we are trying to get a clear view of the way we are using language so that we don't have to say "I didn't mean it like that" (§ 125). We are talking about more-or-less ordinary nonsense that people try to clear up as soon as it is pointed out to them, as they would a mispronunciation, a bias or a bad habit.

Wittgenstein is certainly aware that he has come down from a height and is taking a completely different, mundane approach. In *On Certainty* § 532 he accuses himself of doing philosophy like a forgetful old woman (not like the heaven-storming young man who wrote the *Tractatus*).

This thinker has entirely revised his way of looking at language, at the thought-process, at the intersection of self and world – moving from a kind of obsession with fixed structure to a dynamic pragmatism – but he has *not* changed his thinking about philosophy – he has not changed his mind about the activity that he has spent his life engaged in – the very activity that first posited the fixed structure and afterwards learns to be careful, empirical and pragmatic.

Question: why does Wittgenstein continue to talk about philosophy in the same ways – as nonsense, as the disease, as elucidation, as the cure – even though his views change so much?

Answer: for the same reason that he stated that "The truth of the thoughts that are here communicated seems to me unassailable and definitive" – for the same reason that he says "We must do away with explanation, and description alone must take its place" – not following the principle "don't think, but look!" – not actually *looking* at the variety of philosophical work.

Extrapolation

Wittgenstein describes bits of language that serve different purposes; they are like the saw, hammer, nails, glue-pot, and straight rule in a toolbox; he is trying to make the point that we use expressions in different ways in trying to communicate. If we look at the variety of philosophical work, we see philosophy as a big collection like this. Defining our terms, generalizing from examples, extrapolation, citing counterexamples, looking for applications, combinatorial expansion or compositionality, conceptual analysis, conceptual metaphor, etymology or philology or historical linguistics, tracking presuppositions, systemization, deconstruction, practicing skepticism, drawing analogies, symbolization, demonstration, working through formalized restatements of arguments, intellectual experimentation, overthrowing assumptions, building connections, pruning connections, theorizing and making constructions of all kinds – these are all tools of philosophy – so is imagination and much else in the inventory of human powers of mind. Wittgenstein, if we may correct him and use his thinking to take next steps, moved from the picture theory to a behavioral conception of language, and by this analogy we should think of philosophy as a toolbox with glue-pot, rule, saw, hammer – tools that solve different kinds of problems – and thus overturn his idea that philosophy is the disease and must heal itself by undoing all the knots that it has tied by misunderstanding things.

Philosophy is the mind at work in thinking. The mind in this conception has no single belief network. It is more like a toolbox with many sorts of tools. Just as color and shape are handled by different parts of the visual system, so myriad distinct networks contribute to the behavioral system – all of which domains remain separated in human cognition. The mind has pathways – it is like a city, just as Wittgenstein says that language is like a city with a maze of little streets and squares, with old and new houses, and houses and additions from many periods, surrounded by many new neighborhoods with straight regular streets and uniform houses (PI § 18). These pathways offer opportunities for thinking, but just as easily lead astray; they are simply powers of mind, from which all good and bad ideas emerge. The point is that we are not hardwired into any *single* metaphor when thinking about a problem, but can switch among them or take a completely new approach. Pragmatism gets us back to the idea that our thoughts are about things in the world, so that we are not just trapped in a self-referential circle of thoughts and thoughts about thoughts. Beliefs about the world can be true or just believed, driving us to test and prove them. We have to pry our conceptual models free of the domains they were designed for and apply them as analogies and in new combinations to new problems – we have to depart from the natural mindset – we also have to pry evaluation away from traditional authority, to ensure the free exchange of ideas and (as Habermas expressed it) follow the "unforced force" of the better argument. Wittgenstein feared that when we move words from their native contexts and let "language go on a holiday," we create problems for ourselves; we tie mental knots that we will later have to untie. But the only reasonable way to let thinking work through problems is to offer it up every human power of mind, in whatever combination, in perfect freedom of argument.

Backsliding into instinctive conceptions and narrowly reigning in abstraction come easily to us. Wittgenstein might have worried just as much about an inherently conservative principle in thought as he did about wayward extrapolation. He was too focused on letting things stand as they were: "Philosophy leaves everything as it is," "Philosophy may in no way interfere with the actual use of language" (§ 124). The idea that philosophy is a check on human ignorance makes great sense, but philosophy is also a spur, an aspiration, trying to overturn the shortcomings of our instinctive ways of looking a things. We have to overturn our models and keep finding new ways to make use of them as we encounter new problems in experience.

My extrapolation is that Wittgenstein did not think enough about fighting off the gods that normally rule our reactions. He did not look carefully enough at the way in which the past predisposes us to make similar choices in new situations; the way past goals become active and guide behavior; the way past perceptions and emotional reactions motivate our searches. He did not look hard enough at everything that is done under the automatism of tacit knowledge. I am thinking of the ways in which emotion-software, and social-interaction-software, and cognitive programs steer our way through the environment, warning and alerting, detecting predators and in-group kin and adversaries, assigning causes and meanings and perceiving wholes. These are completely ordinary uses of human powers of feeling, socializing and thinking. Wittgenstein's distinction between ordinary uses of terms and terms that are stretched into odd shapes – the contrast between humble uses of language and analogical uses – language at work versus language on a holiday – draws us to this same baseline of ordinary use. "What *we* do is to bring words back from their metaphysical to their everyday use" (§ 115). These ordinary uses of human powers represent a baseline, but we also have to look at what ordinary human powers do *under the stress* of powerfully eruptive existential crises – in face of suffering, in confronting violence, injustice, incalculable loss and, ultimately, the stark fact of death – we also have to consider what ordinary human powers of mind are able to accomplish *in the quiet* of reflection. I am extrapolating from Wittgenstein's identification of ordinary language as a baseline for thinking about the way in which human beings navigate through life. He tells us that the problems of philosophy crop up when we get too fancy in our thoughts and get too far away from the humble circumstances in which we first learn to talk and interact. This really is a *first* step in the survey of man's reflection on and interpretation of experience. But there are at least two further steps:

- Ordinary circumstances of life; ordinary language – "this is how things are" (§ 114)

- Stressed conditions of life; religious language; the world of wishes, personifications, rituals, ceremonies, observances, myths – the magical world

- Reflected conditions of life; philosophical language – seeing the world as a problem

Wittgenstein tends to conflate religion and philosophy. He says that *ethics is supernatural*; that *in ethics we are looking at the world as a miracle*. He sees religion and philosophy as equidistant from humble uses of language – equidistant from the straightforward use of language we see in the sciences – both make the mistake of departing from ordinary usage – both are nonsense. But he also holds that these departures carry all the important things we want to say about our experience.

Religion and philosophy redirect ordinary human powers of feeling, socializing and thinking from real-world applications into imaginary-world constructions. Asking someone to pass the salt is quite different than asking God for forgiveness; but asking God for forgiveness is also different than asking Socrates if virtue can be taught. The redirection of ordinary powers, from humble, unproblematic circumstances and everyday communication to a metaworld, happens in different ways. Using Wittgenstein's terms, religion and philosophy are different kinds of language-games. They define different moods, life contexts, they take different departures. Religion is a departure into fantasy, under the stress of suffering; philosophy is a departure into interpretation, in the quiet of reflection. Plato makes this point in the *Sophist*. Religion treats us like children who like to hear a story (μῦθόν τινα διηγεῖσθαι, 242c). Philosophy is for adults. In philosophy we are trying to reach understanding by our own efforts – every single one of us must take up this problem for ourselves – or live an unexamined life not worth living.

Philosophy is the entirety of human powers of mind at work wrestling with conscious mortality.

Or perhaps the value of philosophy lies only in uncovering one or another piece of plain nonsense.

Important Nonsense

The conversation carried on between Frank Ramsey and Ludwig Wittgenstein looks closely at the philosophical enterprise and forces those of us who listen in on the conversation to try to disabuse ourselves of pretension, separate our confusions from real problems in the world, and pose again the question about the nature of philosophy and the role it should play in our lives.

Ramsey and Wittgenstein end up agreeing that philosophy has a very mundane purpose (the clarification of thought) and that we do better to deflate its high-flying ambitions (its expression of the aspiration of transcendence – the kind of philosophy that earns our respect because it aims very high) and emphasize instead its pragmatism (becoming more self-conscious, less self-absorbed, more empirical and less dogmatic). Both tried to take philosophy back to *this* world and to clearing things up here – especially to clear up the way people think – as a basis for action.

Both saw the old problems, the traditional philosophical questions, as nonsense.

Ramsey and Wittgenstein, despite their recommendations, both exemplify the passionate, powerfully moved, deep-diving spirit of inquiry – an uncompromising, high-minded, unsurrendering commitment to truth – a powerful seriousness that is unwilling to set it sights lower – an inspiration to think about the hardest things in the world with commitment and focus – to uphold the high calling of philosophy. That is, these thinkers incarnate the very kind of philosophy that earns our respect because it aims so high, and not at all by its pragmatism.

The philosophical archetype made visible in Ramsey and Wittgenstein is nearly opposite to their recommendations. Philosophy *recommended* by these thinkers is a kind of hygienic exercise. It is a check on human ambition. Philosophy *embodied* by thinkers is a great reach for the whole, from the very limited prospect of human life. It is unyielding, restless, radical questioning.

Ramsey's and Wittgenstein's pronouncements about ridding ourselves of philosophy or bringing philosophy to an end seem ridiculous now. Philosophers before Ramsey and Wittgenstein argued about belief, knowledge and like matters. They are arguing about these questions today. They will argue about them in times to come. Surely Ramsey and Wittgenstein knew this.

The idea that philosophy takes place in every human being seems to be missing in the Wittgenstein-Ramsey discussion. The idea that philosophy will last as long as human experience – the idea of philosophy as reaching beyond present experience to clear a space for thinking – is missing.

I draw the conclusion that the real contribution of these philosophers on the subject of philosophy is not anything that they say about it. This appears to be the most important fact to interpret in their dialogue. They say a good deal of nonsense in their remarks about philosophy and their ideas on this subject are not persuasive. Yet their dialogue is alive – it is a model of philosophic interrogation – it builds the philosophic mind and brings new life to questioning.

I begin to see that the point of going on with the philosophical enterprise is not to resolve traditional questions in the field or to define 'reality' for all time but to develop the capacity to *think* beyond present contexts and clear a space in which wakeful living becomes possible.

If this is the point of work in philosophy, then it especially striking that these two gifted thinkers argued about the value of philosophy, and even accounted it as nonsense, during a period of unprecedented political disaster. Their thinking seems quite disconnected from the startling events taking place in their lifetimes. This is another aspect of powerful fact to interpret in their dialogue.

Long before Wittgenstein, Plato conceived philosophy as a form of therapy (θεραπεύειν, *Charmides* 156b). His discernment (*diagnosis*) of the illness (*asthenia*), uncovers a kind of ignorance (*amathia*) and an inversion (*anastrophe*) or distortion (*paramorphosis*) of the soul. This upside-down condition leads to psychological conflict, unhappiness and vice in the individual, and a whole range of disasters for social and political life. Philosophy offers a *therapeia* (treatment), which is a course of education (*paideusis*), working through the process of destructive scrutiny (*elenchus*) that purges (*katharsis*) ignorance, brings about a conversion (*metanoia*) and, ultimately, salvation (*metastrophe*).

Plato's arguments, dispersed around the dialogues, are highly complex, and he often appears to be rethinking his position. He explicitly denies that there is anything like "the philosophy of Plato." The best we can do is to follow a few hints and make a provisional statement of the general direction of his thought – thought which seems continually under revision. In brief, he seems to be concerned with the body – *soma* – and what this does to the soul – *psyche*. The worst results for a soul incorporated into a body are, in Plato's thinking, that the things of the body distract the eye of the soul. Psychic attention gets diverted from its natural object – ideas – and instead gets dragged down to mere stuff, and especially all the trifles, charms and wiles of beautiful bodies that stir our desires. Philosophy on this conception is a way of life, a discipline, meant to restore the focus of psychic attention, which puts knowledge in place of ignorance and harmony in place of self-conflict; the soul is restored to its healthy condition of searching and political life is reestablished as justice. Plato emphasizes in virtually every passage where he discusses these issues that the kind of knowledge he is talking about is a *decision* – an act of will takes hold of attention and directs it from the things of the body to the realm of ideas – the soul is *self-convicted* of error and *self-persuaded* of truth – the soul restores itself by a *choice* to do so and thus allows its underlying urge to know, which was dethroned by desire, to resume its rightful leadership of the mind.

Compare this to what Wittgenstein is saying in the *Investigations*. Philosophy, he says, is a kind of therapy and is the treatment of an illness. The work we have to do is on ourselves, and we can only convict ourselves of a mistake if we truly feel and realize that we are making one. Therapy is a slow process that gets us to see by degrees that the problems that were troubling us were caused by looking at things the wrong way – we were seduced by a picture or captivated by a picture – but by following many twists and turns of argument we can get over this puzzlement – now we know our way around – now we can see what lies directly in front of us – everything lies open to view (§ 126).

The comparison suggests that Wittgenstein like Plato is trying to get our attention reoriented back where it belongs – he is talking about work that we have to do for ourselves and that depends on our will, decisions, choices – but for Plato doing so is the beginning of a discipline that we have to enact every moment of our lives – which determines our happiness and the health of the state. For Wittgenstein, therapy does not inaugurate a life of philosophical search but instead just the opposite – the philosophical problems completely disappear (§ 133). All our attempts at explanation turn out to be completely empty and, since everything lies open to view, there is in fact nothing to be explained (§ 126). There is really nothing out of the ordinary to get worked up about –

at last we can stop chasing Chimeras and other mythical beasts – we can also stop babbling about these idiocies to other people (§ 94).

To me the comparison demonstrates that Wittgenstein the patient has much more to offer us than Wittgenstein the physician. The kind of philosophy that earns our respect because it aims very high, that engages us in work on ourselves and articulates a path from self-examination to political participation, is much more likely to be of use than a ban on metaphysical speech.

A poor understanding of philosophy helps to create a climate in which political disaster is possible. Philosophy cut short is no longer philosophy – is no longer the public space in which ideas appear and vie for influence – no longer a model for free discussion and a gradually emerging rational consensus. A quiet respect for the mystical – especially one we are barred from unveiling – can neither help us live examined lives nor improve society.

The only way that philosophy can serve its intended, mundane purpose of "clarifying thought" is through its extension to the widest possible context – to the ultimate frame of reference in the fact of existence itself – in order to challenge the various forms of stupidity that darken thought in our world. Philosophy must drive to the extreme, break all ranks and trespass all borders. That is how it saves.

It is more evident today than at any time in the past that human beings need philosophy in all its aspirational power to detach wisdom from any connection to systems of uncritical loyalty and offer it instead as an intellectual, moral and spiritual project for individuals.

Philosophy is not merely useful or therapeutic. Philosophy is an existential life-struggle to keep thinking in a world of fanaticism, greed and boundless stupidity. Philosophy is indeed important nonsense.

Some notes

Suffering (1-46)

(page 15) The terms *suffering, suffere, passio* (to undergo, to be subjected to, to bear, to submit, to be acted upon) help to motivate the thing called 'religion.' In the religious response to suffering – in ancient times especially the inspiration of religious transport was taken to be an autonomous intrusion of force into the life of a passive recipient – the believer has the religious experience or receives the message – undergoes, bears, submits.

To suffer is to be a passive recipient; not to invent but to be given; not to be the source but the destination. I receive the message; I carry it; I become the messenger. If I am a messenger, then I am not the *author* of the message; I am receiving the message and passing it along. Thus I am modeling the relation in which another person can stand under the message just as I do, so that we both submit to something else – something more than human, an external agency. I have effectively struck out my authorship of the message – my responsibility for it – and I have hit upon a solution to the problem of making my message binding in society, by modeling obedience.

I have done this by *dividing myself into parts*. Part of me is saying 'this is not me, this is a message from the Big Other' and part of me saying 'we cannot question this message, this is a message from the Big Other.' I am recipient and proclaimer at once.

→The point is that the religious response to suffering works by dividing the self into parts.

→Stepping back again: the religious response to suffering provides suffering a new kind of context for resilience (coming back from the break). The religious response to suffering calls up new sorts of psychic energies to ward off pain (broken body, broken connection, broken meaning). These energies may be greater than those lost in the traumatic event – lost in, consumed by, or taken up with managing this event or the shock it has created. They may also be more plentiful (there may be more of them).

This response works by *staking out a value* (defining a value, attaching to a value, upholding a value). The self is divided into 'participant in transcendence' and 'bearer of suffering.' In the light of the transcendent value, the provoking event is placed in an expansive context; the weight of suffering is lifted and the broken connection is repaired. The response is an extrapolation from suffering and has all the problems and opportunities that emerge from extrapolating from complex life episodes to simplified conceptual abstractions

In some traditions the action of staking out a value is given an explicitly 'otherworldly' interpretation, so that the faith response to suffering looks like a transfer to another realm. The weight is lifted because I have entered into a magical realm of light, healing, love, *mana* or spiritual power. I am transported, the veil is lifted, I set foot in the other world, I am reborn, the clouds part.

In some traditions the action of staking out a value is 'worldly' rather than 'otherworldly.' I enter the temple or travel to the sacred territory, sanctuary or retreat; I perform the sacred action, e.g. ritual mourning or purification or quest or ethical doing; I may even travel to a special place 'in us' – 'in me' – e.g. a special trance, a meditative state or form of mindfulness; in effect a special self.

The religious response to suffering 'goes somewhere else' – this is a common element in the religious 'transcendence' or 'overcoming' of suffering – religiosity 'transports.'

Uncontroversially the religious response to suffering may actually *succeed* in reframing the painful situation and 'rise above' the immediate circumstances of pain, finding comfort in a larger context of meaning. There is no distinction here between traditional religions and cults. The commonsense observation that very odd belief systems sometimes help a person overcome pathological behavior is also relevant to this point. As

William James expressed it, "the cure for dipsomania is religomania."

This represents a juncture point for interpretation. Given the event and suffering that follows, the religious response works by staking out a value; by participating in transcendence, the bearer of suffering is comforted. If we are suspicious about this value and regard the participation in transcendence as a fraud, then the comfort will also seem delusory. On this interpretation the religious response to suffering represents an elaborate hoax – a state of denial in which the reality of suffering is explained away or otherwise made to disappear – i.e. not the result of an honest confrontation with loss; not genuinely a case of 'rising above'; instead, a mental disorder. This tack portrays the religious response to suffering in terms of splitting or fragmentation or dissociation or compartmentalization of the personality. The personality manages the traumatic event by breaking into parts; in cases like these we are looking at a pathological response to trauma. Thus the relief that the patient may feel is dismissed as delusory or merely transient – we deny that the religious step has offered any real help.

Some options for reflection here are (1) acknowledging that the value may be a fraud but dismissing the importance of this kind of judgment; emphasizing the opposite idea of respecting 'whatever works' for the patient (the agent who experiences suffering and responds to suffering with a religious interpretation) – i.e. whatever lessens his or her trauma and helps to get through suffering is, for that reason, self-validating; (2) looking more thoroughly at the idea of responding to suffering via psychological fragmentation; raising questions about *identity* and the relations of parts or pieces of the personality (if such things exist) to the whole personality or the integrated personality (if there is such a thing) – in a sense we are looking at the special sense of self formed in a religious matrix and how this compares to alternatives for identity – in particular, whether this is borrowed functioning or whether it is or can be an authentic emergence of this particular self; (3) forgoing a skeptical approach to religious valuation – accepting the religious value offered in the religious response to suffering at face value, simply as another kind of comfort offered to sufferers; 'bracketing' its existence claims and having a look at it as a form of therapy or pain management; looking at its effectiveness; or (4) asserting the religious claim.

A sign that we have to do with mental disease rather than health – psychological denial and delusion rather than honest confrontation and adaptation – shows itself when the disaster no longer registers as *suffering* (it disappears in the larger context of religious construal). In such a case it does not make sense to call this 'rising above' the painful events, because the system of interpretation in this case appears to deny that the painful events ever took place.

The fact that the subject responds to trauma by 'breaking up into parts' is probably not enough to motivate a diagnosis of mental disorder. A person may experience something very powerful and feel strongly moved in several directions. Perhaps I have to divide myself up a bit for a moment, for some period of time, before I can collect my thoughts and reconstitute myself. I need some time to put myself back together as the shock sinks in and I get a chance to think things through.

Arguably, skepticism (which takes a bit of critical distance from a given belief) already invokes a mild form of dissociation. As simple a thing as a moment of reflection and suspended judgment may resemble a kind of dissociation – in these kinds of cases there is no autonomous intrusion into the personality (from an outside agent or force) – in these kinds of cases the intrusion is willed and conscious. One of the findings here is that disorientation is a goad to creativity.

A middle case might be a kind of temporary psychosis that helps to purge overwhelming feelings of grief. The Ancient Greeks, for example, carved out the idea of healing madness, *theia mania*.

Suffering feels like a trap, an enclosure – we cannot see our way out of it – captivity, entrapment, loss of control, disempowerment – and if I cannot leave any other way then (perhaps) I will leave magically. That is: a part of me will leave, and a part of me will stay – e.g. my body is still here. We are looking at a set of circumstances in which a person might undergo, be subjected to, bear, submit, or be acted upon, to a dissociative result. Under the pressure of the event, a coherent sense of self is lost – some strains of connection between thought, memory, feeling, action or normal identity are severed – somehow the mind has created a measure of distance from an experience that is too difficult for the psyche to process. Symptoms might include dissociative amnesia, fugue states, depersonalization – the subjective experience of unreality, a narrowing of attention, disruption in memory, changes in reasoning and perception – psychic numbing, disengagement, a general inability to adjust. The inner witness, the agency of control, the inner autobiographer, fall out of joint with one another, and the connecting links between memory and expectation are severed.

The agent gets into a mode of regression – the situation becomes frozen – the question becomes how to unfreeze this frozen state – how to get past the trauma and into adaptive states of being.

The upshot is that the religious response to suffering is in some cases like *rising above* and in others like *sinking under* – healing the break or breaking apart; a healthy, honest, accepting and adaptive response; or an unhealthy, dishonest, delusive and sick response. Part of the indication is whether suffering is acknowledged or 'explained away.' Another part may be simply how long the agent remains in the dissociated state. Arguably there are at least two further indices for the healthy or unhealthy response to suffering: whether the response rests upon making an outlandish, counterfactual or untestable claim; and how this claim is held, i.e. dogmatically or openly, subject to test and revision. In brief: the best indication of mental health is a sense of humor.

(page 17) The religious response to suffering – taking the position of the value X and claiming it; serving the cause of the value X; taking it in, taking it upon one, grasping that the thing we believe in is at stake, at risk. This cause and risk is modeled in the figure of the 'suffering servant,' who willingly gives himself for sacrifice; a morally blameless man who offers himself to repentance; a figure modeling moral endurance and moral courage through suffering; a figure exemplifying the transition from religion as ritual sacrifice to religion as moral action. The ethical standpoints of self-possession, will and heroism include the idea of courage (being able to withstand pain). The religious response to suffering includes the idea of 'aiming high' (articulating an ideal in the face of the merely 'real'). Connecting this ideal to a demand for justice offers the prospect of God in search of man. This new prospect expands the vocabulary of suffering to terms like 'following through in action' (realizing the value, following our own advice, doing what we say, walking the talk) or 'breaking faith' (hypocrisy, moral failure).

(page 20) Gandhi conceived a new and special kind of religious response to suffering – i.e., a special kind of response to suffering by holding on to a value – attaching to a value but *renouncing any claim to a special absolute*. The defining appeal in this case is not to the (still unconverted) layperson, who may not have heard the message or understood it – who still remains outside the circle. Instead the defining appeal is to *oneself*. This is an example of a person who is trying to hold on to the value X – here is a would-be moral agent – here is an active human will – here is someone who stands up for the value X – but in this case, the aiming concept, the aspiration is not just to hold up X, but to be honest, to make the appeal honestly, to stake out a value but not step over any boundary of strict honesty. Honesty trumps even the value X we are trying to uphold. The agent is trying to live fully in accord with honesty, i.e. bearing it and carrying it through without exception. The ethical position here includes some of the ideas above – being able to withstand pain, the note of aspiration or 'aiming high,' the importance of following through and of matching words to actions; the focus on honesty emphasizes a new idea of humility in which the battle against suffering and various mistakes that might arise from it is conducted entirely within oneself. The social impact of an idea is not the result of making an address to society. The impact comes from living the idea perfectly at the personal level. This shows itself so brightly that the world cannot but take note.

(page 29) What I am calling 'Axial' terms that become important in the analysis of suffering include *humanitas*, suffering as story or narrative or journey, the 'great transformation' and the explicit choice of happiness, and wisdom and disowning wisdom. There are others: the razor's edge, the two infinities, the infinity below and above; the inward turn, making an island for oneself, becoming one's own refuge, 'reigning within'; also selfless action, mindful action, 'knowing fate' (knowing *ming*) and 'doing for nothing.' These three latter groups of terms seem to indicate the characteristic existential *situation* of the moral agent, the characteristic subjective *focus* of the moral agent, and the characteristic practical *attitude* of the moral agent.

Some 'modern' terms in the analysis of suffering – unlike the 'Axial' terms above – include fact, meaning, anxiety, grief, gloom; authenticity; serving both suffering *and* beauty; taking ownership of meaning-making; grace, elegance, thankfulness. The 'modern' vocabulary is sparser, the prospect looks bleaker, the agent appears less empowered, the jump to a transformative vision seems more of a stretch – there is less hope. Hope in this context is more of an achievement.

(page 39) Abraham J. Heschel: No one wants to learn a new word for suffering, but everyone is fated to learn a new word and try to bear it. *The Prophets*, 1962.

Hope (47-81)

In conversations with Brice Tennant, Rachel Pikar, Dennis Higgins, Rob Bremmer, Gary Cox, Wendy Daegas, Osam Edim, Susan Frances, Gary Wolfe, Eric Springsted, Erin Murphy, Larry Dutton, Alex Garklavs, Les Gould, Michael Aaron, Maria Kwong, Robert Hampton, Lew Ayres, my mother Gloria Strelitz and my wife Claudia Kritz, I found my way to the kind of thinking about hope recorded here. Thank you, my friends. My patron George Graham and the YP Collective helped me in innumerable ways during my many philosophical apprenticeships. I am in their debt.

I wrote an early draft of this essay while working on Sen. Barack Obama's

Presidential campaign in 2008. Mr. Obama had written a book about hope and had chosen 'hope' to be his campaign theme. From many conversations with fellow campaign workers, it struck me that it was important to think through the difference between true and false hope.

My friend the poet and filmmaker Marilyn Zornado was kind enough to invite me to present a version of this study of hope to a group of young people studying storytelling, filmmaking and animation. The comments from Ms. Zornado and the class were very helpful to me in exploring hope.

Striving (82 – 161)

(page 118) Nietzsche is not the first person to pose himself the problem of living without gods. Even in his own epoch, many other thinkers were exploring this idea and thinking through its results. Marx and Feuerbach, for example, set down thoughts very like Nietzsche's in the generation before him:

"Religion is consciousness of the infinite. Religion therefore is nothing else than the consciousness of the infinite in our own consciousness; or, in the consciousness of the infinite, the conscious subject has for his object the infinity of his own nature. Therefore God is nothing else than man: God is, so to speak, the outward projection of man's inward nature" (Feuerbach, *The Essence of Christianity*, 1841).

"God is the alienated essence of human reality; at a later stage of history, wealth becomes this alienated essence; at a final stage of history not yet accomplished, human reality will assert its *own* essence. It will cease to worship an external image and placeholder for its own creative power" (Marx, *Theses on Feuerbach*, 1845).

Nietzsche's thesis that *God is dead* has also outlived him in several surprising ways. Nietzsche (despite his dark themes) was an optimist; so were all the thinkers of his age, including Feuerbach and Marx; they all foresaw a happy future in which a new kind of man would stand on his own two feet, without crutches – without creation myths, earth mothers, sky fathers, or other fairy tales. Man's prehistory seems to point to a shamanistic religion, gradually replaced by monotheism and disciplines of religious devotion – the Victorians thought that human civilization would surely continue this line of progress in the direction of reason and scientific experimentalism. But all these thinkers were mistaken – this is not what history appears to be showing us. After Nietzsche, succeeding generations of thinkers, having lived through world wars, pandemic outbreaks, vast natural disasters, social crises, economic swings, assassinations; – the Holocaust, the Iron Curtain, the Cultural Revolution; after all this, new generations of thinkers no longer held this faith, and gave up the claim that history shows steady progress. Religiosity retook much of its lost territory, reversing the evolution towards secularity noted by Victorian scholars. Today the picture is much more complex. We have normalized atheism and fanaticism, and most people live lives that weave both these strands together.

Karl Jaspers defined the standpoint of his 1919 work *The Psychology of Worldviews* as the "philosophy of existence." He cited Nietzsche as his inspiration. Jean-Paul Sartre renamed this philosophy "existentialism" and had great success in popularizing it. Existentialism came into its own in the aftermath of the World War II. Existentialism was an attempt to come to terms with the real world – the real, concrete, tangible, physical world – the cruel and absurd world we live in – what exists rather than what we wish for or believe in our religions.

Jaspers held, in particular, that Nietzsche drew his attention to the problem of death and the idea that our ideals are fragile – that the eternal, God, turns out to be mortal – that ideals ultimately are human creations. Jaspers did not take this to mean that our ideals are frauds; he concluded that we are *responsible* for them. They are as much as we can make them.

God is dead – Jaspers read this to mean: we have to confront death; we have to confront the fragility of everything we care about; we have to accept the responsibility of making our ideals into principles of action – to make them felt in the world. God will no longer do this for us.

The same change, from optimism to facing hard reality, swept over theology a generation after Jaspers' work, for example in the writings of Thomas Altizer and Paul van Buren, who also took their inspiration from Nietzsche's thesis, that *God is dead*. This came to be known as "death-of God" theology (Altizer's work created a good deal of controversy; he even received a number of death threats from religious fanatics). (*Descent into Hell*, 1970; *Living the Death of God*, 2006)

Several generations later, the same ideas, ignited by the same source in Nietzsche's works, took form as something called "weak theology," for example in the writings of Gianteresimo Vattimo and John D. Caputo.

Altizer argued that Nietzsche showed us the danger of maintaining traditional ideas and practices of faith in a radically new historical situation; their very life is sucked out of them by failing to respond to their times. *God is dead* – this means: the old myths cannot satisfy us; our faith will not allow us to comfort ourselves with childish stories. God exists in the actions of men or He does not exist at all. Faith shows itself in the fullest development of human consciousness and reasoning, not in irrationalism or by hiding from reality behind a screen of rituals or empty formulas. War and the record of human cruelty call to us – to believe in a gracious and providential God after Auschwitz is an insult to humanity – Nietzsche was right to call us back to our humanity, to live up to it, to try to make a home for ourselves on the earth.

Altizer's works reached their widest audience in the middle 1960s – a cover story in *Time* magazine (April 8, 1966) brought this theology some celebrity by asking the question in bold red letters on a plain black background, "Is God dead?"

A second Nietzsche-inspired tradition called "weak theology" began in the 1980s – some thinkers associated with this school include Harvey Cox, Mark C. Taylor, Jean-Luc Nancy, as well as Vattimo and Caputo. Caputo writes that *God is dead* – God has no power and cannot rescue us – God is not strong but is weak – God is an ideal and He cannot become real without man. God is "an unconditional claim without force." Caputo reads Nietzsche as showing us the power of desire – the desire to live and fulfil one's life as a human being – the desire to live fully on the earth. God, and all our ideals, all the things we care about, exactly like desire, exists in the space between what exists and what does not; God is hope in the sense of dynamic potential; God is not a force that intervenes in nature but a claim that a human being feels the pull of and incorporates by practicing mindfulness, humour and charity (*The Weakness of God*, 2006).

Vattimo's approach credits Nietzsche with the key discovery of "the great lie" – the discovery that values, principles, ideals are merely *forces* – merely what we are able to put forward and make real – the big lie is that God is powerful – in truth, *God is dead* – that is: God is weak and needs us. God's "weak thought" must become ours, which we will make strong (*Dialogue with Nietzsche*, 2008).

The most important thing in the world has died – this means, it is up to us to bring it back to life. But it is also true that when we bring God back to life and own our responsibility for protecting God, this is fundamentally a new God, an uncertain God, a mortal God, and not the only one.

(page 127) Freud as a Nietzschean. A selection of Nietzschean concepts developed in Freud:

Ego, defining a continuum between dispersion (*Id*, instinct) and obsession (*Superego,* conscience) – opposite principles fight against one another and reach intervening periods of reconciliation –sometimes the fantasy-mechanism is dominant; sometimes reality.

The Unconscious – some thoughts are brought forward and are 'conscious,' others fall out of awareness and recede back into memory or are forgotten – these are 'unconscious.' The relation of the focus of awareness to the content of awareness is a *practical* relation; the decision as to which contents should come forward and 'be conscious' and which others should be forgotten and 'unconscious' consists in excluding. This is the interest in *not being aware of something*. Freud held that the phenomenon of "not knowing" in this connection is a "not wanting to know" (*Standard Edition*, volume 2, p. 270). Consciousness is an *accomplishment* in which the individual marks off the range of what he wants to accept as his own being.

The value that the ego sets on erotic needs instantly sinks as soon as satisfaction becomes readily available. Some obstacle is necessary to swell the tide of libido. The capacity for rational thought attempts to overtake biological urges: yet whenever it succeeds, new information arises from the senses and the process begins again. The situation keeps playing itself out.

Nietzsche develops these ideas from his study of Greek culture. My thesis: behind Freud and Nietzsche stands Homer – the first poet, philosopher, scientist, journalist, psychologist.

Odysseus sails eternally from the war in Troy towards his home in Ithaca but never arrives. He lives his life between these two eternities – he discovers eternity in the moment of pursuit.

(page 143) Rudiger Safranski, *Nietzsche: A Philosophical Biography*, translation by Shelly Frisch (New York: Norton, 2002), p. 291.

(page 149) S. Kierkegaard, *Concluding Unscientific Postscript*, translated by David F. Swenson and Walter Lowrie (Princeton: Princeton University Press, 1941).

Sources for this essay:

Friedrich Nietzsche, *Samtliche Werke: Kritische Studienausgabe*, ed. Giorgio Colli and Mazzino Montinari, 15 vols (Berlin: de Gruyter, 1980).

The Birth of Tragedy (Die Geburt der Tragödie,1872); published in English with The Case of Wagner (Der Fall Wagner, 1888), trans. Walter Kaufmann, (New York: Vintage, 1966).

Untimely Meditations (Unzeitgemässe Betrachtungen, 1873-1876), trans. R.J. Hollingdale (Cambridge: Cambridge University Press, 1983).

Human, All Too Human (Menschliches, Allzumenschliches [vol. 1], 1878 and [vol. 2], 1879-1880), trans. R. J. Hollingdale (Cambridge: Cambridge University Press, 1986).

Daybreak (Morgenröte, 1881), trans. R, J. Hollingdale (Cambridge: Cambridge University Press, 1996).

The Gay Science (Die fröliche Wissenschaft, 1882; with important supplements to the second edition, 1887), trans. Walter Kaufman (New York: Vintage, 1974).

Thus Spoke Zarathustra (Also Sprach Zarathustra, bks I-II, 1883; bk III, 1884; bk IV [printed and distributed privately], 1885), trans. R. J. Hollingdale, (New York: Penguin, 1973).

Beyond Good and Evil (Jenseits von Gut und Böse, 1886), trans. Walter Kaufman (New York: Vintage, 1966).

On the Genealogy of Morality (Zur Genealogie der Moral, 1887), edited with important supplements from the Nachlass and other works by Keith Ansell-Pearson; trans. Carol Diethe (Cambridge: Cambridge University Press, 1995).

The Case of Wagner (Der Fall Wagner, 1888); published in English with The Birth of Tragedy (Die Geburt der Tragödie,1872), trans. Walter Kaufmann, (New York: Vintage, 1966)

Ecce Homo (Ecce Homo, 1888, first published 1908), trans. R. J. Hollingdale (New York: Penguin, 1992).

Nietzsche contra Wagner (Nietzsche contra Wagner, 1888, first published 1895), trans. Walter Kaufmann, in The Portable Nietzsche, ed. Walter Kaufmann (New York: Viking, 1954).

Twilight of the Idols (Götzen-Dämmerung, 1889); published in English with *The Anti-Christ* (Der Antichrist, 1888), trans. R. J. Hollingdale (New York: Penguin, 1968).

The Will to Power (translation by Walter Kaufmann and R.J. Hollingdale; edited with commentary by Walter Kaufmann) (New York: Vintage 1967).

Nietzsche commentaries consulted:

Habermas, Jürgen. Der philosophische Diskurs der Moderne (Frankfurt: Suhrkamp, 1985), available in English under the title, The Philosophical Discourse of Modernity, trans. Frederick Lawrence (Cambridge, MA: MIT Press, 1987).

Heidegger, Martin. "Nietzsches Wort'Gott is tot,'" in Holzwege (Frankfurt: Vittorio Klostermann, 1952 [written in 1943]). "Nietzsche's Word: God is dead" in The Question Concerning Technology and other essays, trans. William Lovitt; co-edited J. Glenn Gray and Joan Stambaugh (New York: Harper, 1977).

Heidegger, Martin. Nietzsche I-II (Pfulligen: Neske, 1961).

Heidegger, Martin . Nietzsche, vol. I-IV, trans. David Farrell Krell, (San Francisco: Harper, 1979ff).

Heidegger, Martin. "Platons Lehre von der Wahrheit,"(written in 1930, revised in 1940), published in Wegmarken (Frankfurt am Main: Klostermann, 1967); "Plato's Doctrine of Truth," in Pathmarks, ed. William McNeill (Cambridge: Cambridge University Press, 1998).

Heidegger, Martin. "Was Heisst Denken?" (Tübingen: Niemeyer, 1954); "What is Called Thinking?," trans. J. Glenn Gray and Fred Wieck (San Francisco: Harper, 1968).

Heidegger, Martin. "Wer ist Nietzsches Zarathustra?" in Vorträge und Aufsätze (Stuttgart: Neske, 1954); "Who is Nietzsche's Zarathustra?" in Nietzsche vol. II trans. David Farrell Krell, (San Francisco: Harper, 1979), 209-233.

Jaspers, Karl. Nietzsche. Einführung in das Verständnis seines Philosophierens (Berlin: de Gruyter, 1936); Nietzsche: An Introduction to the Understanding of His Philosophical Activity, trans. Charles F. Wallraff and Frederick J. Schmitz (Baltimore: Johns Hopkins University Press, 1997)

Kaufmann, Walter. Nietzsche: Philosopher, Psychologist, Antichrist, 4th edition: (Princeton: PUP, 1974).

Klossowski, Pierre. Nietzsche et le cercle vicieux (Paris: Mercure de France, 1969),

Lambert, Laurence. Leo Strauss and Nietzsche (Chicago: University of Chicago Press, 1996)

Montinari, Mazzino. Reading Nietzsche, trans. Greg Whitlock (Urbana: University of Illinois Press, 2003).

Nehamas, Alexander. Nietzsche: Life as Literature, (Cambridge, Massachusetts: Harvard University Press, 1985).

Schacht, Richard. Nietzsche: The Great Philosophers (London: Routledge, 1983)

Strauss, Leo. "Note on the Plan of Nietzsche's Beyond Good and Evil" in Studies in Platonic Political Philosophy (Chicago: University of Chicago Press, 1983).

Vattimo, Gianni. The End of Modernity trans. Jon R. Snyder (Baltimore: Johns Hopkins, 1988)

Vattimo, Gianni. Nihilism and Emancipation (New York: Columbia University Press, 2004).

Peace (162 -186)

Abbreviations used in this section to indicate citations from works by and about Wittgenstein:

PI = *Philosophical Investigations*, Third Edition, ed. G.E.M. Anscombe and R. Rhees, trans. G.E.M. Anscombe (Oxford: Basil Blackwell, 1958)

CV = *Culture and Value*, rev. ed., ed. G.H. von Wright in Collaboration with H. Nynam, trans. By P. Winch (Oxford: Basil Blackwell, 1998)

PO = *Philosophical Occasions*, 1912-1951, ed. J. Klagge and A. Nordman (Indianapolis: Hackett, 1993)

LE = "A Lecture on Ethics," 1965, *The Philosophical Review* 74:3-12 (lecture delivered in 1929)

BB =*The Blue and Brown Books*, ed. Rush Rhees (Oxford: Basil Blackwell, 1958)

Ms, Ts = *Wittgenstein's Nachlass: The Bergen Electronic Edition*, ed. The Wittgenstein Archives at the University of Bergen (Oxford: Oxford University Press, 2000) (by manuscript or typescript number followed by page number)

NM = Norman Malcolm, *Ludwig Wittgenstein: A Memoir* (London: Oxford University Press, 1958)

vW = G.H. Von Wright, *Wittgenstein* (Oxford: Basil Blackwell, 1982)

M = Ray Monk, *Ludwig Wittgenstein: The Duty of Genius* (New York: Free Press, 1990)

F = K.T. Fann, *Wittgenstein's Conception of Philosophy* (Berkeley and Los Angeles: University of California Press, 1969).

LC = L. Wittgenstein, Lectures and Conversations on Aesthetics, Psychology and Religious Belief, Edited by Cyril Barrett (Berkeley and Los Angeles: University of California Press, 1966).

PB = L. Wittgenstein, *Philosophische Bemerkungen* (Oxford: Basil Blackwell, 1965).

(page 166) Von Wright through Cavell. See G.H. Von Wright, *Wittgenstein* (as above); Marie McGinn, *Wittgenstein and the Philosophical Investigations* (London: Routledge, 1997); Oskari Kuusela, *The Struggle Against Dogmatism: Wittgenstein and the Concept of Philosophy* (Cambridge, Mass.: Harvard, 2008); Richard Rorty, *Objectivity, Relativism and Truth: Philosophical Papers, Volume I* (Cambridge: Cambridge University Press, 1991); Norman Malcolm, *Thought and Knowledge* (Ithaca: Cornell University Press, 1977); Stanley Cavell, "Declining Decline," *This New But Unapproachable America* (Albuquerque: Living Batch Press, 1989), here p. 57.

(page 167) Wittgenstein following the ancients. Plato, *Apology* 30a; Plato, *Symposium*, 210a-b; Aristotle, *Nicomachean Ethics*, VI, xii, 15; see also *Nicomachean Ethics*, VI, xii, 9.

(page 173) "Philosophy is a tool which is useful only against philosophers and against the philosopher in oneself." Quoted in Kenny, "Wittgenstein on the Nature of Philosophy," in Anthony Kenny, Brian McGuiness, J.C. Nyiri, Rush Rhees, G.H. von Wright, *Wittgenstein and His Times* (Chicago; University of Chicago Press, 1982), p. 13.

(page 176) *The Foundations of Mathematics and other Logical Essays*, by Frank Plumpton Ramsey (New York: The Humanities Press, 1950).

(page 176) NM, 39-40.

(page 179) Stanley Cavell, *The Claim of Reason: Wittgenstein, Skepticism, Morality and Tragedy* (Cambridge, Mass.: Harvard University Press, 1979).

Important Nonsense (187-218)

(page 192) Avrum Stoll, *Wittgenstein* (Oxford: One World Publishers, 2002), pp. 50-51. See also Ray Monk, *Wittgenstein: The Duty of Genius* (London: Penguin, 1990), p. 118. Monk quotes a note from Wittgenstein dated September 29, 1914: "In the proposition a world is as it were put together experimentally (as when in the law-court in Paris a motor-car accident is represented by means of dolls and so on)." Wittgenstein returns to the theme of traffic patterns in *Zettel* (1945-1948), edited by G.E.M. Anscombe and G.H. von Wright (Oxford: Basil Blackwell, 1967), § 440. The earlier idea (important for the *Tractatus*) begins with the observation that a proposition is like a picture; this becomes the idea that significant language pictures something; this becomes the idea that language must work in a certain way and that everything that does not follow the required pattern is nonsense. The latter idea (developed in the *Zettel*) is that if we are worried about regulating traffic patterns, we may be able to make some improvements, but it would not make much sense to talk about an *ideal* ordering of traffic; this becomes the idea that when we are thinking about problems we can perhaps make some adjustments and improvements and some progress towards a specified goal, but we are not pointing at any *ideal*; we are not approximating to anything; we are just trying to solve a simple problem and there is no reason to talk about ideals; talk about ideals get us off the track and leads us into confusion. Stepping back from these passages: it is possible that Wittgenstein drew the wrong conclusion in both cases.

(page 193) Ludwig Wittgenstein, *Tractatus Logico-Philosophicus*, translated by D.F. Pears and B.F. McGuinness, (London: Routledge & Kegan Paul, 1961).

(page 197) Rudolf Carnap, *Philosophy and Logical Syntax* (London: Kegan, Trench and Trubner, 1955), p. 37f. "[Wittgenstein] seems to me inconsistent in what he does. He tells us that one cannot state philosophical propositions…and then instead of keeping silent, he writes an entire philosophical book."

(page 197) Holding in awe. Louis Sass, "Deep Disquietudes: Reflections on Wittgenstein as an Antiphilosopher," in *Wittgenstein: Biography and Philosophy*, edited by James C. Klagge (Cambridge: Cambridge University Press, 2001), pp. 99-155, here note 86, p. 151.

(page 199) Frank Ramsey, "Facts and Propositions" (1927), in *The Foundations of Mathematics and other Logical Essays*, here p. 155.

(page 199) Frank Ramsey, "Philosophy" (1929), in *The Foundations of Mathematics and other Logical Essays*, here p. 263.

(page 199) Frank Ramsey, "General Propositions and Causality" (1929), in *The Foundations of Mathematics and other Logical Essays*, here p. 238.

(page 199) Frank Ramsey, "Epilogue" (1925), in *The Foundations of Mathematics and other Logical Essays*, here pp. 286-7, 290-2. Ramsey suggests that, since no facts weigh in the case, the thinker who is depressed by the world (presumably Wittgenstein) is someone we can pity or feel sorry for (because that is what we feel for such people) and the thinker who is thrilled by life and excited by its prospects (presumably

Ramsey) is someone we can cheer and congratulate (since that is what we feel about happy people). Perhaps he is a bit inconsistent on this point, since he says that we pity a depressed person with reason, "because it is pleasanter to be thrilled than to be depressed," and also that it is "not merely pleasanter but better." If there is no fact to correspond to, it is hard to see how one feeling can have reason on its side and another not; it is also hard to see how we can assert a proposition such as "it is better to be thrilled than to be depressed." George Pitcher makes a related point by noting that in Wittgenstein's universe the philosopher is a helpless victim surrounded by madness (i.e., nonsense); but "the same logical terrain" can be a playground or a battlefield. To be tortured or be delighted by the world – if the terrain is a-factual – are of a piece. Pitcher seems to be saying that delight trumps despair – which seems true enough – however if we grant Wittgenstein his a-factual universe, this preference no longer makes any sense. George Pitcher, "Wittgenstein, Nonsense and Lewis Carroll," in *Ludwig Wittgenstein: The Man and His Philosophy*, edited by K.T. Fann (New York: Delta, 1967), pp. 315-335, here p. 335. At a distance, both arguments reveal the emptiness of the positivist account of the emotions.

(page 200) K.T. Fann, *Wittgenstein's Conception of Philosophy* (Berkeley and Los Angeles: University of California Press, 1969), pp. 32-33.

(page 200) K.T. Fann, *Wittgenstein's Conception of Philosophy*, pp. 34-35.

(page 201) Frank Ramsey, "Facts and Propositions" (1927), in *The Foundations of Mathematics and other Logical Essays*, cited above, here p. 155.

(page 202) Ludwig Wittgenstein, "A Lecture on Ethics," *Philosophical Review*, LXXIV, no. 1 (1968), pp. 4-14.

(page 203) Frank Ramsey, "Philosophy" (1929), in *The Foundations of Mathematics and other Logical Essays*, p. 268.

(page 203) Ludwig Wittgenstein, *Culture and Value*, edited by G.H. von Wright in collaboration with Heikki Nynam, translated by Peter Winch (Oxford: Basil Blackwell, 1980), this note on page 17e.

(page 203) Ludwig Wittgenstein, *Culture and Value*, here p. 3; *Tractatus* § 6.53.

(page 203) Ludwig Wittgenstein, *Culture and Value*, p. 16.

(page 204) Moritz Schlick, quoted in Monk, *Wittgenstein: The Duty of Genius*, p. 282.

(page 204) Ludwig Wittgenstein, *Philosophical Investigations*, third edition, translated by G.E.M. Anscombe (New York: Macmillan, 1953), p. vi.

(page 204) Ludwig Wittgenstein, *Philosophical Investigations*, § 81; also Ludwig Wittgenstein, *On Certainty*, edited by G.E.M. Anscombe and G.H. Von Wright, translated by Denis Paul and G.E.M. Anscombe (New York: Harper, 1969), § 422.

(page 131) Language a cage – see the "Lecture on Ethics," quoted above on page 4. Language not a cage – see Friedrich Waismann, *Wittgenstein und der Weiner Kreis*, edited by B.F. McGuiness (Oxford: Basil Blackwell, 1967), here p. 117. Here Waismann records what he remembers of a conversation between Wittgenstein and Moritz Schlick that took place on December 17, 1930.

(page 205) Ludwig Wittgenstein, *Philosophical Investigations*, § 43.

(page 205) Frank Ramsey, "Philosophy" (1929), in *The Foundations of Mathematics and other Logical Essays*, p. 268.

(page 205) Ludwig Wittgenstein, *Remarks on the Foundations of Mathematics*, edited by Rush Rhees, G.H. von Wright and G.E.M. Anscombe (London: Basil Blackwell, 1967), part IV, § 53.

(page 205) Ludwig Wittgenstein, *Philosophical Investigations*, § 66, 109.

(page 208) The illness. Ludwig Wittgenstein *Culture and Value*, p. 44. "Philosophy is a tool which is useful only against philosophers and against the philosopher in oneself." Quoted in Kenny, "Wittgenstein on the Nature of Philosophy," in Anthony Kenny, Brian McGuiness, J.C. Nyiri, Rush Rhees, G.H. von Wright, *Wittgenstein and His Times* (Chicago; University of Chicago Press, 1982), p. 13.

(page 210) Wittgenstein is certainly aware that he has come down from a height and is taking a completely different, mundane approach. In *On Certainty* § 532 he accuses himself of doing philosophy like a forgetful old woman (not like the heaven-storming young man who wrote the *Tractatus*).

(page 218) An important conclusion of Jonathan Glover's study *Humanity: A Moral History of the Twentieth Century* (New Haven: Yale Note Bene, 1999), pp. 1-7; also a principal theme of Kant's 1795 work *Perpetual Peace*.

(page 218) Thought has to drive to the extreme. Aristotle argues that although moral virtue strikes a mean between excess and defect, intellectual virtue does not. Intellectual virtue has to drive to the extreme, in order to discover the mark at which moral virtue aims. Skepticism has to be pressed to the extreme – thought cannot and should not stop itself from drawing extreme conclusions, but should drive the argument to the end (*Nicomachean Ethics*, Book VI).

A

Adorno, T. 20
Aeschylus 30-31
Aristotle 83, 84, 167
Arjuna 33
Asanga 1

B

Batchelor, S. 2
Bloch, E. 140
Braithwaite, R.B. 190
Brandes, G. 140, 150
Buddha 1-11, 42-45
Burg, A. 26
Burkert, W. 18

C

Camus, A. 33, 52, 64
Cavell, S. 167
Carnap, R. 197
Confucius 29, 31, 34, 66

D

De Chardin 47

E

Eckhart 9
Einstein, A. 36

F

Fann, K.T. 200
Freud, S. 27, 49, 76, 96-99, 117, 127-8, 136, 178-180, 230, 236
Frye, N. 27
Fung, Y.L. 34

G

Gandhi, M. 6, 20-23
Griffin, J. 11

H

Hegel, G.W.F. 49
Heidegger, M. 37, 41
Heschel, A. 18-19, 39
Homer 11, 14, 27

J

Jaspers, K. 29, 35, 59, 95, 143, 149, 159

K

K'ang, Y.W. 30
Kennedy, R.F. 79
Kierkegaard, S. 41, 54, 149-159, 204
King, M.L.K., Jr. 21-23
Kołakowski, L. 48, 78-81, 187

L

Leibniz, G.W. 20
Locke, J. 83

M

Malcolm, N. 176-7
Mandelstam, N. 47
Mannheim, K. 67-74
Marx, K. 70, 83
Moltmann, J. 48, 54, 63-4
Morris, I. 24
Murdoch, I. 39

N

Nietzsche, F.W. 6, 10, 42, 44, 87-161
Novalis 24
Nussbaum, 143

O

Oedipus 13
O no Yasumaro 15

P

Pandora 50-53
Plato 86-89, 167, 214, 216-217
Po, J. 2
Pythagoras 31

R

Radin, P. 29
Ramsey, F. p2, 187-218
Ruhala, W. 3
Russell, B. 79, 90

S

Schmitt, C. 38
Schopenhauer, A. 8-20, 42
Seneca 11
Shakespeare, W. 36
Socrates 29, 31, 44, 45, 48-49, 79-80, 85-89, 139, 143, 146, 157, 164, 167, 183-5, 214
Solomon 31
Sophocles 14
Spinoza, B. 40-41
Story, F. 2
Stroll, A. 142

T

Trungpa, C. 2

V

Vasubandu 1
Vyasa 33

W

Winnicott, D. 76
Williams, B. 144
Wittgenstein, L. 36, 163-218

Made in the USA
Lexington, KY
26 April 2012